TERROR HAS NO DIARY

ANNALS OF A GAY JEW AND HIS COMRADES
BEHIND A HOLY WALL IN NAZI EUROPE

MICHAEL MELNICK

DEER MOUNTAIN PRESS
"a writers' and artists' co-op"
Los Angeles   New York

Copyright © 2013 Michael Melnick.

All rights reserved. No part of this book(text only) may be reproduced in any form or by any electronic or mechanical means, including information storage and retrieval systems, without permission in writing from the publisher, except by a reviewer, who may quote brief passages in a review. Direct inquires to deermountainpress@gmail.com

The photographs presented in this work are either of obscure provenance, recently made by the author, or part of the author's ancestral archive. In all cases, they are free of copyright assertion.

The author presents this work as a *Yahrzeit* (memorial) for his family members who were murdered by the Nazis in Libau (Liepaja) and Riga, Latvia. In their memory, all proceeds from the sale of this work in any form, including film or theatrical rights, will be donated to MAZON: *A Jewish Response to Hunger.*

DEER MOUNTAIN PRESS
"a writers' and artists' co-op"
deermountainpress@gmail.com

ISBN: 978-0-9759485-1-4 (sc)
ISBN: 978-1-4566-1732-5 (e)

Library of Congress Control Number: 2012952902

Because of the dynamic nature of the Internet, any web addresses or links contained in this book may have changed since publication and may no longer be valid. The views expressed in this work are solely those of the author and do not necessarily reflect the views of the publisher, and the publisher hereby disclaims any responsibility for them.

The design, composition, printing and binding of this book
is by LuLu Publishing Services (LuLu.com).

Lulu Publishing Services rev. date: 09/18/2013

DEDICATION

KALMAN LINKIMER
(1912-1988)
A Moral Witness

AUTHOR'S NOTE

You die twice. First, when your brain turns off and your heart no longer beats; second, when not a soul on earth recalls your life, even your name or face. It is then that you are but a statistic in a government ledger, in a necrology, or on a faded cemetery headstone that receives no visitors. The Shoa sharply focused this almost universal reality. Europe is a vast unmarked Jewish graveyard, from Kiev to Amsterdam, from Hamburg to Salonika. The continuing tragedy is that relatively few can be rescued from a second, and final, death.

This cataclysm intensifies our obligation to those who survived as targets of the Germans and the local gentile populations that collaborated in and profited from the genocide of the Jews. That obligation is to permit survivors their memorial remnants with all the idiosyncratic nuances that cannot be gleaned from administrative documents. To "pierce the smugness of scholarly detachment," as survivor-historian Saul Friedländer tells us. To bring the story to notice and allow us to infer. To tell it true.

The story you will read is my attempt to vivify a small number of the many Jews who resided in the Baltic seaport of Libau (Liepaja), to provide a forum for them to reveal their hopes, fears, and, most of all, their reactions to the destruction of their community. More than two decades ago, Aharon Appelfeld, survivor and Israeli literary lion, erected the guidepost: "Everything in [the Shoa] seems so thoroughly unreal, as if it no longer belongs to the experience of our generation, but to mythology. Thence comes the need to bring it down to the human realm.... to attempt to make the events speak through the individual and in his language, to rescue the suffering from huge numbers, from dreadful anonymity, and to restore the person's given and family name, to give the tortured person back his human form, which was snatched away from him"[1]

The outcome of my effort is solely my responsibility and is not to be construed to represent the views or beliefs of those who may have assisted me in any manner. In attempting to measure up to Appelfeld's high bar, I have sometimes had to draw inferences from diaries, testimonies, and the like that may be wholly different from those that others might draw. To "give the tortured person back his human form" is neither simple nor without detractors, particularly those bewitched by the myth of objective historiography and/or repulsed by the Jewish tradition of transcendent history. Notwithstanding, I very much hope to have achieved some measure of success in distilling the truth of the matter from the facts of the matter. Still, whatever is contained in these pages, good or otherwise, is my responsibility and only mine.

* * *

First and foremost, I want to acknowledge the great generosity of Edward Anders, Professor Emeritus, University of Chicago. Professor Anders (né Alperovich), as a young man, survived the destruction of the Jewish community of Libau. He and his mother immigrated to New York City after Germany's surrender; his father and brother did not survive. Over the past decade or so Professor Anders has dedicated a considerable portion of his life to documenting and memorializing the destruction of Libau's Jews. He worked tirelessly to construct a memorial to the thousands who were murdered, a dignified monument prominently placed in the Jewish cemetery of Liepaja (Libau). Professor Anders has written and lectured extensively on Libau's Jews, notably his memorial book "Jews in Liepaja, Latvia, 1941-1945" and his English translation of Josifs Steimanis' "History of Latvian Jews."

Most central to the book in hand, was Professor Anders' great effort to make "The Diary of Kalman Linkimer" accessible to the English-speaking world. Initially translated from the Yiddish by Rebecca Margolis, Ed Anders edited the diary with care and sensitivity to produce "Nineteen Months in a Cellar: How 11 Jews Eluded Hitler's Henchmen." This was a frustrating effort for many reasons. First, Linkimer began the diary on the day of Germany's invasion, left the diary behind when he escaped from Paplaka, and reconstructed it after he arrived at Sedols' cellar. Second, the diary abruptly ends more than two months before liberation. Third, it appeared to Ms. Margolis, based on the uniform handwriting of the "original," that the diary was rewritten, or at least recopied, sometime after liberation. Fourth, the diary is a diary: it is highly subjective and considerably stilted in its prose, with little to no narrative flow. As a consequence of all this, the English translation is an important primary source, but neither complete nor literary.

All this notwithstanding, unrestricted use of Professor Anders' English translation of Kalman Linkimer's diary was invaluable to me in preparing the book in hand. I was deeply moved eight years ago when Ed Anders offered me the opportunity, as he put it, "to prepare a shorter, more dramatic and faster-moving version of the diary that will have wider appeal." Professor Anders, to be sure, bears no responsibility whatsoever for what appears in the book in hand. The present work is not an edited version of the edited English version. Rather, the diary is an important source among many other sources. Still, I shall always be indebted to Professor Anders for his offer and generous willingness to consign Linkimer's story to an unknown telling.

I am most grateful to Ada Israeli (née Adinka Zivcon) and her husband, Yosef. They were my hosts in Israel, and made all the arrangements for my visits with Hilde Skutelsky and Aaron Vesterman. Ada and I have had many hours of conversation in person and by email about her mother, Riva Zivcon. In addition, she has provided very many of the photographs in the book. Most importantly, she was kind enough to read an earlier draft of the book and to encourage me over and over to completion. I am also grateful to Hilde and Aaron for hours of conversation that provided important facts and insights to events and personalities in the story. Aaron has also given me three key photographs, including the most moving picture in the book which he snapped clandestinely, that of the matronly women in the marketplace with square Jew patches sown on their dresses.

I am also grateful to my cousin Elias Hirschberg and his twin brother Jacob, the sons of Zelig Hirschberg, one of the eleven in the cellar. Elias spent a week acquainting me with Riga, its environs, and the countryside between Riga and Liepaja. In Liepaja, both Elias and Jacob helped me explore the city in detail, including a stop at 14 Kauf Street (now 22 Tirgonu). Together we made an emotional visit to Zelig's grave and to those of our great grandparents, Meir and Beila Hirschberg. Elias and

Jacob were invaluable in helping me put the events of the book in a physical and geographic context.

I wish to thank the University of Southern California Shoah Foundation Institute for Visual History and Education, and to humbly acknowledge those whose interviews most informed the book in hand: Shoshana Kahn (née Rosa Sachs); Jeffrey Lowenson (né Efraim Levenson); Efraim "Fred" Neuburger; Max Solway (né Soloveichik). I thank my friend and colleague, Professor Abraham Yaari, who provided the initial rough translation of the previously untranslated Yiddish poems of Kalman Linkimer. I mostly wish to thank my scientific collaborator of 35 years, Professor Tina Jaskoll, for her invaluable assistance in preparing a complex manuscript.

To conclude, I thank Anita, my wife of 47 years. She has enthusiastically supported all my peregrinations save one—running with the bulls in Pamplona.

                                        Michael Melnick
                                        Professor
                                        University of Southern California
                                        January, 2013

Whichever word you speak—
you owe to destruction.

Paul Celan, "Whichever Stone You Lift"

PREFACE

Zachor . . . remember. Remember that you were a slave in Egypt, that you stood at Mt. Sinai, that you were attacked from behind by Amalek, that Haman sought to kill you, that you were exiled from your land by the Romans, that you were massacred in the Ukraine; in the Jewish experience there is no end to remembering, it is central to it. Indeed, it was ancient Israel that proposed history as decisive and introduced a world-view that human history provided meaning to Divine revelation and purpose. Still, historiography, a precise chronicle of historical events, an immanent understanding of recorded events, has been largely alien to the way in which Jewish collective memory has been addressed or evoked.[2]

Thus, the primary custodian of Jewish collective memory is not the historian. It is the storyteller, just as it is among most other ancient peoples. This Jewish midrashic tradition, and by extension the central Jewish experience, filters the facts to arrive at the truth by a functional dynamic that relies on the way events are seen (or imagined) by those who participated in them. In essence, the central Jewish experience is a transcendent history in which not all "facts" are meaningful or worthy of detailed recollection, and not all poetic evocation's are fictions. This history is literary history, or what contemporary writers refer to as narrative nonfiction, using strategies and devices of the novel to distill the truth of the matter from the fact of the matter. The story recounted here is told very much within this ancient tradition.

If you, the reader, venture beyond this introduction to the narrative, you will be accompanied by a most remarkable narrator, Kalman Linkimer. When the Germans invaded the Baltic port city of Libau, Latvia, Kalman was just shy of 30. He was already a veteran of the Latvian army, a broadly educated teacher and poet who tutored wealthy gymnasium students, and an habitué of cafes where he endlessly played chess, consumed espresso, and smoked cigarettes. He was also Hitler's nightmare . . . a gay, religious Jew who was an avid socialist.

Avishai Margalit has made a very important observation: "The notion of reliving the past involves, I believe, various ideas about remembering emotions and especially about remembering emotions with respect to the events and the people remembered. It is not only the sense of the past that we try to recover in our memory but its sensibility. What was it *like* to be in that situation or with those people there and then?"[3] Conveying the sensibility of evil events, say the transcendent history of the Holocaust (Shoa), requires a special agent of collective memory, what Margalit terms the moral witness. He proposes Anna Akhmatova (1889-1966)[4], the Russian poet, as the paradigmatic moral witness:

> No foreign sky protected me,
> no stranger's wing shielded my face.
> I stand as witness to the common lot,
> survivor of that time, that place.

"Requiem 1935-1940"

Thus, the paradigmatic moral witness is one who witnesses *and* experiences *both* evil *and* suffering; one or the other is not enough. A moral witness is one who clarifies the endless night of murder, torture and humiliation inflicted by evil actors entirely empty of empathy. The moral witness transmits the pain of evil to those who were not there.

Kalman Linkimer is a moral witness. Not protected by a virtuous social contract, Kalman throws off the mask of the gentle aesthete and exposes his true grit. His emotions and his assertions are no longer parallel, they intersect. He concedes to no one the mission of storytelling; he is consumed with a clear sense of being a witness. Kalman Linkmer is not a *tzadik* (saint), he is a moral witness.

PART ONE

And what about God? According to the settlement
Of divorce from the Garden of Eden and from the Temple,
God sees his children only once
A year, on Yom Kippur

Yehuda Amichai, "The Jews"

We are in *yenne velt*, the other world, where Satan sets traps for the unprepared, and demons are so familiar we know them by name. Just eleven of us now, buttoned up in a cellar beneath the heat of baking ovens: the tailor, the shoemaker, the butcher, the jeweler, the electrician, two glaziers, two wives and a widowed mother. And me, Kalman Linkimer, a teacher, a poet. Zionists, Bundists, and Communists all together, fasting. It is Yom Kippur Eve, 26 September 1944.

Misha has drawn watch. The others slumber, but I remain in its antechamber. A black sorrow is never lonesome, for soon enough it conjures up a multitude. Just a year ago the ghetto was emptied. My mother, my sisters . . . . We often tell one another that our evasion is a manner of resistance, but this is delusion. Resistance signifies confrontation, evasion is avoidance. Resistance is certain death. Evasion, with the help of comrades like the Sedols, is the possibility of survival, of bearing witness. Without witness, what is worth fighting for?

Yom Kippur sunrise steals through the chinked cover of the cellar window. We still fast, most of us. Eight men, three women. In *this* sanctuary we are a minyan. We say *Yizkor* for our dead. To avoid the severe decree we pray: *teshuva, tefilla, tzedakah*. Obviously, You have been listening. Our story, after all, is one of miracles. Inscrutable miracles, cast naked upon the ruins by men and women of courage and cunning, not saints. We are students again, and the current of events has always to teach us that a drowning man is not troubled by rain . . .

Libau yesterday

THE NIGHTMARE BEGAN

On 22 June 1941 Hitler betrayed Stalin. Purgatorial fire set upon Libau without delay. The air was screaming. By turns high-pitched and guttural. A cat's tail stepped on; a mad dog barking. Next day, the Germans encamped at the gates. Entry proved far more difficult. For five days the Nazis were held at bay by Soviet forces and the volunteer Workers' Guard. At the while nearly 300 Libauer Jews fled by rail. Zelig Hirschberg's sister, Bunya, the banker's wife, was one; she went to Moscow. By the evening of 28 June, the Fascist troops breached the perimeter. Libau was occupied by dawn. When I was but twenty-nine, evil erupted like the sparks of a summer storm, and the Jews were consumed by the fires of hate.

The sunny morning of 30 June, barely 24 hours later, saw Hitler's SD men tear into Chaya Minkowski's home on 12 Hücke Street. There lived eleven Jews, one being Walter Hahn.[5] A beloved musician born in Vienna, Walter, just 30, was conductor of the Libau Opera. All were ordered into the garden: ". . . lie down . . . stand up . . . lie down . . . ." Then an officer barked, "Stand up! Who among you fled from Germany . . . three steps forward! Quickly, or all will be shot!" Walter Hahn advanced without hesitation. Standing stiffly, he firmly announced, "I fled from Germany."

"Over to the fence," shouted the SD officer. Somewhat ceremoniously, Walter placed himself by the fence and adamantly called out, "Shoot, life with you is worse than death!" A bullet to the neck put an end to his life. More shots rang out, but they were directed skyward. "Your turn will soon come! Now bury this garbage in the garden. Quickly!" The Germans left as swiftly as they came, but not before taking everyone's watch.

I loved Walter Hahn. He never knew it. No one knew it. For me, Walter's death blew a trumpet. So, in the dark dawn, when words fade and ghost-markers come alive, Hirsch Hirschsohn, Schachne Gatav, and I removed Walter from Chaya's garden and placed him in the Jewish cemetery. No formality, just dignity. You became rather expert at this, in time. And each time, you wondered when you might awake and the night be gone . . .

Not far away, another tragedy was unfolding at 17 Ulich Street. There lived the chief accountant of the Kursa Watch Factory, Jeannot Yankelson, with his wife Sara and two teenage daughters, Riva and Betty. Nearby lived the Latvian building janitor, Gerke. Just this day, he invited three SD men to board in the Yankelson's apartment. Each took a room for himself, forcing the Yankelsons into the single remaining room. Late that evening, one SD officer barged into the Yankelson's room and demanded that Riva bring him tea. Jeannot offered to bring it shortly, but the officer imperiously demanded, "*Your daughter* will bring it, and no one else. I give her fifteen minutes to get me tea."

Riva took the tea to the officer. Sensing that only ill could come of this, the other Yankelsons remained tense and agitated. Not ten minutes later, they heard a muffled voice, "Papa help!" Without hesitation, Jeannot dashed to the officer's room and struck the German's head with an axe. He dropped to the floor bloodied and screaming wildly. Riva scurried to her mother and sister as the other German housemates came running. Jeannot quickly exited through the window into the yard and scrambled to the attic. The janitor, Gerke, saw him climbing up the stairs and gladly directed the SD officers. They cornered Jeannot, dragged him down the staircase to the courtyard, shot him, and dumped his body in a large bomb crater opposite the Yankelson home. Meanwhile, Sara and her daughters fled to 19 Bade Street. There they remained until 15 December, when they were humiliated and shot in the dunes of Skede.

Two days later, on 2 July, Misha Libauer and Hanan Kandler were snatched off the street and held prisoner at the Prefecture. In the afternoon, the police sought two volunteers for a work detail. Hoping to somehow escape, Misha and Hanan seized the opportunity. The police led them to the bomb crater facing 15 Ulich Street. Under the watchful eye of a German SD officer and the Latvian policemen, they were ordered to dig up all the bodies. Doing so they quickly uncovered Jeannot Yankelson and the Blechman brothers, Elias and Leib, from Catholic Street. In turn Misha and Hanan discovered Ruben Weide, Ulmann, the shoe-uppers maker, and the tailor Avram Portnoy. It was the next and final body that so disturbed Misha Libauer he could feel his rage gnaw at the root of his reason and nearly topple his restraint. It was the young Mordechai Sand from Helenen Street, whom the SD had castrated before murdering him.

Each body was put in a truck. When all were assembled like logs in a pyre, Misha and Hanan jumped in with two policemen. The SD officer and his driver rode up front. Upon arrival at the Jewish Cemetery, Misha and Hanan were ordered to dig a single, large grave. This took quite awhile and soon it was dusk. They took each body from the truck and placed it in the grave, incessantly murmuring *El Malle Rachamim*. As they began returning earth to the grave, the policemen went off to another task, leaving the SD officer and his driver who was dozing in the truck. Within moments, Misha Libauer's shovel shattered the officer's prerogative. The right side of his face collapsed on his nose; his own knife entered his chest as he lay helpless. Misha and Hanan fled into the dark streets between the cemetery and the sea.

Women's prison

    Back to 30 June, for the worst was last. That evening, SD men, joined by Latvian police, set upon the Jewish homes of Helenen, Jakob, Ludwig, and Unger Streets. Torn from home and family, maniacal shouts and vicious beatings herded scores of Jewish men to the Women's Prison—ostensibly for work assignments the next morning. Hapless Jewish men, unable to defend themselves, were at the mercy of feral Germans and cowardly neighbors. Jewish men we all knew: Yisrael-Aaron Gutman and his grandfather, Yossel; Lemech Schapiro; Boruch Levenson; Leib Silberman; Iser-Elya Feldhun, father of Arya, an infant; George Michelson; Noah Jakobson; Samuel Herzfeld, whose son Leib had fought the Nazis as a workers' guard and died just days before. For many days there were only rumors about the arrested fathers and grandfathers, husbands and sons. On the morning of 5 July, as I emerged from my home, I was snatched by the police and forced to join a group of Jews who marched along at gunpoint—the teacher Moishe Rosental, Leib Glikman from Hasenpot, Gassul and others. We were all certain that this was a work detail, but when we were led across the canal bridge to the Rainis Park pavilion and given shovels our thoughts turned foreboding. Standing in a clearing of this urban forest of birches, lindens, chestnuts, pines and black alders, our mind's eye saw us digging our own graves.

Glikman threw down his shovel and proclaimed, "If you want to shoot me, then do it here, do it now! I will not dig a grave for myself." Leib's protest was answered with a rifle stock to the back, forcing him to the ground. The other policemen raised their rifles in our direction and we froze. Then a Latvian worker, who was standing by with his truck, told us we were only there to dig up and remove corpses. He was to transport them to the Jewish Cemetery and we would re-inter them there. We believed this citizen and set to work.

We dug into the freshly turned earth not more than twenty centimeters when corpses began to appear, heads split open like overripe melons, all with bullet holes in the back of their necks. It was quickly evident that we were tending to those arrested some days earlier. We absorbed the tragedy and, without discussion, undertook our solemn obligation to make note of those who died. Some we immediately recognized, but most were distinguished solely from their identification cards. I don't know how many there were, but it seems no less than a hundred bodies.

The victims were stacked on the open truck and driven to the Jewish Cemetery. We, of course, made our way there on foot. We buried the corpses in a mass grave. It is inexplicable, but the Latvian police allowed us to erect a makeshift memorial with the names of those we had previously identified. We murmured *Kaddish*. All of us but Gassul were sent home. To Gassul fell the task of having to go to the Central Cemetery to bury five Latvians whose names we could not determine. As we later learned, Gassul dug a grave for them, threw them in, and then was shot himself.

From the cemetery, we brought awful news of those who were beaten and arrested on that grim evening of 30 June. In merely two weeks, our lives spun upside-down. The systematic extermination of the Libau Jews had begun. Our families and friends had distressing news for us as well. The military commandant of Libau, *Korvettenkapitän* Fritz Brückner, issued a new set of rules for the Jews: Jews must wear a bright yellow 10 cm by 10 cm patch on their outer garment, front and back; all men between the ages of 16 and 60 must assemble in the Firehouse Square at 7 AM every day for assignment; otherwise, Jews may only leave their homes between 10 and Noon, and 3 to 5 PM; Jews must surrender weapons, radios, typewriters, and all means of transportation; Jews are forbidden to change address, use sidewalks, use public transportation, enter parks, cinemas, and libraries, and attend schools; Jews are forbidden to attend public events and to walk on the seashore; all shops owned by Jews must be so designated in 20 centimeter letters in the front window. This was clearly the endgame. You had to make each move with care.

Jewish women in the marketplace

The next morning, I joined my comrades at the *Hauptwachplatz* at seven, ostensibly to await work assignments. Before long the crowded square was turned into a perverse and terrifying slave market. Dozens of trucks stood ready to take the slaves to their assigned jobs. However, first the *Musterung* (selection), an exercise in which the life or death of hundreds, if not thousands, was decided. SD officers accompanied by Latvian police would meander among the Jews staring and prodding at random. If you looked back without sufficient deference or simply had a nose they did not like, they would bellow, "A ha! Communist! *Marsch raus*!" With great pomp and ceremony they would viciously beat the "offenders" and drag them away to the Women's Prison. Tortured until the next morning, the half-dead victims were tossed into trucks, taken to the lighthouse dunes, ordered to dig their own graves, and shot.

The lighthouse

There was no shortage of other atrocities invented to humiliate and torment the Jews who gathered each morning at Firehouse Square. SD *Scharführer* Erich Handke especially distinguished himself in such creativity. His favorite was a version of "damned if you do, damned if you don't." Handke would randomly select a small group of Jews and order them to sing the Internationale or Hatikva. If they feigned ignorance of these songs, he would beat them into submission. When they began to sing, Handke would be even more enraged and, with his aides, would beat them to near collapse, whereupon he would then order the Jews to beat each other.

The heavy artillery bombardment during the night of 28 June until early morning the next day left considerable damage in central Libau. Only two synagogues remained intact, the Beit Midrash and the great Choral Synagogue, both on Peter Street. As expected, the Nazis needed to destroy these as well. They could not simply burn them down or blow them up, they were surrounded by many wooden homes filled with Latvians. So the SD arranged for the Jews to tear them down, plank by plank, brick by brick. Among the local people salvaging the planks and bricks, was the apartment house manager, Robert Sedols.

The destruction of the Choral Synagogue provided a new outlet for Handke's creativity. On the morning of 14 July, several bearded Jews were singled out from among those in the Firehouse Square and dragged away to Peter Street. There Handke's accomplices ordered them to put on prayer shawls, take two Torah scrolls each, and return to the Square. When they arrived, Handke's aides unrolled the Torah scrolls and Handke demanded that these bearded Jews walk on the scrolls and proclaim, "Our God is dead, long live Adolph Hitler." The Jews refused and were severely beaten.

Not satisfied, Handke turned to the elderly Chief Rabbi of Libau, Isser Polonski, and made the same demands. Rabbi Polonski walked alongside the scrolls, but not on them. The only words from his lips were *"Sh'ma Yisrael . . . ."* He was, of course, brutalized for his defiance, and was taken unconscious to the Women's Prison along with the other bearded Jews. Later that day, together with scores of others, they were removed to the lighthouse dunes and shot.

The morning theatrics completed, their sadistic souls sated, the SD set about organizing the forced labor: cleaning the streets of rubble, making uniforms in the old Cork Factory, working on the Naval Base, demolishing the synagogues, or covering the mass graves near the lighthouse. While the work was orderly, the brutalities at *Hauptwachplatz* were wild and whimsical, as were "*khapenes*," the snatchings, in the streets. Serendipity ended on 22 July with the arrival from Riga of the Latvian SD Commando under Viktor Arājs. The specter of the blue buses signaled designed escalation.

For three days the bloody *khapenes* were as predictable as the rising sun. For me it began promptly the morning of the 22nd. The previous day we heard rumors that those who went to Firehouse Square for their daily work assignment were taken directly to the Women's Prison. It was 6 AM and I could see from my window that Jews were being snatched and led away by the police. I decided that slavery has no reward. I stayed home. I would spend the next three years as prey giving the slip to predators.

I shared an apartment with my sisters, Ita-Hinde and Shayne Feinstein, and my mother, Malke. And there was my mate, Moishe Hirschhorn. He was the taller, older, wiser and more throaty of the peacock pair who nightly two-stepped in their corner of the housetop. Over coffee and rolls, Moishe and I devised a plan. We would spend our day in the kitchen. If the police began pounding on the door, the women were to create confusion before opening it. By then Moishe and I would be back in the flat's concealed attic. Not twenty minutes had passed, when the police began banging and shouting and threatening to shoot. The women panicked and opened the door quickly, but we managed to scramble to the attic anyway.

The police searched everywhere, but could find no men. "They were taken days ago," Ita-Hinde declared. The police didn't believe her. They thrust Ita-Hinde and Shayne against the parlor wall and menaced them with cocked rifles. The initial panic fled and they revealed nothing. Agitated and anxious to fill their quota of "Zids," they left. From a small portal in the attic, we could see the building next-door. Moments after they left our flat, we saw police snatch up the soccer-playing brothers Aisik and Itzik Josefart, and Jechiel Genson.

After awhile, we left the attic. As we re-entered the flat, Hava Skutelsky appeared at the door behind us, hysterical that her husband, Michael, with whom I once worked as a glazier, had been dragged away in the morning's *Aktion*. "Please, Kalman, you must come with me to save him," she cried, rocking to and fro, wringing her hands without stop. "Hava this is not possible," I implored her, "It is too risky now . . . we will be arrested." After two days of Hava's constant pleading, my mother spoke up: "Go, Kalman, today is the day! If you will help him today, perhaps he will help you tomorrow."

On 24 July my life took a new turn. As soon as Hava and I entered the street, the phantasma of death enveloped us like a fog. In my mind's ear I could hear my mother: *"Az me muz, ken men!"* When you must, you can. We stole from yard to yard, from alley to alley, from doorway to doorway. We could hear the raging police and the wails of the victims. Far off I spied a group of maybe fifteen young Jews heading to Firehouse Square. Facing them was Aaron Schwab, the eminent Jewish doctor, motioning the men to go back home. Wearing a white armband with a red cross, this almost disembodied arm motioned frantically. The young Jews quickly scattered. Dr. Aaron Jacob Schwab would pay dearly for his kindness.

Hava and I continued on our journey to the prison, dodging police leading groups of Jews at gunpoint. We were clearly on a fool's errand. But Hava was delusional: "Be calm, come quicker, they are just leading the men to work." My adrenalin subverted common sense.

"Jude—Hände hoch!" Jew, hands up! I was blindsided by two Fritzen who drove me like an errant cow into a column of Jews on their way to the Women's Prison. Hava was numb, almost catatonic, but untouched. She faded from sight. She did not live to celebrate Chanukah.

Hell has three gates: lust, anger, and greed. The middle one opened to the prison yard. A hard rain of rifle butts and clubs beat upon your head as you ran to join the others packed like tinned fish into 200 square meters. The sounds of the victims' cries and the tormentors' tattoo was *schrecklich*, horrifying! Young men, old men—like chickens come to slaughter. In the chaos, my run of luck pushed me beside Michael Skutelsky, the initial object of my ill-fated sojourn. From behind I whispered in his ear, "Michael!" Surprised, he turned and gasped, *"Oy vay iz mir, Kalman,* you too! *Gottenyu!"* In a perverse way, befitting this nether world, we took pleasure in our mutual discovery. The joy was fleeting.

It was that voice again, the madman Handke: *"Wo ist der Jude mit dem weissen Mantel?* Where is the Jew with the white coat? Suddenly, Handke was dragging Dr. Schwab by the hair, screaming: *"Du Verräter, Spion! Du wirst mir meine Arbeit stören, warte, ich werde mich mit dir abrechnen!"*

You traitor, spy! You dare to disturb my work, wait, I shall get even with you! Handke's henchmen inflicted the well-rehearsed thrashing: the club to Schwab's head buckling him to the ground, then the dragging about the yard by his legs, all the while beating his head until it bursts forth as raw liver, eyeless and boneless. Dr. Schwab pleaded with the cowards to shoot him. They just laughed. Finally, half-dead, he was thrown into the prison basement for later disposal.[6] Blood was in the air and the raptors were ravenous. Aaron Schwab was only the first. This went on for two hours. Ben-Zion Lapidus from Peter Street and others. Screams, blood, Handke's mania, flesh on the floor. Dozens of lifeless lives tossed into the basement. When it was over, the freshly hatched barbers set about cutting everyone's hair with a cross in the center, one by one marking another Jew for crucifixion. The base cruelty was enigmatic. Just weeks ago the policemen and barbers were our neighbors.

While awaiting my Jewmark, not far away stood Fricis Klāsons, erstwhile owner of "Italia" on Korn Street, a rather lively ice cream parlor. Now he was the prison chief. He was walking about selecting a small group of Jewish craftsmen skilled as mechanics, tinsmiths and the like. Among them were Yerachmiel Simson, Schloma and Yossel Schefkind, and Markuse. I thought perhaps Michael and I could join them. I bolted from the crowd and informed Klāsons, "I am a craftsman as well, a glazier." He slapped me so hard I fell back in line. My appeal to the fat German nearby was met with, "*Marsch*, back with the others!" Still, our only chance was to join Yossel's group. I grabbed Michael and we joined the line of eight skilled Jews. Our *chutzpah* went unnoticed. Individually, each of the others was called before a seated Latvian woman who properly registered them and told them to leave the prison. As they gathered by the gate, the rather puckish adolescent, Efraim Levenson, bolted from the packed prisoners and joined the exodus of the skilled with impunity. The guard seemed to look the other way. Michael and I remained. Knowing the woman would not call our names, I approached her with considerable glibness.

"Who are you? What do you want? You're not on the list."

"Linkimer," I answered calmly.

"Which Linkimer?" She was quite agitated.

"No need for a fuss, dear lady, we are glaziers—Kalman Linkimer and Michael Skutelsky."

"Where are your instruments, if you are a glazier?"

"At work," I responded, "but perhaps I have a diamond in my pocket." I carefully searched for what I did not have. "I am sorry, the diamond is at work as well."

"So you are a glazier," she said with dismissive disdain. "We all know what kind of glazier you *really* are!"

"We work together," Michael assured her, and he showed her his diamond. The woman softened. She registered us and we emerged from Sheol. With stealth and bribery we made our way home. Moma and Hava Skutlesky shuddered at the sight of us. Hope, no longer an emotion, was now an illusion.

Still, there were many Jews who would not relinquish the ghost of German civility. They were convinced that those arrested were merely being sent to forced labor outside of Libau. As proof they would proudly show the letters received from husbands, fathers, brothers, sons. The police who delivered these missives were always most pleased to accept large bundles for delivery to the "workers." Of course this was a ruse. The letters were coerced before the slaughter.

Such a letter was delivered to my sister, Shayne. It was from her husband Martin Feinstein, a watchmaker. The note was rather short, feebly written in Latvian not Yiddish: "I am with 250 other Jewish men 50 km east of Libau. We are doing roadwork. I am fine. Send money, clothes, and white underwear." *White underwear*, a shroud, was our prearranged metaphor: no work, only death! Awakening from self-delusion was painful for hundreds of families; it was slow in coming and not without haunting doubts. I shall always recall the agony of my dear friend, Aaron Vesterman, when he came to believe without reservation in the true fate of his brothers, Baruch and Raphael. He was a bird without song, an artist without hands, a soul vaporized.

The day following our return home, Michael and I resumed work at the destroyed Kursa Watch Factory, digging burned machines and watches out of the rubble. We had begun as a work detail of about 50. On 25 July only nine of us remained: Morduch Waisfeld, Zev Grinfeld, Plutzes, Scholem Wulfson, Nachman Tevelov, Ruben Gutman, Aaron Imerman, Michael Skutelsky and I. We had not been there an hour when five policemen arrived. "On the truck, all of you. Take your shovels. Quickly!" We were taken to Skede, about 10 km north of Libau on the seashore. They marched us several kilometers through the forest until we arrived at a very large clearing overlooking the Baltic. The debris of a fierce battle was everywhere. Artillery in large bunkers were regularly placed. Munitions, empty artillery shells, mines and dead dogs were strewn about.

Soon enough an SD officer ordered us to dig a large pit. All of us froze, certain of our imminent death. Nachman, Aaron, and I had decided to scatter, each in a different direction. Our taut bodies and searching eyes revealed our intention. "If one of you runs, all of you will be shot!" bellowed a German soldier. Sensing our mistrust, the SD officer assured us we would simply be burying the detritus of war. And so we did, until the evening.

After awhile a truck arrived to take us back to Libau. Quietly, the driver confided that this day had been particularly bloody in town, we needed to be exceptionally cautious. Our escorts were two young German sailors, both decent. They agreed to sheppard us through town with raised rifles, making it seem as though we were seized Jews on our way to prison. Adorning their raincoats to hide their rank and unit, they eventually brought each of us to our home. Everywhere we passed Jews shoulder to shoulder, faces to the wall, hands over their heads. At the last, were Ruben, Michael and myself. As we approached our homes, we ran afoul of a sizable police *Aktion*. The sailors agreed to lead us further to calmer streets. Ruben and Michael quickly ran off together, and I took refuge in Chaim Sachs' apartment on Tomas Street.

Chaim was witless. There he stood, a rucksack across his right shoulder, crammed with socks, shirts and food. An accountant by trade, careful and precise and thoughtful, he had become reckless. Such impetuosity was endemic.

"Chaim, what are you thinking?" I bellowed.

"I've prepared to leave for work."

"To work? There is no work! Only slaughter! Chaim, I dug the graves myself."

"Tomorrow, then, I shall go to the Firehouse Square," Chaim calmly announced. "It will not be pleasant but at days end I shall return to Sophie and our girls."

One of the girls, Rosa, stood watch downstairs, ready to signal danger's approach. Rosa was a tall, thin, lovely girl of 18, intelligent and witty. Though eleven years her senior, I found her maturity engaging. That night she was an early warning as I encamped by an open window, ready to flee upon her signal.

"Chaim, listen, yesterday Michael Skutelsky and I were at the Square, trapped in Handke's hell! Only *chutzpah* and luck brought me here tonight. Chaim, *hof oif nissim noz farloz zich nit oif a nes*. Hope for miracles but don't rely on one!"

Chaim silently avoided my eyes. He put down his sack and withdrew to his bedroom. No answer was also an answer. The night was dark and quiet, a new moon. Dawn brought Chaim's folly. Together with the pharmacist Israelson, he lumbered to the Square, Rosa scouting ahead and I behind in the shadows. The two "workers" entered the Square; Rosa and I separately meandered to our homes. It was the 26th of July, the 1st of Av, Chaim's last day.

For Rosa, Miriam and their mother, Sophie, life was now more than uncertain on Tomas Street, it was delusional. Rosa cleaned gardens for the Germans; Sophie and 8 year old Miriam remained at the flat to affect domesticity, all the while certain that Chaim toiled at forced labor. Mrs. Kronberg, an elderly Baltic German, brought food to the Sachs family, as she did for other Jewish families on Tomas. She even managed already forgotten delicacies: marinated mushrooms, cookies, cakes.

Sophie worried about Chaim's health. It was August, but perhaps he was not warm enough. "Rosa, take this coat to the prison." Or, perhaps he was too warm. "Rosa, take these sandals to the prison." Concerned for her father, she would journey to the Women's Prison, ring the bell, and the guard would admonish her to make contact with reality and quickly run home. Sophie and Rosa knew the truth of Chaim's fate, but they had rather not believe it.

Perhaps the capstone of July 1941, *ne plus ultra* as we were taught in Latin class, was the murder of Leib Soloveichik. Leib was a fine man about 60 years of age who owned a shoe shop near the Rose Garden in central Libau. He had several children, the youngest being Mordechai, or Max as they called him. Max had been preparing for his Bar Mitzvah for over a year. Regularly, after school, he went to the *cheder* to study Torah and Haftorah with Rabbi Michelson. But now the synagogues lay in ruin and Jewish religious practice was dangerous. Nevertheless, his veiled Bar Mitzvah was scheduled for Thursday, 31 July, in the family flat. All was well-prepared and a small number of close family and trusted friends were invited. Thus, before all and with some joy, did Max celebrate the transition to adult moral responsibility. Leib blessed Max in a near whisper: "*Barukh shepatrani me-onsho shel zeh*." Praise God who has released me from the responsibility of my son! A small toast to Max, a little schnapps, some bread, a few cookies. And then a knock on the door. The Soloveichiks were betrayed. The Latvian police grabbed Leib, marched him out of the flat, down the stairs and out to the front of the building. There they pushed him against the wall, shot him in the head, threw his lifeless body on a waiting cart, and promptly departed. Max saw it all from his bedroom window. God is most often ironic these days.

Inexplicably, as July ended, so did the mass murders. For nearly two months hence, only little horrors that defined the character of the Germans and their Latvian volunteers. None more so than the fate of Adolph Salmonson on Tisha B'Av. Ada, 12, lived with his mother, Musja. This day he strolled on the sidewalk, not in the street with the horses, as required. Before long he was facing an SD officer not 30 meters away. Ada turned and ran. The officer pursued him, threatening to shoot. Ada, young and agile, had little trouble putting great distance between himself and the angry officer. As he neared home, he was certain of his escape . . . . until a Latvian policeman laid hold of him. Arrested, he was taken to the Women's Prison. Days later he was dead.

The "quiet" was shattered at the end of September, precisely on Rosh Hashanah. In an organized *Aktion*, Latvian police and German SD simultaneously raided several workshops and factories where Jewish women labored. The women were packed into *khapoyto*, the snatching vans. This day, Rosh Hashanah, marked the moment women and children were consigned the same fate as the men. All illusions that German culture, Libau's culture, would not countenance the murder of women and children, crumbled like the sands of Skede.

Even *alte Juden* were not unsubject. All the synagogues destroyed, so it was that scores of men, hobbled by age and circumstance, gathered in homes about the city to *daven* the Yom Kippur prayers and remember dead family and friends. From one home and then another, these elderly men, each still wearing his tallis, were herded in the *khapoyto*. Hundreds of *alte Juden* did not live to hear the sound of the *shofar* at nightfall.

It became clear that Rosh Hashanah and Yom Kippur were special days for the Nazis as well. But, then again, so was Chanukah.

HAPPY CHANUKAH: 15 DECEMBER 1941

You looked all over hell for a sign, any sign. You poked around, pried about. Ransacked, rummaged, scoured, and combed. You stalked every conversation, cataloged every whisper. To stay alive you have always to take the temperature, listen to the wind, and know the signs. At the dawn of December there came a sign: whole companies of Latvian police with shovels in their hands drove north from Libau in the early morning. They did not return until nightfall. The dunes of Skede soon became our focus.

The Baltic beach at Skede is about 10 kilometers north of Libau. In years past, the Latvian army used the dunes as a practice range. There were military barracks for an artillery battalion and a wooden stable for their horses. Not a hundred meters from the now empty stable, nearby the shoreline, the Latvian police were preparing killing ditches of varying sizes: 50 x 4 meters, 100 x 5 meters, 250 x 8 meters. On Chanukah these ditches would inter nearly 3000 Jewish men, women and children, more than two thirds of the remaining Libauer Jews.

Certainly, weeks earlier you could only guess at the meaning of trucks full of police with shovels. Still, you sensed death on a grand scale. It had become more and more difficult to hide. Trust was long-lost. Shortly after the Yom Kippur murders, Moishe and I fell out over my decision to put myself in the hands of the goldsmith Ducmanis, a close and long time Latvian acquaintance of mine. Ducmanis and I shared political sympathies. Before the Germans arrived, he was a member of the Communist underground, an enthusiastic Stalinist. Ducmanis, expressing concern for my fate, promised to help me throw-in with the partisans. In actuality, his intent was to betray my trust. On the evening I was to meet with two partisans at Ducmanis' flat, two SD men awaited my arrival. My *comrade* had set a trap for me. Fortunately, my friend Mordechai Nai had a flat in the same building. As I approached from the street, Mota warned me off. It was now more clear than ever that options were retreating with the tide.

I recall that the American poet, Emily Dickinson, taught us that suspense is more hostile than death, for death cannot increase but suspense does not conclude. Such was our conundrum: the bow too tensely strung is easily broken; the bow too loosely strung is wholly feeble. Buck up, you admonished yourself.

Latvian police with shovels were always ill-omened. You sought to confirm your suspicion that the coming dread might be your last. You tapped your usual sources, even policemen you knew to be sympathetic. Nothing. A close friend, David Zivcon, was one of many Jews who worked for the German SD as electricians, mechanics, glaciers and at all manner of other skills. David was particularly gifted and was assigned the most complex tasks. There was a grudging respect for his extraordinary abilities, and this brought him access to important SD officers. So much so that he had been able to ransom many people from death—a life could be exchanged for a Leica camera! Despite David's wire pulling, he learned nothing about the men with shovels.

In the evening after work and dinner, it had become my habit to remove my yellow patches, defy the curfew, and walk to David Zivcon's flat two blocks away. There he had hidden the *sanctum sanctorum*, the holy of holies . . . the radio. Slowly stealing parts from the SD, David built it himself. Night after night the BBC supplied hope. We eagerly followed the battle for Moscow. By November's end, the Germans had camped within twenty to thirty miles of the city on three sides—north, south and west. December 1 they began their all-out assault. Within a week, the Germans had been stopped everywhere along the 200 mile front around Moscow; General Zhukov commanded 100 divisions in a savage counterattack. The myth of German invincibility was crushed! On December 8 a ray of light pierced the darkness.

It was our custom that whoever heard a bit of good news about "the front," would rush to share the joy with friends. On this evening I ran from David's to Voldemar Dolin's flat on Bade Street. At this teacher's home sat the usual gathering: Dr. Ber Grinman, director of the Jewish high school; Jenny Sebba, the dentist; Nina Rapoport and her mother, Rosa. As I passed through the front door, I deflated. Anguish hovered on the wings of despair. There was a sense of fear. All was known. Rosa Rapoport, whose husband Moshe was murdered in the July *Aktion*, had learned from a Latvian policeman of long acquaintance that there was soon to be the *Grosse Aktion*. The ditches at Skede were to be our new home. As with the other towns and villages of Kurland, Libau was to be *Judenrein*, Jewless!

Mrs. Rapoport smashed our idols of illusion. For in truth we already knew, or should have known. Remember those young men with sculpted bodies and wildly erect bearing, the Jewish lads who passed through Libau maybe five years earlier on their way to Palestine. Do you not recall their stories and the "Brown Book" with the photographs of what befell Jacob's children in Germany, the anguish of soul and torment of body! Comfort and riches left us looking out the window. In but a day, both were lost forever. All that remained was Jeremiah's hollow promise: "He shall curse them and shall make them a shame among all the nations." So you see, in almost unearthly calm you have always to calculate your survival, for you are obligated to be the thin end of the wedge, to bear witness and exact revenge.

Within days of Mrs. Rapoport's alarm, on Saturday, December 13, an announcement appeared in the Latvian newspaper, *Kurzemes Vards*: "Jews are forbidden to leave their homes on Monday, December 15 and Tuesday, December 16. Station Chief of SS and Police, Dr. Emil Dietrich." Dr. Dietrich had resolved to give the remaining Jews of Libau a Chanukah present—an outing to the beach at Skede. There, whole families could undress and stand together at the precipice, looking out upon the sea, imagining their imminent arrival in Heaven.

There were, of course, exceptions. To be sure, all Jews were filthy swine, but some were a bit less filthy than others. These were the skilled craftsmen with special permits from the Gestapo, and often their families as well. I held such a permit. Indeed, I was working for Dr. Dietrich. There were about 40 of us, men and women, who were building Dietrich's personal *Luftschutzkeller* [bomb shelter]. On that fateful Saturday morning, Emil the clown devised an entertainment for us. After all, if you were not to be killed just yet, at the least you should experience a bit of anxiety: *Di katz shpilt zikh mit der moyz, ober oplozn lozt zi zi nit op* (The cat plays with the mouse, but never lets it get away).

Dietrich sent his lieutenant to announce that as of tomorrow only 8 would remain at the *Luftschutzkeller* site, the rest were needed elsewhere. By now it was easy for us to define "elsewhere." When he asked for volunteers for "elsewhere," there were none. Alternatively, we decided to draw lots from the cap of one of us. We made 40 lots, eight of which had the number "8" inscribed. Each worker was to draw a lot. About midway in the drawing, it was halted by the lieutenant. He apologized for his mistake, but the eight workers were actually for "elsewhere" and the others would continue constructing the *Luftschutzkeller.* The drawing resumed for several minutes and the German halted it again. This time he deeply apologized, but he had forgotten the rules—Jews were not permitted to draw lots. All chosen lots needed to be returned to the hat and he would draw all forty. This sadistic *divertissement* went on for several hours, until the notice arrived informing us that the whole affair was a great misunderstanding and we were all to remain working at the *Luftschutzkeller* until it was complete.

As we endured Dietrich's amusement that Saturday afternoon, Jews were in a panic throughout Libau. Many searched for safe places to hide, others attempted to flee, and still others sought out protection from Latvian friends of influence, or at least those married to such. For most, no fruit was borne. In the end, some chose suicide by turning on the gas stove, even entire families. Berman, the pharmacist, and his wife chose Veronal, a fashionable sedative. This white crystalline powder was now much coveted. Odorless with only a slightly bitter taste, Veronal induces a soft, floating, somewhat hypnotic effect. Ten, twelve grams will surely bring on death, an exit that is slow and pleasant, even euphoric.

On Sunday evening, December 14, the first night of Chanukah, my dear friend Aaron Vesterman did not light a candle. Instead he put on his finest coat, new shoes and a fedora. Without his yellow stars, he strolled the sidewalks of the city. From time to time, there passed by trucks with pickled policemen. The *shikkers* sang anti-semitic songs in Latvian. These Latvian men had finally found their balls, willing to face danger and expose the cowardice of naked women and children.

Aaron walked the streets until 9 o'clock, the start of curfew. A cold rain was falling. He stood alone. Unable to return to his flat, he took shelter in the cellar of a bombed-out house on the corner of Korn and Post. Night was timeless, morning a dodge. After a tract of time the future arrived, cold and numb like Aaron's fingers and toes.

The cloud gray dawn was wet and frigid. Aaron emerged from the cellar frostnipped. Collar and hat carefully postured against the elements, he trudged upon the sidewalk, directed to the park. Aaron was not alone. Men, women, and children carrying small bundles were being herded to the Women's Prison by swaggering Latvian police. No one seemed to notice Aaron, even as he slowed to give ear to the desperate chatter of doomed Jews, sometimes conversation, more often soliloquy.

Among the many Aaron glimpsed, was Rosa Sachs, her mother, and her sister Miriam. As it happened, their fate on this day was quite the exception. *Tante* Mina, Mrs. Sachs' sister, was not arrested with the others. Indeed, she was a close acquaintance of Emma Kronbergs, a very special member of the Libau Latvian SD. Dear Mrs. Kronbergs was the translator, interpreter, and lover of SS *Untersturmführer* Wolfgang Kügler, the Libau German SD chief. Kügler commanded all in Libau; he could be bribed, if done properly. Emma drew upon her intimacy with Wolfgang to occasionally help Jews of her acquaintance. Mina rang up Emma. Before long Handke not only released Rosa, Miriam and their mother from the prison, but he ordered two Germans to drive them back to their flat. Handke saw no need not to be solicitous of Emma, this was merely a stay of execution.

Aaron made it to the park where he exercised a bit, regaining some feeling and limberness in his extremities. It was now later in the morning. The rain and cold had eased. Aaron became increasingly anxious about his brother Leo and his wife. He resolved to return to the flat the three had shared. The windows of the building were almost all lit. As he neared the front door, he heard the Latvian police barking. In an instant, he retired from sight behind a large gate across the street. Before long, Aaron watched a dozen or so Jews, even the obviously ill, being driven away from the house. There was little Molly Blumberg crying, "Papa, I don't want to go!" Pesach, her father, tried to assure her, "Come, *shayne maidel*, today is Chanukah. A miracle will happen!"

Perhaps thirty minutes passed and all was silent. Aaron entered the building. Searching about, he found no one. Aaron readied himself to enter his shared flat. The door was not entirely closed. He quietly pushed it open and softly advanced. "Who's there?" called his brother Leo. He and his wife had not been taken away. Both were among those working on Dietrich's *Luftschutzkeller*. They were part of the water pump team. Libau being a port city on the mighty Baltic Sea, the water table was high. So day and night water had to be pumped out in order to pour the concrete for the bomb shelter. As the three rejoiced in reunion, others entered the flat. They froze, open-mouthed. It was Aaron's sister, Frieda, and her child. Without reason, the Chanukah *Aktion* had passed over them.

Nearly 3000 others were not so fortunate. There was Mirele Polonski, the frail wife of Rabbi Isser who was murdered by Handke in July. There was the family of Chaim Epstein, the banker exiled by the Soviets: Malka, 18, Max, 15, Aaron, 11 and their mother Emma. There was Fanny Jacobson, the running champion of Latvia, and her sister Dora. There was Zelda Purve, an accountant at the "Kursa" watch factory, and her mother Fruma-Yetta. There was Hava Skutelsky, my dear friend Michael's wife. And there was Moishe Hirschhorn, my erstwhile mate who insisted on fate.

And, then, there was Leib-Judel (Julius) and Muscha Hirschberg, my comrade Zelig's uncle and aunt. Julius was like a father to Zelig, taking care of his family after Zelig's father, Julius' brother Jacob, walked out the door and vanished. It was Julius who supported Zelig's enthusiasms like Maccabee soccer, and gave him an important job in his wholesale meat business. And now Uncle Judel and Aunt Muscha are sprawled ditch dead at Skede. Perhaps they needed help. It was expected that after their brains spewed forth from above their eyes, they would simply twitch and jiggle hindward into the pit. But Jews are a stiff-necked people, often ungrateful for a day at the beach. They would just slump in place. For these Jews there was the "kicker."

The mass murder continued through the first three days of Chanukah. Just before the fourth candle would have been lit, the *Aktion* drew to a close. Those who stayed in the shadows for three days evaded death. Most relied on cunning, *chutzpah*, and luck. Some, like Efraim Neuberger and his mother, found an angel in unexpected places. In their case his name was Navy Captain Friedrich Kroll, supervisor of the Navy Uniform Warehouse, *Marine-Bekleidungskammer*, in the old Cork Factory. Shayne and Efraim had decided on the first night of Chanukah to gather up some food and water and take themselves to the cellar of the bombed-out building next to theirs. When all seemed quiet by mid-morning, they returned to their flat. Shayne soon learned from a Latvian neighbor that Kroll was protecting all his laborers. Shayne and Efraim had been working at the Navy Warehouse for some time. A walk to the old Cork Factory was risky, no more so than holding one's breath at home. So they journeyed transpicuously to Kroll's Warehouse and joined a large number of other Jews, some gleaned directly from prison. For three bloody days Kroll permitted no one to work evil on "my Jews."

Now a strange quiet girdled Libau. Slowly the Jews emerged from their lairs. There was little more than a thousand of us remaining. By Chanukah's end all of us resumed our assigned jobs. Thousands were swallowed at Skede but murder did not have a face, that is until David Zivcon's discovery.

David, I mentioned before, was one of those Jews with technical skills highly valued by the German SD. David was an electrician who had evolved into a talented radio technician. One late December day, SS-*Scharführer* Karl-Emil Strott summoned David to his flat and ordered him to install an electric outlet near a dresser mirror. As he was about to complete the task, David noticed a key left in the lock of a drawer. Curious about the contents, he opened it.

There it was, a roll of developed film. "Let's see what girls Strott has photographed this time," he thought, as he lifted the negatives before the light. David was shaken, his lips dried, his eyes moistened. The lens had clinically captured the condemnation of the helpless at Skede. He looked at his watch. It was 2 o'clock, the precise moment when Germans take their lunch. As always, they will remain in the dining room until 4.

David rushed downstairs to his friend, Pesach-Meir Stein, who worked in the photo lab. Not thirty minutes later, he strung a dozen wet prints to dry.... Hundreds of people in a ditch. Women stripped naked, in passage to execution. Some David knew—Fanny Jacobson, Mia Epstein. Old men and children confused, awaiting death. After awhile he placed the dry prints in a metal box, soldered it shut, and secreted it behind a loose brick in a wall of the auto repair pit. By 3:30 the roll of negatives was back in the drawer, the key back in its lock. It fell to David to bear witness. Heine's illusory claim that humans are the "aristocrat amongst the animals" was well and truly foreclosed, evidenced, as it were, in Meir Halevy's memorial poem, Amber Footstones....

Baltic beaches evince
mighty confrontation:
adamantine earth
abutting wave and tide.
Harmonic intermezzos unshroud
the sun glistened wet sand
comfortably enveloping
golden glint signals tossed
in a war of elements.
With each triumphant arrival
of the ceaseless future,
dune grasses sing
of Avraham, Yitzak, and Yakov,
of Sarah, Rivka, Rachel, and Leah,
of all those bone-cold
in their moonless night.
And those who walk
through the vast valley
of the shadow of death
now presciently chant elegiac:
Az me grubt a grub far yenem,
falt men alain arein!

---

*If you dig a ditch for someone else, you fall in it yourself!

Terror Has No Diary | 27

THE GHETTO

By February 1942, Wolfgang Kügler determined there were still too many Jews for the planned ghetto . . . . about three hundred too many. The *khapenes* resumed, and Jews were snatched up daily. In the evenings, small groups of ten or fifteen were taken as usual to the Women's Prison. Since there were several unusually large snowfalls during these weeks, the Jews were transported to Skede in horsedrawn sleighs. They were made to kneel with their hands tied behind their backs and their heads on the floor, arriving in Skede half-conscious from the head-knocking journey. The slaughter was all the more efficient.

Those who had somewhere to hide quickly disappeared. I slipped away with my mother and sisters to my brother Meier and his wife, Rosa. With other families in the building, he had prepared a large, concealed basement room that was accessed through a trapdoor in Ita Bernitz's flat. So it was that we vanished: the Linkimers; Jankel Zinn, the shoemaker, his wife Mina, and daughter Etta; Yeta and her children, Itzik and Sheva; Ita Bernitz; Rosa Neuburger and her youngsters, Lipman and Getzel. Even the chic Rosa Sachs joined us at the last moment. Bizarre happenstance had driven her near our flat *in extremis*. The police smashed and ransacked every flat but found no one. Their consolation? All they could carry away with two hands.

Though the February *Aktion* slaughtered 200 Jews, there remained too many for the projected ghetto. Still, there was quiet for some weeks. You could concentrate on ordinary living, such as it was, and on your historical enemies. March 3 was Purim. I imagined David Zivcon as Mordecai, Rosa Sachs as Esther, and Handke as the wicked Hamen. *Pesach* arrived on Thursday night, April 2, without matzah. There were more than four questions, and several answers to each question. You were a slave to Kügler in Libau, but God had not smote the Germans and set you free. Perhaps you were not a slave long enough? The answer came soon enough. A week after *Pesach*, there was another *Aktion* to cull the numbers to ghetto size. Among 50 or so others, Ita Bernitz and Rosa Neuburger were chanced upon and murdered. Now at less than 800, mostly women and children, we could fit neatly into our quadrangular cage.

By April's end, the Libau newspaper, *Kurzemes Vards*, noted: "The Jewish problem in Libau is completely solved. We are rid of the Jews.

However, should we from time to time stumble upon a Jew, we are obliged to show him the place he deserves." A month hence, the newspaper acknowledged that *Judenrein* was not quite accurate: "It is necessary to be rid of the enduring Jews among us." This was a preamble to the published order requiring all Jews to move to a ghetto by 1 July.

In the month that remained before entry, we were forced to prepare our prison. Under Kügler's direction, a *Judenrat* had been formed as a "governing" council. At the head was Solomon Israelit, a distinguished and respected businessman in his 50s. Assisting him was Menashe Kaganski, a young lawyer about 35. All Jews were required to register with the *Judenrat*, and it was they who assigned each a dwelling place.

The Libau Ghetto was about one rectangular city block. It was bounded by Herren, Garten, Espen and Waisenhaus Streets. There were about a dozen tumbledown buildings, mostly two stories, mostly wood. They were entirely unoccupied; the Latvians had left months earlier to occupy the flats of exterminated Jews. In the evening, after the usual forced labor, we Jews prepared the ghetto. Fortunately, most of the surviving men were skilled craftsmen of one sort or another. We began by building a barbed wire fence around the perimeter, as would befit a ghetto. The condition of the flats were dismal, so we spent most of the month of June cleaning and repairing everything.

Johanna Sedols and daughters   **Robert Sedols**

Among the chief foremen, was my dear friend David Zivcon, the *Über-Jew* of the German SD. Late one fog-chilled evening in June, David went to see his Latvian friend, the onetime sailor, Robert Sedols. They had been close since childhood. Self-control and risk taking was their bond. Robert was a rather handsome, rugged-looking man of about 35. He worked as the building manager and janitor at 14 Kauf Street. When David arrived long past curfew in his threadbare coat and workman's cap pulled down about his eyes, Johanna Sedols was shocked. "Aren't you afraid!" she shrieked in place of a greeting.

"Afraid . . . . What should I be afraid of. Didn't you see the notice? The first of July all of us will be penned in a ghetto. Use your imagination. How long do you think the Fritzen intend to take care of 800 hapless Jews?"

"Bastards," Robert sharply declared. "Listen, David, let's go to the cellar . . . I have an idea and I need your thoughts. Anna, could you prepare something for David? Surely he's hungry."

Robert lit a candle and they carefully navigated the old wooden steps of the substructure. The cellar was a maze, with many recesses, and all sorts of junk tossed about. At a spot where three walls formed a niche, Robert stopped and pointed: "Look, if we build a fourth wall here we'll have an isolated room. Only a floor plan and careful inspection could betray this deception. We'll use those bricks piled over there. They're the holy bricks of the Choral Synagogue. I collected them last July."

David was stunned by the offer. He was more stunned by the symbolism. He was a communist, an anti-fascist, an atheist, but at the last he could be saved by the synagogue, his grandfather's *shul*. "It seems I am a Jew," he mused in silence. Bricks burnished by fervent prayer now radiated a common destiny.

After some moments, he reconnected with Robert, "This is a really fine idea, but how do we go in?"

"Do you see the workbench? Under it we can make a small hatch, just big enough to crawl through, and then camouflage it with various odds and ends."

"Then we'll have to be quick about it. Once we are locked in the ghetto, I won't be able to help you."

"Not to worry. You only need run electric wires under the plaster, I'll do the rest."

"Robert, frankly I'm puzzled. Why do you want to involve yourself in such dangerous business. What about Johanna and the girls?"

"Sailors are not afraid of risk," was his terse and only response. Robert disliked idle chatter, explanations, and second guessing. A decision was a decision, no turning aside. This decision was for David and his Jewish comrades. It was for the Bolshevik future he and Johanna longed for, a tribute to her father.

On the first day bombs fell on Libau, Robert had swiftly arranged to have Johanna and their daughters, Irida and Indra, transported 50 km from the city to Asīte, where Johanna's parents lived. Weeks later, returning to his flat one evening after a day of scavenging, he was surprised to find Johanna sitting at the kitchen table. All looked tidy again, and the girls were asleep in their beds. Johanna looked spent.

"So, how was your visit?" Robert asked almost rhetorically.

"Father has been arrested," was Johanna's grim response.

The news had not shocked Robert. Among the bourgeoisie of Asīte, Zanis Preiss was reviled as the "Red." Zanis was a tough, broad-shouldered farmer whose hands seemed never to rest. From sunup to sundown, he battled the poor earth of his small, swampy farm. A bushel of grain here, a bale of hay there. From the first months of Soviet domination in 1940, Zanis was devoted to raising Latvian communism. He was an enthusiastic speech maker and member of the land use commission, a group whose job it was to unmask the tricks of wealthy farmers and more equitably divide the land, or as these prosperous farmers viewed it, confiscate their private property.

Robert liked Zanis from the first, even if he did not always share his enthusiasm for politics. Zanis would often admonish him, in a teasing sort of way, "Once life grabs you, and thoroughly mashes you, your eyes will open to the beauty of socialism." Slowly they did. What Robert had seen on the streets of Libau these weeks had solidified it. And then the arrest of his old father-in-law, a man who never hurt anyone.

"How did it happen?" asked Robert.

"All was tranquil. We had no idea the Fascists had come near us. But then Bērzins appeared in an *aizsargi* (civil guard) uniform with the new red and white armband, you know the ones supplied by the Gestapo. He had a rifle in his hand and he walked about with disdain. Remember

Bērzins? Father was given some of his land by the commission. We clearly understood. Father immediately hid in the forest, but for days no one came to the farm. Father decided the danger had passed and he returned home. It was a trap. That night, drunk, they crashed through the front door screaming, 'Say your prayers, you Red scum . . . soon you will rot in a pit.'"

"Where did they take him?"

"To the cellar of the parish office. Mother went there, hoping to leave some bread and milk for Father, but they shoved her aside with rifle butts. Yesterday we learned that Father and his comrades were sent here, to Libau. Mother asked me to return to ask for your help in finding him."

"I will try," Robert promised, all the while having visions of the prisoners being herded into the Women's Prison.

The next morning he found himself embedded in a crowd of desperate women holding parcels for their husbands, fathers, sons. The guard room door opened and there emerged a short, barrel-chested German with disgust in his eyes. He pushed aside the women and crossed the street. Just then he spied Robert in the crowd.

"Haven't we met before?" he demanded.

"A few years ago," Robert answered. "Copenhagen to Rostock. Olsen and Sons. You were boatswain, I was sailor."

"Ha, sure . . . So now we meet again. Why are you standing here with all these whores?"

"An acquaintance mistakenly got into trouble," Robert slowly responded, noting the disappearance of the friendly smile from the fascist's face.

"Nobody gets here by mistake. You're not one of those Reds, are you? No . . . you're too smart for that. Reds, Jews . . . one, two, three, against the wall. Finished."

"Anna, I'm not hopeful," Robert announced upon his return home.

Nearly a year had passed when David visited them that June evening when they hatched the secret shelter. Zanis Preiss, Johanna's father and Robert's beloved father-in-law, was still in prison. They were more politically committed than ever.

Libau ghetto houses

Precisely on schedule, on 1 July 1942, the remnant of Libau's Jews found themselves relocated within the barbed-wired, and rather grim, ghetto. Each to his or her assigned dwelling place. The quota was 4 square meters per Jew, and so several families had to crowd into a single flat. Partitions had been erected to provide each family a private corner. It was intimate, and it was your concluding days of family life. But for a few in hiding, we were all there. All that remained of Jewish life, indeed Jew-life, was concentrated in a square city block. In just one year, 7000 became 800, and a century-old social contract was in shreds.

L'dor v'dor, from generation to generation, they walked through the gates. There was Max Soloveichik, a year beyond his tragic bar mitzvah, and his mother Sarah. Each with a simple bundle of clothes and personal things, they settled into a room shared with an odd couple who spoke little and smoked much. The only furniture for Max and Sarah was a bed, not even a chair. There was Efraim Neuberger, but a few months from his imagined bar mitzvah, and his mother Shayne. They crowded into a single room with two other women and three children. And then there was the romantic, Rosa Sachs, her sister Miriam, and her mother Sophie. They shared a room with several surviving members of their extended family. Such a familial arrangement proved less tense than the others. When not working, Rosa was with a novel, or her boyfriend

Leibl Schalminis, a Jewish ghetto policeman, or sometimes both. Miriam attended the one room ghetto grade school. Sophie Sachs tended the ghetto vegetable garden and improvised one hundred ways to cook a potato, even as cake.

Among the others, were the families of comrades. I arrived with my 65 year-old mother, my sisters, my brother Meir, and his wife Rosa. David Zivcon entered the ghetto with his wife Henni, his mother Sarah, and his mother-in-law Tzilla Friedlander. Zelig Hirschberg came with his mother Sarah, brother Yudel, and sister Rachel. Michael Skutelsky entered with his wife Hilde Zik. They recently married in the only way one could in the last year, Biblically. Michael's wife, Hava, was executed in the December *Aktion*; Hilde's husband, Mendel, had been murdered in the July *Aktion*. Michael and Hilde shared a flat with my brother, Meir, and his wife. Schmerl Skutelsky, no relation to Michael, arrived with his wife Henni and their three handsome sons. Riva Zivcon, David's cousin by marriage, came with her beautiful 2 year old daughter, Ada; Riva's husband, Leo, was murdered in the July *Aktion*, two months before Ada's first birthday. Yosl Mandelstamm arrived with his wife, Nechama, and their 4 year old son. Misha Libauer entered with his wife, Hani, and their 5 year old son, Avram. Aaron Vesterman came alone. He was accommodated in the *Junggesellen-Heim*, the bachelors' hostel. It was a large room with two dozen or more beds. There were some true bachelors like Aaron, but most were men whose families had been murdered while they were at forced labor during an *Aktion*. They had been spared, for the moment, because they were skilled craftsmen.

The ghetto was guarded by Latvian police in black uniforms. Over all was Ghetto Commandant Franz Kerscher, a fat man in his 40s who, compared to Handke and the others, could be described as benevolent. The daily routine was quickly set: up at 5 AM, off to work by 7 AM, and back from work at 7 PM. With few exceptions, everyone from age 12 had to work at hard labor, digging trenches, loading ships, or continuing with jobs they had before entering the ghetto. Each day a small group of Jews were transported to the German SD headquarters, including David Zivcon, Schmerl and Michael Skutelsky, Misha Libauer, and Yosl Mandelstamm. Each evening when you returned from work, you were counted and searched at the gate. Possession of contraband was a death sentence, but this too could be arbitrary.

The official ration was slight, a mere 215 grams of bread per day for each Jew. Not many of us lived on this meager allotment alone. When out to work, you bartered your remaining valuables for food with the Latvians. Some, like Sarah Soloveichik, had made prior arrangements with their sympathetic Latvian neighbors and had already given them the jewelry and silver. Most engaged an *ad hoc* daily exchange with strangers eager to obtain something valuable from the Jews. In this way, food was smuggled in daily and, with facilitation by Israelit and the *Judenrat*, Commandant Kerscher was bribed not to interrupt its passage.

Early on, Robert Sedols visited the ghetto often. As a building manager, he was permitted to requisition the workshop to make keys and repair tools and other mechanical things. Each visit, Robert would pass through the gates with a large suitcase, a friendly wave to and from the guards, and his standard declaration: "Damned Jews, they all should've been shot long ago!" Inside the workshop he unloaded the bread. Then out he came with last week's "repairs," and through the gates with the same curses.

SD Headquarters

David was always a kilometer away at the SD headquarters. Still, he was concerned that Robert's frequent visits might soon arouse suspicions. David asked me to pass a message to Robert, that he needn't come so often, for David had made other arrangements for additional food. He had cultivated a relationship with a most trustworthy fellow, the SD horse groomer. Trofim Torbik was a Russian prisoner of war. This short, disheveled man with little hair and a reddish-brown stubble, had a head that seemed twice as tall as it did wide and bug eyes that looked east and west simultaneously. Publicly quiet and calm, the Germans thought him a simpleton. David, and others who befriended him, privately knew otherwise. Trofim was quick-witted, fond of cutting humor, and especially hateful of his captors.

David made a rather sensible suggestion to his SD masters. They should raise pigs for feasting and feed them with garbage from the ghetto. He recommended Trofim as the perfect "imbecile" to transport all this garbage. The Germans thought this a splendid idea. So that is how Trofim and his two-wheeled cart began to appear several times each day at the main Ghetto gate on Garten Street.

"Open!" he would shout to the guards in black.

"Oh, the simpleton is here," mocked the Latvians as Trofim drove his cart into the ghetto courtyard. Too busy cheering their petty lives, the *real* simpletons had no inkling that under the boxes and tarps were hidden bread and much else. Once he even managed to bring in an entire slaughtered calf, part of which Dr. Schwab's widow turned into an unforgettable veal roast with potatoes. The bread came from a virtuous baker on Republic Street and the other foodstuffs in trade for ghetto inmate valuables. As he came in, so he left. The cart was piled high with ghetto garbage as a cover for tarp-wrapped jewels and clothing.

"Oh, the simpleton is leaving," cackled the Latvians.

Trofim smiled and waved and gently called back what David had taught him: *"Der goyem iz a goilem.* The Latvians are fools!" Ah, David's and Trofim's penultimate jeer.

Life in the ghetto was difficult, but most folks did their best to help each other. As it is with Jews, a social and cultural life was manifest straightaway. When they could, young men and women gathered to play volleyball and soccer, to make music and dance, to read aloud and tell jokes, and to make love. For love takes you from hell to breakfast. Besides, without any expectation of survival, inhibitions were pointless. Still, those of us a bit older gathered to talk of books, listen to clandestine radio, dwell on our losses, and to hopelessly hope. We were habitually sober.

In this strange way, the first few months of ghetto life were unmomentous. But the turn of events, like the Earth's orbit, is relentless. The end of October brought the entry of Jews from the Riga ghetto to our own. They were sent to work at the sugar factory. Too few Libauer Jews remained to fill the production demands. Our new neighbors were greeted warmly. We shared with them our space, our food, and our clothing. They shared with us the truth. The Riga Jews were not only Latvians, they were mostly from elsewhere: Germany, Austria, Czechoslovakia, Poland and Lithuania. They told us about the mass murder in the Rumbula forest 10 kilometers from Riga. They told us of the massacres in their towns and villages, the deportations and the deprivations. Still there was *l'chaim* and laughter. It is perverse to be wholly sad. Comedy is a necessary escape from despair. Even black comedy . . .

GHETTO GARBAGE CAN

I am a garbage can
   in a yard corner,
A lidded black hole fed
   breakfast, lunch, dinner
So rarely the light of day
   is but a shooting star.
At odd times, though, I feast:
   Rescued by Lucifer's minions,
My lid is erectile, the hole
   color-full to bursting.

    Just weeks after the arrival of the Riga Jews, our big ears learned that in the next few days the police would search all the flats. Nearly everyone panicked. They hid their barterable valuables and cast to waste bins the contraband food they so prized. The search was maniacal. The Ghetto was left in a shambles. Nothing was found and life went on.

    David Zivcon is a radio *mavin* (expert). He patiently tried to teach me the way it all works. You see there are short waves and medium waves and long waves. These air ripples made by a faraway transmitter radiate through space. The short and medium ones bounce back and forth from earth to sky to earth. The long ones stay close to the earth, following its curvature. After awhile these radio waves make their way into our hush-hush space and strike the antenna of our ghetto's clandestine radio receiver. The sound signal is extracted by those strange looking tubes from the carrier signal that had been pulsating through the ether.

    That is how it all happened that first week of February 1943 when the little put-together receiver decoded German air ripples. First there was the roll of muffled drums. Then the grim announcement: *The battle of Stalingrad is over. Despite great valor and exemplary leadership, the army has been overcome by superior enemy forces and the unfavorable elements of nature. There shall be four days of national mourning.* After a pause, the second movement of Beethoven's Fifth Symphony was heard. The andante . . . . the quiet dignity of contemplation. God forgive us, we did not mourn. Days later the Riga Jews were transported back to almost certain death. Then we mourned.

It was about this time when a group of us were sent to the SS camp at Paplaka, about 30 km east of Libau. All of us were skilled craftsmen of one sort or another. At first it was just a few of us: myself, Aaron Vesterman, Zelig Hirschberg, Efraim Levenson, two or three others. We were detailed to prepare two large barracks for the Germans, Latvians and Ukrainians. The *Judenrat* chief, Israelit, made a solemn promise it would only be for three weeks. But three weeks became six, we were still in Paplaka, and our group was growing . . . .

SENT TO PAPLAKA

Off to Paplaka
To romp about
Bitter forest mantle
Of frostbound crowbait
Empty of birds and Israelit.
Three weeks, he pledged,
And back to the Ghetto,
A fattened rooster.
    Five times three
    Here we dwell.
    Each day we see
    New ones in hell.
The Jews fare well
At resort Paplaka,
Take the waters and sing
Morning 'til night.
With honor as collateral,
Israelit promised three weeks,
No more, no less,
Save the war will end.
    Five times three
    Here we dwell.
    Each day we see
    New ones in hell.

With the arrival of Purim in late March, it was clear that Paplaka was now our permanent address. By now we were about 30 Libau ghetto Jews, including a small number of women sent to cook, clean, launder, and do office work. I longed terribly for my family in the ghetto, most of all for my mother....

A JEWISH CHILD'S FATE

Barbed circumscription
Of inner Ghetto landscape
Conceals crouching remnants
Devoured by God's wrath.
Young twigs snapped
From the Jewish Tree
Tumble in alleyways,
No homes, no mothers,
Ceded to mad dogs'
Howling necromania
Unsated by butchery.
    Gray clouds, black clouds,
    To where do you scamper?
    Should you come upon mother,
    Pass on a kind reminder.
Chaste children,
Forsake hollow hopes;
Born worst of all evils,
God torments the Jew.
Yes, the God in Heaven
Exhumed matrilineal sins
Warranting penance.
Winds now ever whisper,
"Mother shall ne'er return;
Homeless and motherless, this is
A Jewish child's fate!"
    Gray clouds, black clouds,
    To where do you scamper?
    Should you come upon mother,
    Pass on a kind reminder

The April thaw brought early flowers and improved living conditions for the Paplaka Jews. Instead of the abandoned horse stable on the northeast side of the camp, near the barracks, we now inhabited the abandoned bakery on the camp's southwest side. Doors, windows, running water. What comfort! Still, the food was meager. By now, though, some of us developed other sources for the group. Often we worked some distance from the camp. This allowed us to barter with farmers for food, using valuables stolen from Paplaka. Particularly sympathetic to us was the Vācis family north of the camp and the Brūveris family west of the camp.

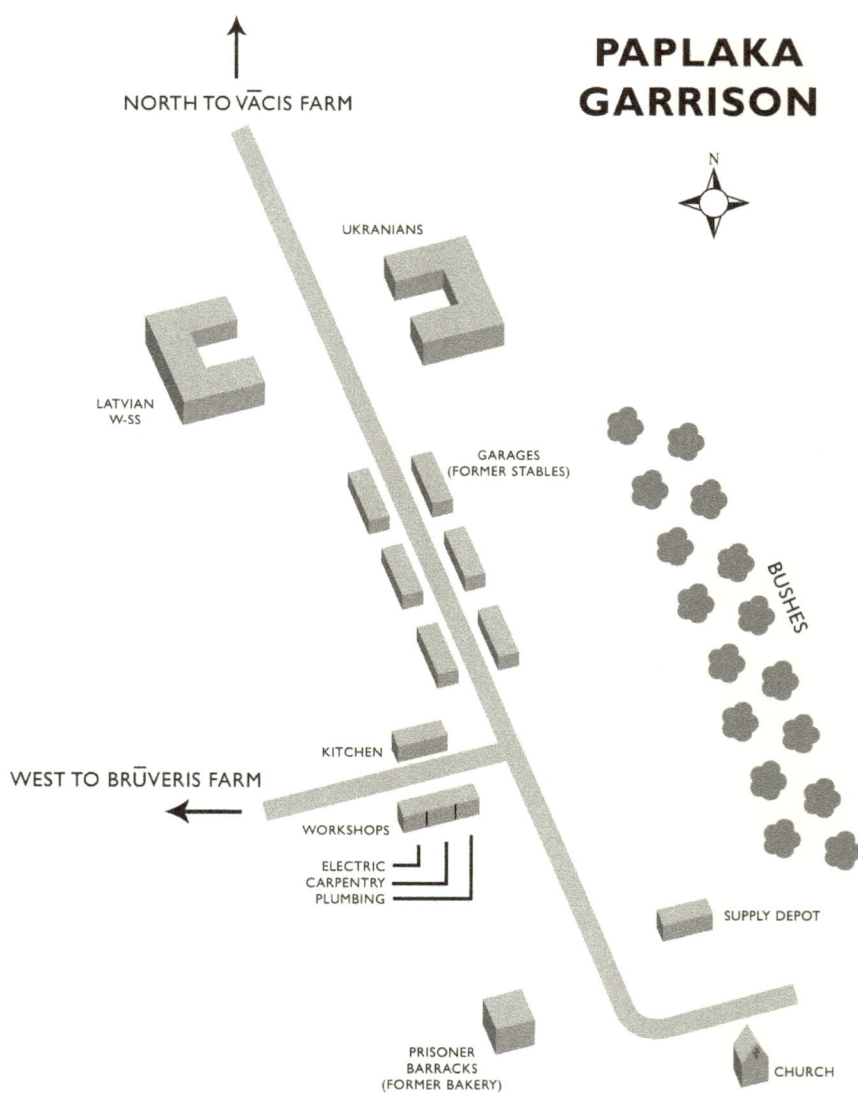

Most amazingly, I managed to persuade the Germans to allow me regular weekend train trips to the Libau ghetto. This was a boost not only to me, but to the others as well. I would always return with radio news, newspaper stories, and detailed reports about family living apart. Before long, I came to be viewed as the "Rabbi." I was older than most of the others and I was determined to exact revenge when this madness ended. I bore secrets, extra food and words of Torah; I did all I could to temper our morale and endurance. We often concluded our evenings with a *Liebeslied* I wrote especially for Paplaka . . . .

PAPLAKA ANTHEM

We are Paplaken Jews
Building "New Europe,"
Hard put for months
In endless drudgery.
    O Paplaka, we've had you up to here
    O Paplaka, let's do away with you.
    O Paplaka, we seek to invert the fear
    O Paplaka, may freedom be in lieu
Commandant's a pig,
More piglets at his side.
May they soon burn,
And deliver us from hell.
    O Paplaka, we've had you up to here
    O Paplaka, let's do away with you
    O Paplaka, we seek to invert the fear
    O Paplaka, may freedom be in lieu
Fear not wind and rain,
Fear not cold and hunger.
Head high, chest out, brave
The high road to fate.
    O Paplaka, we've had you up to here
    O Paplaka, let's do away with you
    O Paplaka, we seek to invert the fear
    O Paplaka, may freedom be in lieu

> Food is quite unpleasant,
> Half the Ghetto ration.
> Shake on it with farmers—
> An egg and fattened rooster.
>> O Paplaka, we've had you up to here
>> O Paplaka, let's do away with you
>> O Paplaka, we seek to invert the fear
>> O Paplaka, may freedom be in lieu
>
> O loathsome pigs
> We'll never cower in fear,
> Jewish partisans bear
> Hurt with prescient pride.
>> O Paplaka, we've had you up to here
>> O Paplaka, let's do away with you
>> O Paplaka, we seek to invert the fear
>> O Paplaka, may freedom be in lieu

One evening, not long after we had moved to the bakery, a very drunk *SS-Hauptsturmführer* "*Shikker*" zigzaged into our quarters, waving a pistol.

"Do you Jews realize that I could shoot you all?"

"Certainly, *Herr Hauptsturmführer*," many calmly replied.

"And I am an excellent marksman," *Shikker* added.

"Certainly, *Herr Hauptsturmführer*," we responded.

He twitched and jerked, jigged and jiggled, until he quivered to collapse on a chair beside my bunk. Startled, he rose and ambled to a bookshelf nearby. "Oh, they are in English! So you are an Anglophile! Read to me, Linkimer."

I politely protested, insisting that I had only begun my study and thus knew little. Still, *Shikker* was resolute in his demand. So I opened a book and read, purposely mispronouncing each word as though it were German. The sound of Germanified English seemed to entrance *Shikker* and before long he was back in the chair, dead asleep.

We pained to seem unwelcoming, but we concluded it was in everyone's interest, including his, that *Shikker* play out his drunken stupor in his own quarters. So Aaron and Efraim lifted *Herr Hauptsturmführer* by his arms and legs, carried him to his flat, softly placed him on his bed, and removed his boots. I unloaded the pistol and placed it on the night stand, the bullets neatly aligned like SS in the morning. Carefully, we returned to our quarters.

The next morning several of us encountered a rather droopy-eyed *Hauptsturmführer*. With a paresthetic tongue and a reluctantly appreciative tone, he remarked, "You did the right thing last night." He quickly moved on. *Naronim un kropeveh vaksen on regen*. Fools and weeds grow without rain!

Days later, on the eve of Passover, *erev Pesach*, 4 Jews from the Riga ghetto arrived: Arkady Scheinker and Kasriel Zwicker, both born in Riga, and two German Jews, Hans Levy from Hannover and Max Gunzenhäuser from Bamberg. The overnight trip was exhausting and they were given little to eat or drink. On *Pesach* we always would say, "Let anyone who is hungry come and eat." It is a holy deed, a *mitzvah*, to invite a needy guest to share one's repast, more so that it was meager. Gratefully, Arkady, Kasriel, Hans, and Max made it possible for us to perform at least one *Pesach mitzvah*.

To be sure, there was no *matzah*. I replaced this with a story of *matzah* and *mitzvah*. It was a well-known parable told by the *Chafetz Chaim*, a saintly giant of the last generation, Rabbi Israel Meir HaCohen: Once on the eve of Passover, the Rabbi had gone to retrieve his order of *matzah*. With curiosity and some chagrin, he watched as the baker added pieces of *matzah* to make the weight ordered. Piece after piece and still no success. Finally the baker added a whole *matzah*, and that was success. The *Chafetz Chaim* looked at the baker and gently taught: "The same holds true in matters of the spirit, in fulfilling a *mitzvah*. Some folks are charitable in order to boast, or because others have embarrassed them into it. Others pray without meaning it, or learn Torah for *their* honor. These are broken deeds, *mitzvot shvurot*. They are sterile and useless. Only a whole *mitzvah*, like a whole *matzah*, can leave us undiminished."

For me, Passover concluded with the very acme of SS cruelty in Paplaka. By then many of us were allowed to return to the Libau ghetto every other weekend to visit family. Others and I journeyed on the Passover weekend. When we alighted on Paplaka that Sunday evening there was a surprise search of the returnees. It was directed by the commander of the German SD in Latvia, *SS-Sturmbannführer* Rudolf Lange, a man who hated Jews so much that he could barely look at them. Food and cigarettes were found on several of my comrades. Lange commanded that since I was the elder I was responsible and was to be punished accordingly: 25 blows with a cane on my bare ass. Before all, Lange ordered me to drop my trousers and he personally administered the punishment, requiring that I count aloud each blow. Now *Pesach* was truly complete. This was my *maror*, my bitter herb.

May brought flowers and Italian soldiers, not quite prisoners, not quite free. They were reluctant warriors, always befuddled by their fate. Inexplicably, these soft soldiers sought solace among the Jews. Long without libido, I received an unanticipated message: *Der kleyner shlang shtelt zikh oyf* (The little snake is standing up). "Italian" was ready-made . . .

ITALIAN'S LAMENT

In Paplaka, our resort,
Is imprisoned Italian,
Who cries and complains,
Totally wretched.
Near him sits a Jew
Enjoying the lament,
Listening open-mouthed
To all that's insipid.
  O'Bizerta, O'Tunisia,
  O'sweet towns by the sea,
  O'Italian Africa,
  The bell tolls for thee.
Tripoli gone, so too Tunis,
What does it matter?
Still, Italian's on fire
With bitter apprehension:
"With Africa lost,
Rome soon to follow,
Tell me dear friend
Where sits my new pension!"
  O'Bizerta, O'Tunisia,
  O'sweet towns by the sea,
  O'Italian Africa,

> The bell tolls for thee.
> The soft-hearted Jew
> Gives advice to Italian:
> "There's a place nearby
> You're most welcome to stay.
> Simply put on Jew-rags,
> Yellow patch and all.
> Be with me in comfort,
> In our Ghetto hideaway."
> > O'Bizerta, O'Tunisia,
> > O'sweet towns by the sea,
> > O'Italian Africa,
> > The bell tolls for thee.

Since his arrival on Passover, Arkady Scheinker and I became fast friends. That May, Arkady came to me with an alluring conjecture: "Kalman, I think between the two of us we can count three *beitzim* (testicles)." I thought about it for some minutes and then answered, "Arkady, it certainly is surprising to me that you have three." My carnal preference confirmed, we both laughed. Sadly, there were no women for Arkady in Paplaka.

But for one small, but hopeful, incident, the early days of Summer were routine. In June, shortly after *Shavuos*, several Soviet planes flew over Paplaka at night for the first time. They dropped flares, perhaps to take photographs. The Frizten and their Latvian recruits ran from their barracks into the rain and mud. Wearing only their nightshirts, these heroes of Europe threw themselves to the ground, looking every much like windswept laundry on a field.... An air raid in Paplaka, a welcome guest!

The arrival of August witnessed anger; the departure of August despair. The official food rations alloted to laboring ghetto Jews and their families were centrally delivered to the *Judenrat*. Their designated "shopkeepers" distributed the foodstuff weekly from the Center for Food Distribution, known to all as the Ghetto Shop. All allocations were equal, but by August it was clear that some allocations were more equal than others. Crowds gathered regularly to angrily complain, and just as regularly they were dispersed by the police, always with a promise to harshly punish cheaters or take the matter up with Israelit. Yes, there were protocols and decrees, endless words with the same result ... *bupkis*!

As August waned, the mood in the Libau ghetto was grim. Rumors began circulating that the Riga ghetto had been liquidated, and the Jews sent to the Kaiserwald concentration camp. There the guards were heartless German criminals, sent from civil prisons to torment and murder Jews. Libauer Jews were convinced that liquidation of their ghetto would surely come soon.

Despair was greatest among the elderly and women with young children. Wherever they were transported, their fate was sealed, for the Nazis were not about to build homes for the aged or kindergartens. Though anxiety was deep and palpable among all ghetto residents, they wore an intrepid mask of normalcy as the official and unofficial leaders sought to avert the evil decree.

By September, the *Judenrat* elders, Israelit and Kaganski, had been notified by Ghetto Commandant Franz Kerscher that the ghetto was soon to be liquidated and its residents transferred to Kaiserwald. Concealing this, Israelit and Kaganski tried to raise the ghetto morale with assurances that many were interceding on the ghetto's behalf because employers needed the skilled Jewish workers. The stories, true stories, circulated: *Gebietskomissariaz* official, Dr. Dorffel, strenuously argued with the SD that the Jews were absolutely essential, and would be difficult to replace by an equal number of skilled Latvian workers; Ghetto Commandant Kerscher offered a plan to house the Jews at their workplaces if the ghetto buildings were needed for other purposes.

For some time, David Zivcon and the Jewish ghetto police had been making counterplans. In secret, they decided to acquire weapons, and if the decree came they would stage an uprising. Better to die a lion than a lamb. For this task David prevailed upon Trofim once again. In early August 1943 Trofim traded ghetto valuables for pistols. They were wrapped in oil-soaked rags and hidden in the SD yard coal pile. Once a week for the next several weeks, Trofim, ignoring the presence of SD men in the yard, calmly took the wrapped pistols from the pile, placed them in his cart, and covered them in the usual manner. David waited for him in the ghetto, where they hid the pistols in a mostly collapsed shed paid attention to by no one. Fate was unkind. In the close of September, a routine inspection by Latvian guards stumbled upon the hidden cache. The Germans chose to ignore the find. Perhaps Ghetto Commandant Kerscher prevailed with an argument that it was an old Soviet cache, unknown to the Jews.

About then, I arrived from Paplaka for my biweekly visit. It was the 25th, the Saturday before Rosh Hashanah. David was quite skeptical that an uprising could still be equipped and organized in time. He had other plans, private plans. He invited me to take refuge in Robert Sedols' cave of holy bricks, along with himself and Michael Skutelsky and their wives. I pledged to return from Paplaka in several days, regardless of the situation, by whatever means, in order to effect the escape.

That evening I visited with my dear mother and sisters. When all was quiet, in the dead of night, I wrote a song for the comrades I would leave behind . . . .

UNTIL TOMORROW

Dolorous Jew-songs
May cut to the heart
For the sake of
Satiating sadness,
But arced bodies belie
Steel-hard souls forged
By dim apparitions
Of eternal passings.

Black clouds gainsay
Sunshine in dirty places,
Even tormenting despair,
But put in mind
A self-reliant future,
An *aria di bravura*,
A stiff-necked dignity
That boasts of prevail.

Beloved friends, I say
Farewell, *zei gezunt*:
Gey gezunt, cum gezunt;
Ess gezunterhait!
Though our fate is chaos,
Baruch Hashem, we shall meet
When and where our hearts still,
Here or There . . .

The next afternoon, shortly before departing, I spoke with my Paplaka mate, Shmuel Hackel, who had just been told by *Gebietskomissar* Alnor that the ghetto would almost certainly remain intact. I returned that Sunday evening and stayed in Paplaka, entirely in the dark.

By Rosh Hashana it was settled. The ghetto closure was certain, all appeals were exhausted. The traditional Days of Awe took on new meaning. The dialectic was dead. Talk of suicide was everywhere. Mothers rushed about the ghetto and elsewhere exchanging valuables for Veronal. With this sedative, they were determined to spare their children and themselves a cruel execution. For over a week, the authorities shut off the gas line every evening after 10. Still, folks were determined. Old Mrs. Mandelkorn hung herself in a stairwell. With each day, gold was increasingly less valuable than Veronal. Some who possessed the elixir of death meandered about the ghetto euphoric, others resentful of their good fortune.

Late Monday afternoon, 4 October, Michael Skutelsky chanced to meet Hinde Foss returning from work at SD headquarters. She told Michael that the men working at the SD would be back at the ghetto later than usual, and that by nightfall there would be a major inspection. Michael rushed to tell his wife, Hilde, and then proceeded to bury his pistol and other valuables. In the early evening, he made his way to the Zivcon's flat. He found Henni, but David had still not returned. Rushing back to his own flat, he came upon Avram Hirschovich and Aaron Herzbach returning from the SD. He inquired of David. David, they said, was staying at SD awhile longer to deal with important matters.

David had been summoned to repair the SD teletype, which had ceased mid-line. Milking a rare opportunity, he expressed the seriousness of the breakdown and worked slowly. Though ordered to leave the room the moment the teletype was operative, David had managed to read the fragment "liquidate 8 Oc . . . ."

In the early evening, David huddled with SD driver Barnitzky. He trusted Barnitzky, having known him since childhood. A Baltic German, he had been conscripted against his will. For some time he had been helping David with food and cigarettes. Now David needed the truth.

"Is it so?" David gasped, almost shooting the question.

"It has been for weeks," Barnitzky responded. "I don't know what they plan for you, but regardless you must escape."

"Escape to where, with what?" David shot back, disingenuously.

"Here," Barnitsky replied, pulling a pistol from his pocket. "Take it, you will need it!" David was stunned.

"One more thing, David, the ghetto guard will be reinforced by midnight, and all who remain will be deported in but a few days. Where, I don't know. How I don't know. But gone, I do know!"

David returned to the ghetto. Before going to his flat, he spoke with the *Judenrat* elders, Israelit and Kaganski. David recounted his conversation with Barnitzky.

"What do you intend to do?" queried Israelit.

"Flee with my wife," David responded.

"Do as you must," replied Israelit. "The collective was inspiring, but it is done with. Now, we are each on our own. David, our lives are a bitter lesson: *Ganaiden un gehenem ken men baideh hoben oif der velt* . . . In this world there is both heaven and hell!"

David left Israelit and proceeded to the Skutelsky flat. He told Michael and Hilde of his conversation with Barnitzky, and with Israelit. He insisted that they be ready to escape in but fifteen minutes, taking with them very little so as not to be conspicuous. David returned to his flat and told Henni what had transpired and what they had to do. David spoke with Henni's mother, Tzilla Friedlander, who was seated in another room.

"Moma, tonight Henni and I will escape. It is painful for us but we must leave you and my mother behind. You are both too old for this journey."

"Go . . . Go with God," Mrs. Friedlander responded with quiet resignation. "It is the right thing, I shall not hold you back. Please . . . avenge us all."

David promised. Just then Henni arrived. "Until tomorrow, Moma!" Henni cried, unaware that David had given her Veronal. Michael entered David's flat. Henni and Hilde went to wait outside. Mrs. Friedlander kissed Michael and wished him well. David and Michael left to join their wives. Together, they walked to the Herren Street side of the ghetto.

The weather that night was stormy. Clouds, rain, no moon. Faultless for an escape. Michael brought wire-cutters and several hundred cigarettes. Michael set off to intercept the guard and distract him with a long negotiation over bootleg fags. David cautiously cut through the barb-wired ghetto fence. It required fifteen difficult minutes to cleave three rows of wire. At the last, the wire was so tempered the shears broke apart.

The first to emerge from the breach was Henni. She walked directly across the street into the dark alley to await the others. Just then several revelers stumbled by and lingered near the split wire. The others had to wait for some minutes before the drunks were safely out of sight. When they emerged on the street, Henni was gone. To avoid being propositioned by yet another drunken German soldier, she had gone off on her own. David was distraught. He wanted to search for Henni. Michael dissuaded him, "It is better that we send Mrs. Sedols to look for her." The post-curfew walk through night-fallen Libau to 14 Kauf Street, in the center of town, was heavyhearted and perilous.

Arriving at the Sedols' they were surprised and relieved to find that Henni was already there waiting in the shadows with Robert. Taking off their shoes, they all quietly ascended the stairs to take a meal hurriedly prepared by Johanna. After awhile, they went back downstairs and into the cellar to sleep. The cellar was in disarray, the entrance to the hiding place quite obvious. David was shocked, the others confused. They clearly had much work to do. Stacked wood was a more than inadequate camouflage.

The next morning, Robert went to the ghetto to do business as usual. There he was confronted by a desperate and quite agitated Avram Barkan. Avram lived in the same flat as David at Waisenhaus Street near the auxiliary Ghetto gate. The 2nd floor flat had three big rooms and another small one. Avram lived in one large room with his wife and son, his mother-in-law, his brother-in-law Berl Wolfson, and Berl's wife Chaya. David lived in another room with Henni. David's escape with the others provoked complex feelings in Avram of envy, a deep sense of having been betrayed, a fear of collective punishment, and, given David's access to SD headquarters, a trepidation that the Ghetto inhabitants can expect the worst.

"Where is David," Barkan barked.

"I'm not certain. Perhaps he's at the SD," replied Robert. "I don't make work assignments."

"You're a liar," Barkan shot back. "David is with you . . . and so is Michael . . . and their wives. All of us here are in a panic over this. Now we'll surely be shot."

"You've lost your senses, Avram," Robert said with a tone of sadness. "Sure, David is a friend, but how could I risk the lives of my wife and little girls?"

"Wallow in shit, you *and* David," screamed Barkan. "Tell Zivcon the ghetto's fate will also be his!"

Alarmed by such a threat, Robert left the ghetto for home without completing his business. Himself uncertain about the cellar hideout, he led the four escapees to the attic. There they perched for three days, in cold and fear. On Friday afternoon, Robert took them back down to the cellar. Avram Barkan was in a boxcar headed East.

That Friday, just hours before Yom Kippur 5704, 8 October 1943, at 4:00 AM, the Jews were summarily rousted, assembled in the ghetto courtyard beneath the ramshackle flats, stripped of their valuables, and marched to the railroad yard. There they were pushed into boxcars, cramped like cattle. The elderly, the ill, little children with their mothers, little children without their mothers, all the others. No water, no food, a single bucket for excrement. They were on a slow journey to the Kaiserwald concentration camp near Riga, the penultimate portal to dreamless sleep.

Hours passed, a paroxysm of start and stop. It was no longer cold in the boxcars, but hot and damp and fetid. Riva Zivcon and her toddler curled entwined in a corner of the last car. Nearby, Zelig Hirschberg's mother, Sarah, was held upright by her adult children, Yudel on the right, Rachel on the left. It was soon to be Yom Kippur and Sarah mumbled a folksong from her Kapischki childhood in Lithuania:

> *A gantse velt mit ayznbanen iz in undzer tsayt gevorn,*
> *Velkhe firn pasazhirn, orem un raykh,*
> *Loyft zen dem khidesh, nor hot bezikorn,*
> *Az dos iz a moshl punkt kegn aykh.*
> *Mir zitsn dos in di vagonen,*
> *Der lokomotiv iz di tsayt,*
> *Zi shlept mit zikh mentshn milyonen,*
> *Un flit vi di koyln in shtrayt.*
> *Yetrider reltse iz a sekunde,*
> *Yetrider statsye—a yor,*
> *Yeder kusatke iz glaykh tsu a shtunde,*
> *A poyezd iz gantsn a dor.*

Um dem bilet vos er halt in tash,
Dos iz zayn mazl, zayn rayze-plan,
Vi vayt tsu forn un in voser klas,
Bashtimt furn Got, fun direktor ban.

A whole world of railroads arose in our day,
Carrying passengers, rich and poor,
But as we hasten to eye the marvel, recall
It is a mere parable of ourselves.
One and all in the railroad cars,
The locomotive keeping time,
Hauling people by the millions,
A fleet like bullets in a battle.
Every rail a second,
Every destination a year,
Every station house an hour,
A whole train a generation.
And the ticket held in its jacket
Is one's fate, one's path;
How long the journey and in which class
Assigned by God, the trainmaster.

As the sun set on Yom Kippur, the ghetto Jews of Libau arrived at Kaiserwald. Selection began early the next morning: Who shall live, who shall die. Who in threescore years and ten, who in the wink of an eye. Who shall ride at anchor, who a rolling stone. Who erect, who prone.

THE EMPTY GHETTO

As boxcars rumbled to Riga, and after SD *Scharführer* Handke posted notices on the station wall proclaiming Libau *"Judenfrei,"* we thirty Jews of Paplaka found ourselves on a truck directed toward Libau, to the ghetto. The journey seemed endless and you considered the unexpected. After nearly two hours we arrived. Collectively, of course, we embodied a mockery of Handke's enthusiasm. Libau would never be "Jew Free."

Straightaway you were caught off balance. The truck was headed not to the ghetto, but along Kurhaus Street and then down Ulich Street toward the SD. Zelig Hirschberg and I stood up, readying ourselves to escape when the truck stopped at the SD. The others remained seated, in tired resignation. The truck never halted at the SD, but continued on to the construction office before driving on to the ghetto.

Street upon street, there was no Jew to be seen. Grim-faced quiet . . . Aaron, Zelig, all the rest. The closer you came to the ghetto gate, the farther you were from hope. Hope that you would ever see mothers and sisters and brothers and close friends. Before long, we alighted from the truck and received the emetic news from Ghetto Commandant Kerscher, "Good day, fellows. This morning the ghetto residents packed their bags and, quietly and calmly, boarded the train for Riga. It will be better there. There is more room, more services, more opportunity for dignified work."

"But *Meister* Kerscher," I asked, "is this not the same so-called Riga where our fathers and brothers had gone two years ago?"

"Linkimer, you have such an imagination. You have my word, all of you, that your loved ones have been sent to finer accommodations. Not a one will be harmed, not a one."

"So, *Meister* Kerscher, why have *we* come here?" inquired Aaron Vesterman.

"Ah, such a smart fellow, always asking such pertinent questions. You are here, gentlemen, to rescue winter clothing for yourselves. It is October. Before long the snow will fall. So quickly . . . inside . . . do your business. Shortly you will be on the road again to Paplaka."

We entered the ghetto. I stood in the courtyard, spinning like a child's toy, peering at all the windows. A vengeful feeling engulfed me, and my whole body shuttered with anger. My mother's voice halted the tremor: "*Kalman, di klensteh nekomeh farsamt di neshomeh!*" (The slightest thought of revenge poisons the soul!) I was startled. I looked here, there, everywhere. My mother was nowhere to be seen in the square. I did perceive movement in a window nearby. Perhaps they were ghosts of the departed?

With haste, I entered the building corridor. I was struck all of a heap! There was Yosl Mandelstamm, the tailor, and Shmerl Skutelsky, the shoemaker. Through an open door, I spied Misha Libauer, the jeweler, sitting apathetically on the edge of a bed. Yosl, Misha, Shmerl, all close friends.

"Why are you still here?" I blurted insensitively. "What happened last night? This morning?"

"We don't understand," Shmerl responded. "The SD ordered us to stay here. Why? Our children are gone. Confused, crying, stuffed like cabbages in a crate."

Choked with pain, they tried to answer my questions, but their words foundered. I pressed no further. I left for my own flat. The curtains were drawn. I turned on the light. The alarm clock stood on the table and continued marking time as though nothing had happened. I was surprised to see the beds made. Perhaps my mother and sisters had not slept? I sat on the bed of my mother, gazing upon the meager trinkets left behind. Sorrow is an unfillable lacuna.

Soon Shmerl, Yosl and Misha came to fetch me, and together we entered David Zivcon's flat. There was Mrs. Friedlander, Henni's mother, lying on her bed in a pre-mortem stupor, poisoned with Veronal. She was still breathing and had a pulse. She was fully clothed for travel, her bundle lying spilled out next to her on the floorboards. It appeared that at the last she had gathered the courage to end her life on her own terms. At first I thought to revive her, but quickly dismissed this. Instead, I whispered, "Brava, Mrs. Friedlander!"

Moshe Itrof came by and the other three left. I raised the notion of assisting her prompt end. We spoke of the unbearable torment and suffering awaiting her should she awake. Before long, Aaron Vesterman, Efraim Levenson, and others arrived and we left Mrs. Friedlander to her fate.

Zelig and I stopped at our flats to retrieve photographs, before going on to the ghetto workshop. We said our deep-felt good-byes to Shmerl, Yosl and Misha, promising to stay in touch and to pass on any news from Riga. Shmerl gave me a picture of his wife that he had carried for years. "If you see Henni, please give this to her with my love," he quietly requested. Misha and Yosl told me of their plans to escape. They asked if I knew where David was. I knew no more than they did, the speculation that he and the others had gone to Sedols.

Our brief ghetto visit was over. Carrying winter clothing, we all clambered onto the truck for the return to Paplaka. Grim-faced quiet reprised. I sat between Zelig and Aaron. Zelig was lost in his pictures.

There was his mother, his brother Yudel, and the one taken in 1940 with his sister Bunya, who had escaped to Moscow. Then there was the photograph with Yudel and Bunya when Zelig was only three, and the one of Zelig and his uncle Julius with all the smiling Latvians who worked in Julius' business. Mostly he was spellbound by the tiny picture of a father who had abandoned him a decade earlier.

We rambled along back roads and byways as though we were avoiding something. Partway along in the journey, Aaron began to mutter a poem he found pinned to the wall beside Shlomo Feigerson's bunk,

> The hearth is fireless,
> The chamber does quiver.
> No rabbis, no children,
> Both cruelly cast asunder.
>
> Merely a remnant endures,
> But surely it shall flourish
> For the eternal Jewish glimmer
> Has never lost its glow.

We arrived in Paplaka and mourned all that we had lost. Thirty days of *shirim*, songs, of sorrow . . .

> MAMA
>
> Hear O Comrades!
> Our suffering is one:
> Every Jew rendered
> Sisterless, brotherless,
> Mamaless, as if
> An orphaned stone.
>
> God we'll believe our
> World turns for *Your* sake
> If arrival of the future
> Bears our Mama in *its* wake.

Angry, God bitterly
Punishes foolish Jews
Who rely on Him alone,
No direction home,
Mamaless, as if
An orphaned stone.

God we'll believe our
World turns for *Your* sake
If arrival of the future
Bears our Mama in *its* wake.

We planned our escape, and plotted our revenge.

LOOTING THE GHETTO

Not more than an hour after we departed the ghetto, the Germans began their looting. They had a slogan: *"Die Juden sind unser Unglück.* The Jews are our misfortune." Of course, this catchphrase did not apply to Jewish possessions, for in this regard the Jews were their good fortune. The German SD behaved like children. Wherever one went, others quickly followed. Soon fighting erupted, and more than one beating took place. Even gunshots could be heard. While the Germans battered one another, the Latvian ghetto guards quietly set about stealing the choice morsels.

After awhile the Germans exhausted themselves and left. Shmerl, Misha, and Yosl sought permission from Ghetto Commandant Kerscher to stay the night in their ghetto flats. It was not a desire to be in empty rooms with the ghosts of loved ones. They were simply exhausted, physically and mentally. Kerscher did not have the authority to grant their request; he awaited instructions from the SD. In about an hour, the SD driver Barnitzky arrived with a Latvian guard. The order was to take the Jews to their new home in the infamous Women's Prison. Kerscher, a man with some heart, declared that first they must go to their flats and retrieve their necessities.

Through the ghetto gate one more time, each off in his own direction. The sky had turned granite gray and the wind whined and whistled through the boughs of the big tree that sentineled the ghetto yard. Rain slapped at their faces.... Jewish tears perhaps. The dozen silhouettes of Jewish houses were as skeletons, or burnt-out ruins. With dread, Misha turned on the light of his room, and there was the empty little bed of Avram Leib, a "Jewish criminal" of six. Misha toppled down crying, raging at the pillow where Avram's head had lain not long before. In a few moments, he sobered to reality, grabbed Avram's cap and pajamas as keepsakes, and bid farewell to all that was dear to him. Shmerl and Yosl did likewise. Clutching their "necessities," they left the ghetto and were led to their new home . . . prison.

They arrived at the prison and were led through the yard. Once inside, the guards emptied their pockets. Misha, Shmerl and Yosl were placed in a single cell. They settled in and collapsed in exhaustion. At 4:30 the next morning they were roused from slumber and informed that this cubicle would now be home. Here they would eat, shit, sleep, and work. Misha, Shmerl, and Yosl said not a word. They listened, followed orders, and only spoke to one another. At 7:30 the guards arrived with more news. They were leaving prison for better quarters in the SD building.

Kurhaus Prospekt 21 was familiar to them. They had worked there before. It was a well-constructed building with spacious grounds in the rear, large enough for a few cows and the pigpen started by David and Trofim. Yosl, Misha, and Shmerl were taken to their room, ordered to remove their yellow patches front and back, and admonished to never be seen in the streets of Libau. Yosl concluded that since Libau was declared *Judenfrei*, they no longer existed as Jews. Still, they had some value, at least for the immediate future.

For 10 days they were made to sort Jewish belongings. The work was heartbreaking, each item a reminder of family and friends. Seemingly nonstop, heavy trucks drove into the ghetto and returned to the SD with Jewish property: clothes, linens, quilts, electrical items. Fine things the Germans kept for themselves, the rest was set aside for black market barter. The Germans quarreled, sometimes violently, and one often stole from the next. Shmerl, Misha, and Yosl stole from all the Fritzen and gave linens, clothes, and shoes to the Russian prisoners who were their workmates, and to the cooks, Anna and Martha, who provided extra food for them all.

Finally, Misha, Yosl, and Shmerl were relieved from this unpleasantness and sent to work in the workshop, as in the past. Food for the three of them was again meager. Shmerl took it upon himself to duck out of the

SD to barter for food in the shadows of Libau's black market. Whenever possible, he would visit a friend, someone he called "my gentile woman." He knew her for years. She appealed to Shmerl to flee the SD. She was willing to hide Shmerl and his two friends in her flat. He was grateful . . . for her love, her bath, her offer.

As each day gave way to the next, they sensed that their tenure at the SD was coming to a close. They placed locks and bolts on their room door so as not to be taken by surprise. They hid an axe and iron bars for their defense. Each night, Misha, Shmerl, or Yosl drew guard duty. They were determined. They expected death, but refused humiliation.

Shmerl, Yosl, and Misha were not without allies. There was Barnitzky, the Baltic German who was unwillingly conscripted into the SD as a driver, the same Barnitzky who had warned David of the ghetto's impending dissolution. Misha had fabricated a necklace for Barnitzky's wife. When he came for it the last week of November, Barnitzky said he knew of no immediate danger. But the moment he did, he would alert them. Barnitzky, as well, was planning to cut and run.

Then there was Trofim, the SD horse groom, David's friend. Shmerl, Yosl, and Misha began meeting him often in the attic. Ever the watchful "simpleton," he always had timely news and clever insight.

"For you, fellas, your time here will end with New Year. When the necklaces and shoes and other Christmas gifts for SD families in Germany are done, so are you. I heard this from the Fritzen with my own ears. No need to worry. If you are alert and quick-footed you will dodge their grasp."

Trofim had a plan. From the attic there was a gangway to the top floor of the stable. There hay for the horses was stored, a place where only the horse groom went. This "simpleton" would always forget to secure the outside latch, remove the ladder, and lock the gate leading to the street. One, two, three . . . free! Soon enough the bell rang.

On the first of December, SD officer Hans Rode appeared in the workshop drunk, took their work from them, and sent Misha, Yosl, and Shmerl to their quarters. Within minutes Trofim appeared briefly at their door and whispered, "Tomorrow the bosses come from Riga. They will get rid of you before the day is over."

At dusk a pathognomonic truck rumbled into the yard, shovels tossed in the back alongside a burlap bag of bleaching powder. From the attic window Misha and the others observed the preparations. As soon as it was nightfall, each, in turn, crawled the gangway to the hay storage in the stable. Shmerl and Misha scampered down the ladder and onto the street. Yosl stumbled and fell hard to the ground. For a few moments he lay disoriented. When he managed to pull himself aright, piercing pain shot up his leg from his now useless ankle. Still, he managed to drag himself, body and leg, to the street. Misha and Shmerl each grabbed an arm, and all three played the scene in which two buddies return a thoroughly drunk comrade to his home. But, where was that to be?

"Next door to us was a Latvian family. We got on well with them. Maybe they . . . Let's give it a try," Misha suggested.

Before long they arrived at the building where Misha had lived for so many years. Up the staircase carefully, they stood before his flat. Instinctively, his hand searched for the key in his pocket. Red-faced he turned to his neighbor's door and gently knocked. The door opened a crack and a middle-aged woman peered through.

"Misha!" cried out a voice of surprise and fear.

"Can you put us up for the night?"

"Come in . . . quickly!"

Instantly, this kind lady acquired the pain of competing injustices. How could she turn them away to face danger and, perhaps, death on the street. Yet, how could she let them stay and risk the lives of those she loved the most.

"Misha, please forgive me. You and your friends can't stay here long. You know what they will do to my children, my family."

Resting a bit and clearing their heads, they decided on a plan. Each would seek a different shelter. Shmerl to his "gentile woman." Yosl to his wife's old friend, Mrs. Vecīte. And Misha to the Sedols. With Robert's help, the other two would soon be in the cellar at 14 Kauf Street as well.

Shmerl set out for Katerina's flat, Misha for Robert's. Yosl lingered another ten minutes pondering his route. When he finally took off, his lower leg was like a tree trunk, too painful to do anything but crawl on all fours. Appearing the nearly unconscious drunk, was a fortuitous ruse.

A customary knock on the door and Shmerl was securely in Katerina's embrace. He would never forget the smell of her hair that night. Just then, for but an hour, he was in her eyes as one who found peace.

"So, will you stay here now?" asked Katerina as they shared a pot of tea at the kitchen table.

"For just a bit," Shmerl responded. "It will be too dangerous for both of us if I stay longer."

"But where will you go?"

"I am not certain . . . but wherever it is, it would be foolish of me to tell you and you to know."

"But how will I know you are well?"

"We have always managed . . . ." was Shmerl's wistful solution to Katerina's incorporeal query.

By now Katerina had left her chair to prepare Shmerl's favorite winter salad, mostly now a recurring dream. The salted herring fillets were cut into pieces about an inch long. Delicately and precisely she sliced the cooked potatoes a quarter-inch thick, and then cut the slices in half. The apple and cooked beetroot were cut into strips. All was mixed in a bowl with finely chopped onion, oil, vinegar, and crumbled hard-boiled eggs. With the schnapps and the, somewhat stale, dark bread, the meal was mythic.

This fantasy of normalcy endured for but a few days. In the dark of night, Shmerl stole to the Sedols. He was warmly welcomed by Robert and Johanna, happy to see Misha, and overwhelmed to be reunited with Michael and David, and their wives. As he lay in the dark cellar that night, he knew Katerina was lost to him forever. These were guilty thoughts, for they pushed aside Henni and the boys . . . .

When Yosl knocked on Mrs. Vecīte's door, the sun was breaking through the early morning gray. The door opened and he stumbled in pain across the threshold.

"How did you get here?" Mrs. Vecīte asked in a barely audible whisper, shutting the door quickly. "The newspaper announced that no Jews remained in Libau."

"That's a tangled tale best left untold . . . . Thanks for the food you sent to us in the ghetto. It made all the difference."

"Where's Nechama? . . . What happened to your leg? You can barely stand."

"I took a misstep in my escape. I think it's just a bad ankle sprain."

Mrs. Vecīte helped Yosl undress and wash up. She put him to bed and wrapped his ankle.

"It's time for me to go to work. Try not to move about the flat. My neighbors know no one is in the flat during the day and if they hear noise . . . . Surely, I don't have to tell you."

Mostly Yosl spent the day sleeping, occasionally interrupted by pulsing pain. He barely touched the food and water left by his ministering angel. It was dark when Yosl was awakened by Mrs. Vecīte's entry. She was clearly upset.

"What happened?" Yosl asked.

"What happened! What happened! Someone at work came to me and said that her husband had heard of your escape. She thought you might be with me since I was a close friend of Nechama. If she has these suspicions, others are likely to have them. I will be shot!"

"But, I don't see how . . ."

"You will have to find another hiding place, soon!"

It would not be long . . . . Two days later, in the mid-afternoon, the dull thud of an envelope striking a wooden floor caught Yosl's attention as he lay on the couch with his leg elevated. He dared not hobble over to see if something had dropped through the mail slot. When Mrs. Vecīte returned from work she retrieved the note, read it, and passed it to Yosl. It was in Misha's distinctive script: "The patient who has a sore leg needs medicine. That will be delivered on 5 Dec at 1500."

Shmerl, Yosl and Misha in the cellar

The next afternoon, Mrs. Vecite, wrapped in an old woolen shawl, opened the door with suspicion.

"Why have you knocked on my door?"

"I am coming to the patient," Robert responded softly.

"Did you leave a note yesterday?"

"Yes."

"Then come in, please."

Yosl had never met Robert Sedols, but he knew him by sight from his appearances in the ghetto from time to time. Yosl thanked him for coming and began to ask about his friend Misha.

"No questions, please. I'll be back at 6. Be ready. Under present conditions it is a long journey to Lithuania."

Robert returned later with an overcoat and bundled Yosl as though he were a drunk, mismatching buttons and buttonholes. This broad-shouldered former boxer and ex-sailor walked the dark streets with a heavy load. Twists and turns to 14 Kauf Street. Breathless songs, curses, and panting carried him to the courtyard and cellar steps. Now there were seven secreted behind the holy bricks . . . .

Sunrise launched a day like any other at 14 Kauf Street. Robert went to the cellar in the early morning, and soon a fire glowed in the furnace and the waterpump began to rumble. The bakery in the rear yard took receipt of flour and began preparing bread for its twice daily shipments to market. Dawdling over breakfast with Johanna and the girls allowed Robert to organize his day with care. It usually began with deliveries of repaired goods and then a trip down the street to the central market.

Robert and Johanna had quickly gained a reputation as the twosome with "golden hands." Broken watch, worn soles, hot plate no longer getting hot, torn trousers? Take them to Sedols. In a few days, for a modest charge, they would be as good as new. Dead radios were alive again and little girls had new dresses for their birthdays. Robert even peddled his newly invented electric rat trap. The customers would be aghast, were they to learn the secret of the Sedols' success—an artisans' collective behind the wall of holy bricks—an electrician, watchmaker, shoemaker, and seamstresses earning money for their covert upkeep.

If the SD men had an inkling to keep watch over 14 Kauf Street, they would be bemused by only one peculiarity: the janitor's small family consumed inordinately large quantities of food. Nearly every morning Robert left the house with a large suitcase, wandered about the nearby market, and bartered his artisanal wares for all that the farmers had been able to hide from the Germans. Bakers there, as well, knew that Robert never turned aside the opportunity to barter for stolen bread. Usually, these trades aroused no suspicions. Robert was not alone in such activity. The Nazis alloted rather meager food rations and most folks scrambled to provide for their families, building a reserve for hard times that was directly proportional to the skill of the trader.

Still, from time to time there would be a nosy neighbor. Once a woman tenant asked Robert directly if he was hiding someone in his flat. Yes, replied Robert, Hitler's bastard son—his mother is Jewish! Robert and the woman parted in laughter. A few days on, Robert invited the woman to stop by for some tea and evening conversation.

"Come in Mrs. Rolmanis. Welcome." Johanna led her into the kitchen where she prepared tea and made certain to open the pantry widely for all to be in plain sight. When the conversation turned to the difficulty of finding proper clothing, Johanna took Mrs. Rolmanis to each of the bedrooms and explored each wardrobe in detail with her. In this way, "Nosy" had every opportunity to thoroughly inspect the flat and lay her suspicions to rest.

By no means was Mrs. Rolmanis uniquely curious. Every so often her male counterparts would ask to accompany Robert to the cellar when he was attending to the boiler or the waterpump motor. As in the flat, all was transparent: the cluttered workbench with its tools and articles needing repair, the coal and shovels, pipes, boards and the standard mess of a janitor's room.

Behind one cellar wall, camouflaged by the workbench, sat the seven artisans waiting for the signal to emerge. Their cave ceiling heated by bakery ovens, as often as possible, they stayed in the main room of the cellar, reserving the hideaway mostly for sleeping. In the weeks that followed the ghetto liquidation, everything was arranged with care, the routine was established, and space was organized for others who might yet arrive.

Riva and Leo Zivcon   Ada (Adinka) Zivcon

RIVA AND HER CHILD

The last night in the Libau Ghetto had been long, endlessly long, and frightful. Still, Riva Zivcon did not want it to end. She was certain that daylight would reveal a new and fully cruel fate.

For hours she could look only at her little Adinka, just three years old a month before, now asleep, oblivious to the imminent arrival of a tortuous future. Riva thought of her husband, Leopold, and his execution at the lighthouse barely a month after the Nazi arrival two years ago. Perhaps she was seeing Adinka for the last time; perhaps she would soon be carrying her to a sandy grave by the sea. All night her inward eye chased the bliss of solitude.

"*Schneller! Schneller! Marsch! Heraus!*" screamed a hoarse, drunken voice. It was 4 AM. The door banging made the walls shake. Trembling, Riva ran to open the door. There stood *Bismarck*, Hans Baumgartner from the SD, murderer of a thousand Jews. Riva bolted back inside to fetch a swaddled Adinka and the suitcase she had packed the day before.

Encompassed by threats and curses, she hurried down to the ghetto yard.

It was still dark. Scores of black silhouettes with hunched backs seemed to Riva as wakeful dreams darkened into nightmares. Still, she feared losing the substance of her humanity by grasping at the shadows. Despair and helplessness was in eveyone's eyes. But Riva kept telling herself that only courage could save Adinka, and that courage must have hope for nourishment. She was entirely fearful, but she was determined to resist her fear, even master it. All goes if courage goes, she whispered to Adinka again and again.

As the Jews assembled in the main yard, on German orders, the Jewish police confiscated their watches. Soon, they were herded into the street and ordered to line up. When the Jewish police and doctors were directed to a side yard, people broke ranks and began to run to that yard, thinking they might be permitted to stay. Furiously shouting, Kerscher and Baumgartner began chasing people back to the street. They were ordered to line up in a column of threes. Old women and children were confused and could not find their place. Baumgartner was furiously flailing his arms and shouting that he was missing people. With a surreal calmness, the Jewish police restored order and arranged the needed column.

Guarded by eighty Riga SD-men, 750 Jews began their march to the unknown. Children were crying, old women were collapsing, young women were stooped under the burden of children in their arms and bundles on their backs. It was all so pitiful, far worse than most had imagined. After but a few steps, many could not walk and threw away their baggage, afraid that if they trailed behind they would be shot. The young held the arms of the elderly to preclude their collapse. Even Riva's determined body began to rebel, but she clung to her suitcase filled with food and necessities for Adinka. With her last strength she managed the remaining 700 meters to the *Sagerplatz*. There, open-doored freight cars awaited the rather sagging column of Jews.

The climb into the cars was steep and especially difficult for children, the elderly, and those carrying infants, toddlers, and bags. The railway platform was chaotic. Adding to the tumult was Baumgartner shouting aimlessly that the pail with the watches had disappeared. Before long, many Jews were simply thrown into the cars. At the last, all were inside, the outer doors shut, and the locks securely placed. Pressed tightly together, they were mostly on the floor, exhausted and disquieted. The train began to move. It would journey awhile, then stop; journey awhile, then stop. This pattern was interminable.

Riva and Adinka were in the last car. The temper of the train was grim. Everyone was consumed by their own thoughts, imagining the unimaginable. Would they be ordered out at the next station, perhaps to be gassed? Very many had poison in their pockets, determined to rob their tormentors of the endmost domination.

On one occasion, the train halted, the door opened, and several Latvian SD-men entered the car. One of them lifted old Mr. Binder inside. He was in terrible pain. Kidney stones. Dr. Yitzok Baron tried to provide as much comfort as possible. A curtain of coats was made. After some hours of agony, the stones passed and Mr. Binder was relieved. Meanwhile, the other SD-men demanded that everyone turn in their gold and diamonds at once. They refused to believe that all had been confiscated in the ghetto yard. "This cannot be," they snarled. "Jews without money, this is not possible!" Disgusted, they snatched Mrs. Rabinowitz's coat. Her son, Yasha, pleaded that his mother was nearly 70 and ill. "*Saujuden!*" they screamed as they exited the car's door. The train rolled again.

The Libau Ghetto Jews had boarded the freight train about 6 AM. Countless hours had gone by; daylight gave way to darkness. At what some would learn was 2 AM the next day, the train came to a complete halt. Almost immediately, the doors slid open and the maniacal shouts began. "*Marsch, heraus, schneller! Verfluchte Juden*! ("Let's go, out, faster! Damned Jews!) Everyone was confused. Where were they? What awaited them?

As before, from car to ground was steep and difficult to negotiate for the elderly and mothers with children and bags. This resulted in the familiar panic and chaos, which was only heightened when folks realized they were in the middle of a forest, convinced they would soon be shot. Riva's tremors plunged head to toe. Adinka had fallen asleep, oblivious to all. Riva barely had the strength to hold her. On all sides, old people fell to the ground as they jumped in panic from the car. "*Schmeisst die Pakete weg!* (Toss the packages away!)," screamed the Germans. "*Schneller, marsch, voraus!*" Despite the uproar, everyone somehow managed to fall in line and started marching through the forest in deep sand. All goes if courage goes,

Riva again whispered to Adinka. Perhaps this journey was at an end. Lights in the near distance revealed an enormous barrack. Still, the ten minute walk seemed endless to Riva.

Before they could enter the barrack, they had to discard their bags—only empty hands could pass through the door. The barrack was vacant, just a few benches and a table in the center. Most sat down straightaway, either on a bench or on the floor. German criminals, brought to Camp Kaiserwald for construction, now served as foul-tongued and malicious guards. Israelit and Kaganski, the Jewish elders of the Libau Ghetto, approached the supervisor, explained their position, and inquired about their collective fate. The hooligan replied that everyone would be assigned work, with the exception of the elderly and women with small children. They would be sent to the Riga Ghetto until the remaining barracks were ready. Israelit informed the others. Most were a bit more sanguine, but the mothers of little ones remained suspicious.

With dawn, the children began to cry and ask for food. There was none, for the bags remained outside the barrack. Riva implored the supervisor to allow her access to her bag so that she might feed Adinka. The reply was swift—curses and threats. Coatless Mrs. Rabinowitz, no less, provided relief. Somehow she had managed to smuggle a bit of bread into the barrack, and she hastened to divide it amongst the small children. A short while later, others began asking the supervisor if they might step outside to relieve themselves. At first he refused. But after a rather raucous consultation with several fellow guards, he announced a reprieve. Those in need were to line up and go out one at a time. "In two more days everyone will have had a turn!" bellowed the supervisor. Hooligan horselaughs echoed through the eves of the huge barrack.

Outside in the barrack yard, Riva now had a glimpse of where she was. The camp was a rectangle enclosed by a barbed wire fence with guard towers at intervals along the perimeter. Just beyond the entrance were the administrative barracks, like the one with the Libau Jews, and others for the SD and their accomplices. She also saw people in prison clothing, their shirt backs and pants streaked with oil-paint stripes in various colors. Weary and resigned, they appeared to be heading for work in one of those barracks, perhaps in a special workshop. Behind this front area, Riva could easily see separate sections for women and men. The women's section was on the left, and was separated from the men's section immediately to the right by two parallel barbed wire fences between which lay a walkable area about six feet across. Each section had several barracks.

Soon after Riva returned to the barrack, an SD-man arrived and ordered everyone outside. They were to line up in threes, the men facing the women. As usual, the elderly were confused, and ran wherever their legs took them. And, as usual, the SD-man was enraged: "You have five minutes to line up properly. I am leaving and when I return, if you have not done so, you will all be severely beaten!" In moments, the Jews conquered chaos.

First the SD counted the men, asking their ages, how many children they had, and what ages. The men were ordered to enter another front barrack in a brisk trot. Then the SD began to count the women. They started, they stopped. They started again, and stopped again. The women remained standing outside in the cold. The children were crying. They were soon joined by the sterilized Jewish women of Libau: Fleischmann, Gottschalk, Silbermann, Pogantsev, and others. Jewish wives of "Aryans" were initially permitted to reside with their husbands if they agreed to sterilization. Their protected status ended a few days before liquidation of the ghetto when they were arrested and transferred to Kaiserwald.

Once again the women lined up for a count, and again it was terminated part way. They were ordered back to the barrack. A Polish prisoner brought black coffee and the women and children quenched their thirst for the first time since arrival at the camp. Just then a new group arrived, elderly men from the Riga Ghetto and badly crippled young men. The women were ever more certain that they were closer to death, after all the Germans were not about to establish a children's home or build an asylum for the aged and crippled. Before long the dreaded selection began.

Each women was asked her age, how many children she had, and their ages. Single women under 50 were sent to another barrack, and the remainder stayed in place. Riva saw Rivka Stein pacing to and fro with her year old child, gesticulating with her left hand, talking to no one in particular.

"I must do it, there is no choice, I must do it," she murmured. Riva was puzzled by the meaning of her repetitive declarations.

"Hold the baby for a while, I will be right back," Rivka Stein directed her mother. She promptly approached the guard.

"So, I have said goodbye to my mother and I want to return to my barrack now," Stein declared. The guard, unaware of anything untoward, told Rivka to proceed.

Seeing this, some of the other women made the same decision. Mrs. Heller placed her one year old on the large table, said she was coming back, and was gone. Mrs. Itrof and Zisi Vestermann handed their children over to other women and left alone. Mrs. Itrof's son was three, and Zisi's daughters were seven and nine. Klara Stein begged her daughter-in-law, Chaya Klompus, to leave her three year old son, Daniel, with his *Bubba* and do like the others. Chaya refused: "Wherever my child will be, I will also be." Riva's mother-in-law, Elke Zivcon, as well tried to convince her to leave Adinka and save herself.

"Go, Riva dear, you are still young, you can still save yourself. You cannot help Adinka anyhow, leave her with me. I am already old, and there is no hope for me either."

"No, Mama, life without my child would be worse than death. Whatever will happen—life, death—Adinka and I will be together." Riva embraced her mother-in-law, a wordless expression of how moved she was by her concern. As they both cried, Adinka clung to her mother as if she understood.

Within minutes several trucks rumbled up to the barrack. SS-men with rifles got out, entered the barrack, and odiously ordered everyone outside and into the trucks. No one wanted to be first, everyone wanted to gain a few more minutes, perhaps even an hour. The near certainty of death provoked thoughts of a miracle. The SS-men grew furious and began pushing them out the door and into the trucks. In the ordinary run of things, they used wordless violence as the rhetoric of terror and force. As though by the flip of a switch, the barrack mates suddenly became more and more subdued and upright—a collective union of dignity and grace. Riva did not want to wait any longer. She took Adinka in her arms and climbed onto a truck with many others.

As the truck journeyed through the forest, Adinka clung to Riva and cried terribly. Riva imagined the forest as their destination, the mass graves their fate. She closed her eyes and thought only of her past, and all that was beautiful about it. Her childhood, her mother and siblings in Palestine, Leopold, the day Adinka was born. Time stood still, as it always does in the past. The reverie was broken when another woman suddenly screamed out: "Children, there is the city! Riga! We are saved!" There it was, the city, and a bit farther on the barbed-wired ghetto. Elation yielded to quiet tears. They looked at one another as if each had returned from the nether world.

Entrance to the Riga ghetto. This photo was taken from outside the ghetto fence

A sign, in both German and Latvian, warning that people attempting to cross the fence or to contact inhabitants of the Riga ghetto will be shot

Stunned, everyone alighted from the trucks and passed through the Ghetto gate. Yet again, there was in the worst of fortune the best chance for a happy end. As the Libau women milled about, Dr. Klebanov, a well-known Riga Jew, distributed food for the children. After twenty minutes, the German Jewish police arrived and led the newcomers to a large, uninhabited building in considerable disrepair. There they were to settle in until more suitable quarters were found. The Riga women in the Ghetto brought them whatever they could share of their food, clothing, and bedding. They were so kind. After several days, housing assignments were made. Riva and Adinka were directed to a room on the fourth floor of a building in the section referred to as the "women's ghetto."

For the first week, although they had received work cards, none of the Libauers were sent to work. Commandant *SS-Obersturmführer* Eduard Roschmann, his assistant *SS-Scharführer* Max Gymich, German Jewish police chief Rudolf Haar, and most of their underlings were caught up in the dissolution of this very Ghetto. Over the past several months, thousands of Jews had been sent to Kaiserwald, sometimes to *Kasernierung* stations where Jews lived and slept near satellite job sites. All this made little sense: Riga Jews were going to Kaiserwald and Libau Jews in Kaiserwald were sent to Riga at the very moment the Ghetto was being closed. Riva and the others struggled to diagnose the moment.

With the second week, the Libau women received work assignments. The older women were to look after the small children; the younger women were assigned to various jobs, some pleasant, most unpleasant. Riva worked with fifty others sorting bloodied rags with bullet holes returned from the war front. Each morning Riva and her mates gathered in an orderly column and marched off to work with the Latvian women who supervised them. When they could, the women "liberated" usable clothing for themselves and others, just as the women of the potato crew "liberated" potatoes. This was dangerous, but essential. The Libau women had brought little clothing with them, and the daily rations were too meager to live on and too much to die on.

Over the remaining days of October 1943, Riva and the others settled into the routine of their new home. Inescapably, each awoke in sadness nearly every day . . . mistreatment is never as painful as the thought of being mistreated. Life had become an irrational, noncontextual arrangement—purposely. The Libau women were organizing a structured existence in a ghetto that was closing.

As October came to an end, most of the Ghetto inmates had been transferred to Kaiserwald; only a few labor crews like the Libau women, old people, children, and administrative personnel remained. On 2 November clarity emerged. *SS-Scharführer* Gymich organized a hundred-man SS guard that surrounded the Ghetto. The final selection began: Kaiserwald over here, Auschwitz over there. This process continued on and off for 10 days. Everyone yearned for Kaiserwald with its hard labor and vicious guards. The elderly, the sick, children under ten, and the mothers who would not leave them, had no chance.

After the final round of assignments to Kaiserwald, those left behind were ordered home. Not thirty minutes passed when the SS began going from house to house, ordering everyone to make themselves ready to line up in the street with their bundles of essentials. Riva, hands shaking, packed a sack and was downstairs in twenty minutes. The yard was still empty. Only Adinka and Riva, her mother-in-law, and a few others were there. Carrying Adinka, Riva and her mother-in-law left the yard and began to slowly walk the ghetto streets. Riva led the way absentmindedly, not knowing their destination, and thinking little about their fate.

Abruptly, Riva caught sight of an SS detail with rifles entering the Ghetto, and several trucks in the distance. Their intent was certain, as was Riva's reflexes. Without weighing her prospects of success, she parted from her mother-in-law on the pretext that Adinka needed to pee. Slowly, she went in search of a hiding place. Every door she tried was locked. That is, until she arrived at a little house in the "men's ghetto." Shortly beyond the ground floor entrance, Riva spotted a room off the entrance hall. There she crouched with Adinka in a dark recess behind the door. Riva greatly feared that Adinka would cry out. Ceaselessly she humored Adinka with her favorite folk tales. Hours passed in quiet, morning drifted into afternoon. All the same, Riva's whole body trembled as she imagined the consequences of capture.

Mid-afternoon brought voices. The voices grew louder, and through the crack between the door and its jamb Riva saw two policemen with rifles enter the hallway. They were searching the flats. One opened the door and the other entered for the search. At the last, they arrived at Riva's storeroom. Her heart pounded, her body jittered. She placed her hands over Adinka's face to keep her from making a sound. The footsteps came closer and closer. Less than a meter now separated Riva and Adinka from the policeman. Riva pressed Adinka's nose closed, now she was not even permitted to breathe. For an eternity, she prayed to God to keep them safe, to save Adinka.

Daring not to look through the door-jamb crack any longer, Riva relied solely on her hearing. In moments, the footsteps faded further and further down the hallway, until finally the front door slammed shut and there was quiet once again. Riva dropped her hands from Adinka's face. Silently, Adinka looked at her mother with fear and distrust, a child's reproach . . . .

> Mama, dear Mama, speak!
> What have I done
> that you secrete me in concavities
> as though I were a *ganef*?

Am I a sinner,
imposing upon the weak?
Even a mere tot deserves
a word of explanation . . . .

Terror-riven beyond measure,
your threatening glance
peers from a deathmask,
a pupillary lividness.
Your embrace is loveless,
my face buried in your clasp
as if there is air for one,
and it is not me . . . .

Now tears escape their lids
as you beseech pardon
with talk of frenzied rescue
and mad mongrels:
"Oh Adinka, my sweet *mamaleh*,
my lament melts in the air,
for I alone know we are besieged
by angels of death that prowl the shadows.
You inquire of your misdeeds,
of your contemptible crime.
Well, my dear, there is but one:
You were born a Jewish child!"

---

ganef: thief; *mamaleh*: endearing diminutive for a girl, lit. little mother

At dusk Riva and Adinka were once again startled, this time by the sound of gunshots in the street. Were these meant to scare would be evaders? To end the life of those inmates who marched with difficulty to the waiting trucks? Or perhaps it was just another sadistic game? Within the hour, there was again complete silence. When deep darkness enveloped the Ghetto, Riva and Adinka emerged from hiding. Riva searched about cautiously for a refuge more secure than the nooks and crannies she had thus far uncovered. Peering from the shadows, Riva saw a lone man walking slowly nearby. To her joy, it was Mr. Meller, a Riga Jew who had helped her before.

"Mr. Meller . . . Mr. Meller," she called in a loud whisper.

"What are you still doing here?" blurted Meller, clearly taken aback. "How did you manage to elude them?"

"I found an empty storeroom . . . two policemen came round after awhile but I kept Adinka quiet with my hands . . . it became dark and very quiet and I'm looking for a more secretive hideaway."

"Bravo! Well done. Come with me."

Meller led them to the attic of a nearby "atticless" building. She opened the door and was electrified. There was Alya Ring, Rachel Falestkis, Rosa Nieburg, and Jetti Berman. All Libau women who had saved themselves and their children by hiding in this unobvious sanctuary. Unknown to Riva, Alya Ring had planned for this contingency weeks ago. They were joined by Mrs. Glazer and her child from Riga, two women from Dvinsk with their children, a woman from Russia who had smuggled her child to Riga in a sack, and a group of children who were motherless. Meller and several other men brought food, and joined them for communal meals. They lived like this for a whole week.

The afternoon of their eighth day in the attic, Mr. Obermann, an acquaintance of Rachel Falestkis, arrived breathless. He was certain the attic was revealed. They had to pack quickly and leave. Right behind him was Meller. He quietly told Riva to take Adinka and her bundle and come along with him. They hid in one shed and then another. One escape and then the next was planned, but one way or other it came apart. Several days passed. The ghetto became emptier and emptier. Only the inmates of house 66, the workshop, remained.

Meller talked with the Jewish wagoneers who were carting away Jewish belongings, such as they were in the ghetto. They promised to help Riva and Adinka escape, and to provide them with 1000 marks. One morning Meller arrived with the workshop foreman and a Latvian policeman, a corporal named Avots who had selflessly volunteered to spirit Riva and Adinka from the ghetto. Riva and Meller approached the wagon drivers for the promised money, and they refused. They feared Riva would be caught and forced to reveal their names. Pleading with them was useless. Meller was shaken, but not paralyzed. He hurried to his flat to fetch the gold ring he had sewn into his other pants. He gave it to Riva, along with 40 marks, half of all he had saved. The workshop foreman gave her 150 marks. With Meller's help, Riva gathered a few meager belongings and packed them in a suitcase, along with some bread.

At nightfall, the policeman took Adinka in his arms and off they went. He told Riva he expected no trouble from his Latvian comrades, but feared the Jewish police might detain them. When they arrived at the ghetto gate, he announced with clear authority: "Corporal Avots with wife and child." They passed through with merely a wave. But, not a hundred meters beyond the gate, Avots was stopped by a German who was railing at a rather twisted Russian woman. Avots told Riva to take Adinka and stand aside in complete silence. He approached the raging SS-man. The German had caught the woman stealing and insisted that Avots take her to the prison. He assured him that he would, and the German went on his way muttering something about Russian cultural depravity. When the SS-man was out of sight, Avots released the women. Riva, Adinka, and Avots continued on their way.

They arrived at 10 Baron Street, where Riva had a Latvian acquaintance, Mr. Vēstnis. Unfortunately, the building now housed only German soldiers. Riva was distraught. Avots, not at all: "When I start something, I finish it!" He led Riva and Adinka to his girlfriend's flat. They were to present themselves as Russians. And thus they did when they entered the flat in the midst of a rather lively party. Latvian peers were drinking, dancing and singing. Avots took his girlfriend aside to explain. Quickly, they all disappeared to a bedroom in the rear of the flat. Riva put Adinka to sleep, and was obliged to don borrowed clothing and join the frivolity. It was difficult, even repugnant. Still, she steeled her composure and disguised her embittered heart for the sake of her daughter.

Riva and Adinka had been in the flat several days when Avots' girlfriend discovered they were Jews. She overheard Adinka speaking Yiddish, the only language she knew. Avots' girlfriend was frantic. They could stay there no longer. Avots complied. After a day of snooping about, he managed to discover where Vēstnis now lived. That evening he arranged for a coachman to take all three of them to Vēstnis. Vēstnis received Riva and Adinka cheerfully, though his trepidation was palpable. He was already hiding Arnov, the viola-player from the Libau Opera. Poor Vēstnis. Life was three Jews and a blank future.

While Riva battled influenza and Arnov dyspepsia, Vēstnis spent two weeks desperately seeking contact with the underground. His efforts came to naught. It was then that Riva decided to return to Libau, in the hope that familiarity would breed opportunity. Vēstnis agreed to buy her a train ticket. It was only two months since Riva and Adinka had left Libau, but it seemed like two years. Riva hardly expected a warm welcome. Still, she was confident she could arrange something.

On 10 December 1943, they boarded the Libau train at the Riga station without documents and without a ticket for Adinka. The Latvian couple with whom they shared a compartment was most friendly, providing Adinka with endless sweets. This was critical to Riva. Adinka's mouth was otherwise occupied, so she didn't speak any Yiddish. The conductor was also quite decent. Informed that Adinka did not have a ticket, he casually requested that Riva purchase one at the next stop. It was done, with the aid of their compartment mates. The woman insisted that her husband purchase the ticket so that Riva could mind her daughter. Riva and Adinka arrived in Libau at 1 AM. Adinka was firmly asleep. Riva stepped off the train with the little girl in one arm and a suitcase in the other.

Riva stumbled about the streets in the early morning darkness. Blocks from the train station, a kempt passerby offered to help. In desperation, she agreed. They made their way to 18 Valdemar Street, where Riva had lived until entering the Libau Ghetto nearly 18 months ago. The front door was locked.

"Do you have a key?" the young man asked.

"No, my sister was expecting me earlier in the evening, but the train was delayed. I suppose she thought I would come in the morning and she went to bed."

"So what will you do?" pressed the lad.

"I think I will just wait here until daylight. I don't wish to awaken the neighbors with my ringing and knocking . . . . This is not a problem, Adinka is tight asleep and I'm warmly dressed . . . . Thanks for your help . . . . Please, a gift for your generosity." The young fellow accepted the vodka and cigarettes that Vēstnis had given her for just such an occasion, and off he went.

After some minutes, Riva took herself and Adinka to number 32, several houses down the block. There lived Zinaida Stankevich with her husband, Johan, and their nine-year-old daughter, Eva. Zinaida was at first thrilled to see an old friend.

"I can't believe it is you.... After all of this time.... What has happened? How did you get here? I thought you had been taken away to Riga.... And look at Adinka, how beautiful she is, just like her mamma."

"They took us to a terrible work camp at Kaiserwald, and then they took us by truck to the Riga Ghetto. But it was closing and they were killing the old people and the sick and the little children, and I went into hiding with Adinka, and a wonderful Latvian policeman bought me a ticket, and I arrived in Libau not one hour ago, and I need your help...."

Before she could undress Adinka, Zinaida began to cry.

"I'm so sorry Riva, I just can't. Yesterday the SD tore through our flat.... Without a reason someone denounced us to the police.... I feel so badly, Riva. You are a dear friend. But they will shoot us all ... They will murder my little Eva."

Clearly, Riva and Adinka had to leave. It was a bit after 2 AM. She went back to number 18, only this time it was to an alley door that led to the janitor's flat. This door was locked as well. Riva was determined to sit on the steps and wait till dawn. Soon the frigid December air became unbearable, so she knocked on the janitor's door. Her step-daughter opened the window and demanded, "Who is knocking at this hour?" Riva was too frightened to answer, but soon enough she was recognized and welcomed in. "Surely, you can stay awhile until you find something more secure."

The next morning Riva went to see another old Latvian friend, Mrs. Kumels. She was not able to help, but she introduced Riva to a woman friend, Otilija Shimelpfenig, who would be pleased to hide Adinka. Otilija is a tall, thin woman in her fifties, with dark hair and a ready smile. A childless widow, she lives alone on Republic Street, not far from the Sedols. Riva thanked Otilija for her kindness, but she needed more time to think about separating from Adinka, even for a short while.

After several tense days at the janitor's flat, Riva tried again. She went to visit her elderly friend, Jenny Kirstein. Jenny's husband Abram, a Jew, was murdered more than 2 years before. She now shared her flat with Alex Ridnik, a half-Jew who pretended to be Russian and practiced the Orthodox faith. Just two months ago, his Jewish wife, who had been allowed to live with him after agreeing to be sterilized, was deported to Kaiserwald. Jenny was happy to have Riva and Adinka, but Alex was enraged and demanded they leave.

Her last hope was with the close friend of her murdered husband's cousin. With Mrs. Kirstein carrying the suitcase, Riva and Adinka walked to the Sedols at 14 Kauf Street. Johanna and Robert greeted an old friend and her little girl warmly. They shed their coats, hats, and gloves, and settled in for a lunch of cabbage soup and bread. Riva asked Robert about her cousin-in-law, David Zivcon. Robert told her that he had last seen David riding in a truck months ago, but had no idea where or if he was. Riva then recounted her agonizing trek from Libau to Riga to Libau again, and the torment of having nowhere to hide.

"You know how deeply I care, Riva," Robert said with genuine empathy, "but it's impossible to hide a small child . . . . she would expose us all."

Riva and Adinka stayed the night. The next morning Riva tearfully left Adinka with Otilija. She told Adinka she would return in a few days, but in the meanwhile Adinka must be a good little girl. She must not upset "Aunt" Otilija. Riva briskly walked out the door and to the station. As Riva rode the train back to Riga, Otilija initiated her oft-repeated admonition: "All that you remember about your mother is a dream; life with *me* is your reality!" Adinka's name was now Gertruda.

On arrival in Riga, Riva went to the flat of Vēstnis, hoping he could spirit her to the underground. He was shocked and insisted that he could no longer help. He bought her another ticket to Libau and off she went. Anxiety, fear and remorse are terrible traveling companions, they make the journey endless. In hours, she was again a frozen wraith on a Libau park bench. Near panic, her heaviest baggage was a broken heart. As if a tumbling stone reacting to the point of a shoe, Riva found her way back to 14 Kauf Street and the stairway to the Sedols . . . .

A warm glow filled the room. The power shut off again, a small kerosene lamp provided just enough light for Johanna to continue her simple knitting. Firewood crackled in the kitchen stove and heat radiated throughout the small flat. The girls were sound asleep, as was most of the town, creating a welcome quiet, even stillness. The flat was more than a place to hang one's hat, it was a hearth in an expanse of darkness.

Robert sat at the table with an open book in his hand, but Johanna knew his mind was elsewhere. Robert was distraught. He had sent Riva Zivcon and little Adinka away. He had sent them out alone. He was sure there was now no hope for Riva and her daughter. Could he really have been of no help? Could he now only take small risks? Robert's soul was unsettled and his conscience passed harsh judgment. This second evening of painful denunciation was suddenly interrupted by a barely perceptible noise only well-trained ears could have heard.

"Who could that be at this hour?" Robert wondered when he heard soft footsteps approaching.

At that moment there was a knock at the door, a timid and furtive knock.

"Please!" Riva pleaded.

"Shit! The door is stuck," Robert grunted, as he used his proletarian strength to pull the door open.

"Riva! Where is your little girl?" Johanna exclaimed.

"Not now," Riva barely managed to whisper, her eyes reddened and again filled with tears.

"All right, later. Come in, take off your coat," Johanna gently instructed as she embraced Riva and led her to the kitchen table.

"Sit, eat some cabbage and potatoes . . . have some tea."

Almost absentmindedly, Riva did as she was told.

"I must tell you something very important," Robert blurted out like a confession of the guilty. "True, I should have told you last time, when you were here, but I hope you will forgive me . . . . I simply had no right to do it."

Robert made no sense to Riva. No rights? Who has rights? This is a nightmare, after all.

"Remember you asked me where David was?"

"What? Do you know where he is?" Riva screamed.

"Yes, I not only know, but he and Henni and five others are here in this building . . . . in a secret cellar."

Riva stood and headed for the door. Robert retrieved her coat and rucksack, and together they descended to the cellar.

ESCAPE FROM PAPLAKA

The new year arrived, 1944 seemed indistinguishable from 1943. The building at 14 Kauf Street spun out its daily routine. The bakery in the rear yard took morning delivery of flour sacks and twice daily dispatched bread to market. Early each morning Robert Sedols entered the cellar. Before long a fire glowed in the furnace and the water pump began to rumble. Soon he would make his deliveries, a repaired radio, a new blouse, mended trousers, and then be off to the central market down the street. All the while five men and three women, with spartan bedding, scant belongings, and seven loaded pistols on a shelf, made their lives in the concealed cellar cave.

David Zivcon thought often of me and the other captives in Paplaka, but mostly about me. We had been close for years. By now the SS outpost twenty miles from Libau was well developed, two large barracks for Latvian *Waffen-SS* recruits and Ukrainian auxiliaries, as well as officer's quarters, a kitchen, garage, workshops and all the rest. As incarceration goes, I suppose the 30 or so of us had it relatively good. Our quarters had heat and running water, our meager rations were prepared in the soldiers' kitchen, and our unusual freedom of movement allowed us to barter with the Vācis family farm north of the camp and the Brūveris family farm to the west. Life in Paplaka was quite different from that in the cellar at 14 Kauf Street. Life in Paplaka was limital, life in the cellar is open-ended.

Hating fascism with all his being, Robert had chosen a resistance informed by his old and enduring friendship with David. Despite the heavy burden on his family, if the Nazis wished to destroy all the Jews, then he was morally and politically compelled to thwart their intent. And so it was in mid-April, coincident with Passover, that Robert came to the cellar one evening to ask his friend to stand with him once again.

"What do you think, would there be room here for a few more?" Robert asked gently.

"What folks do you have in mind, and how many?" David responded.

"Just yesterday I encountered several Jews in the market. They were loading cattle carcasses onto an open-backed truck. Even though they were guarded by some Latvians, I managed to have a brief conversation with them. They told me they were from Paplaka, and that there are about 30

Jews who labor there . . . You know, David, I feel I must snatch even one of these prisoners from the fascist bastards."

"Robert, what are you thinking? To begin with, you will be arrested or killed if you try this in the market. What will become of your family, and of us? . . . . Then there is the matter of your memory. I have been telling you about the Paplaka Jews and my dear friend Kalman Linkimer for six months. How many times have I needled you to find out about Kalman's welfare, that we had to find a way to bring him here, with us?"

"I'm sorry, David, you're right. What do you suggest?"

"Perhaps you could pass a note to a carcass-loader, or some other prisoner, and have him deliver it to Kalman. We should address it to Mr. Kalish, the *nom de réfugié* he chose when we first entered the ghetto. We could invite him and two or three others to join us."

Robert agreed, and a few days on the note was delivered. I felt assured, but would there ever be a suitable moment? Less than a week later, I received another note: "Mr. Kalish, as I urgently need workers in my shop, please come without delay!" For two days I read this simple sentence over and over again. I became convinced that the end was near for the Jews of Paplaka. I spoke with Aaron Vesterman and Zelig Hirschberg and we struggled with the timing of our escape. It was a sterile exercise for the Germans would make the decision for us.

Friday, 28 April 1944. The trees were grandiloquent with the light green foliage of spring. The sun shone brightly and nature was alive with joyous expectation. I returned from work with Aaron at noon. Feeling poorly all morning, I chose to nap. Aaron retrieved his soup and sat down nearby. Before long I was startled awake by weeping. Hedda Gutmann was sitting next to my bed, her face buried in her trembling hands.

"The SD car is here," she sobbed. "Baumgartner came up to the construction office and asked who the boss was. I don't know what this means, but our chief is very upset. There are another three SD men standing by the car. I can't stop shaking, Kalman . . . . I'm sure they've come to take us all away."

With Hedda's words, I bolted upright. I was not altogether surprised, but I knew that time and chance determined life and death. I jumped out of bed and grabbed my money, 1500 marks which I had saved for just this moment. Aaron and I went from room to room to tell the others.

"So, Kalman, what will you do?" Rachel Brinn asked.

"I don't know yet, Rachel. Whatever it is, they will not take me alive."

"It's crazy to try an escape!" bellowed Moishe Itrof. "We'll all be killed for sure . . . and, besides, we really don't know what this is all about."

I wanted to bid farewell to everyone, but I was heartbroken. I knew what Baumgartner's intent was, and I, "Mr. Kalish," had a better offer. Still, Moishe was right, we didn't really know what was happening. I was determined not to inflict my panic on the others.

"*Az der mogen iz laidik iz der moi'ech oich laidik* (When the stomach is empty, so is the brain)," I declared in self-mockery as Aaron and I left the prisoner's quarters in the old bakery.

Aaron went to hide in the bushes bordering the small forest across the road and behind the supply depot. I rushed to the kitchen to tell Zelig all that had taken place and told him where to join Aaron and me. Before long, all three of us lied in wait, obscured by spring's bounty. Soon Ukrainians began walking about nearby. We had to leave. We ran to the supply depot, where we met Eli Feldman. In a corner was six-year-old Bubi Itrof, left there by his father, Moishe, while he sought answers.

"Come, from the window you can see everything," Eli said in a voice as pale as his face. Zelig crept over to Eli and they both kept watch. In ten minutes or so they observed two Germans, Panpecky and Lange from the construction office, going into the kitchen. Moments later they emerged empty-handed and headed towards the supply depot, fifty meters away. Zelig bolted from the depot and headed across the road and into the forest west of the prisoner's quarters. I followed, and then Aaron. Eli ran as well, but eastward. Bubi's heart-rending shout, "Me too, me too," necessarily went unanswered. To this moment, it has not left my mind's ears.

We ran down a small hill and continued running west through fields and swamps until we arrived at the Brūveris farm. Zelig and Aaron hid on the side of the barn and I went to find Mrs. Brūvers. She was not at home, but as I headed back I saw her walking on the road toward Paplaka. I ran after her, told her about the SD car, and asked if she would find out what was happening. Mrs. Brūvers went on her way and the three of us furtively went to the hayloft and hid in the hay. There we waited. One hour, two hours, three hours, and Mrs. Brūvers did not return. We became despondent. Finally, five hours after departing, Mrs. Brūvers returned, most downcast.

"The German who buys potatoes and cabbage told me that all the Jews had been taken away to Libau to be shot, and that three escapees were caught and shot—perhaps you . . . . The cook of the security police told me that the Russians were not far off and they needed to be rid of the Jews before they retreated to Libau."

"Do you believe what they told you?" Zelig asked.

"I saw a truck, myself, standing with its back door open, and two women and one man dressed in black next to it with bundles in their hands, ready to get in. When my husband returns from Libau, I'll ask him what he saw or heard."

"So it is what we supposed," I declared.

"What do you intend to do," Mrs. Brūvers inquired. "I expect that the SD will come here. You would be so easy to find. Besides, my Russian workhand will be here soon to get hay and she must not see you."

"We will leave as soon as it is dark," I assured her. "We can't risk an escape while it is still light." She was none too happy, but she agreed, and even brought us black bread and milk.

Soon the peasant woman came to get hay, taking it down right above our heads. A few more inches and she would have discovered us. We lowered our heads and dared not breathe, as the hay over us was about to collapse. Fortunately, she did not see us and she left humming and with all the hay she needed.

About 8:30 that evening, Mrs. Brūvers rushed into the barn: "Dear boys, run away. The Germans are searching for you with dogs. You must take pity on me. You must leave here now, before we are all murdered."

At first we thought this was a ruse, a way to hold us to our promise. But through cracks in the loft we could see German and Latvian SS with their dogs searching about the farm nearby. We jumped down from the hay and left the barn, each one separately. First we ran east in the direction of Paplaka in order to slip past the dogs who were being guided west. Then we turned northwest, over hills and through fields and marshes toward Virga.

We walked briskly, with caution and purpose, looking every which way for dogs and SS. In Virga we detoured around the palace in order to avoid the sentries. We were back on the road, 4 miles from Paplaka and 16 miles from Libau. Shortly beyond Virga, we spotted a car in the distance. It drove slowly, stopping at every house. We were certain it was the SS searching for us. Despite their claims, they knew we were alive, and this was unacceptable. We quickly left the road and found ourselves tramping through a peat bog meadow filled with fresh cotton grass. From a house nearby, we could hear a dog bark. A bit farther on we found a stand of tall bushes and we lay down behind the them. Hearts pounding, looking and listening, we planned our new route.

In ten minutes we were off again, only this time not on a road. We headed southwest, in the hopes that we would get to the railroad tracks and follow them to Libau. We trudged through forest and marsh, once again. We cut our way, in a manner of speaking, through an undergrowth of hazel, heather and red huckleberry, the tall spruce and shorter oak and birch obscuring us from above. The moss and grass covered marshlands near the Vartaja River made us more slow-footed. After awhile we arrived at a small isolated road unknown to any of us. We decided not to chance it and continued through the forest until we came upon the Susta railroad station. From there we continued along the tracks toward Libau, ducking in the nearby forest whenever a train passed by.

As we approached the Gavieze station, a little more than halfway between Paplaka and Libau, we were surprised by a POW camp for Soviet soldiers. The area, floodlit and surrounded by many guard towers, presented a new challenge. We had no choice but to risk walking right by it. Aaron and Zelig didn't look particularly Jewish, so they pretended to be two drunks, talking loudly in Latvian. I put a rag around my head in the manner of a woman's scarf, and walked a few steps behind them just waving my arms in disgust. In this way we got by without incident and were once again journeying along the tracks.

Soon we arrived at an iron bridge. It spanned the Otanke River, a wide stream really, that feeds Lake Libau. There are so many lakes, rivers and streams in Latvia. They impress upon your psyche, they are cast in many folktales. Of late, I have a recurring dream: Bare trees betray a dark river unruffled by the tempest . . . my beautiful sisters lie naked on the riverbank . . . our teardrops turn to pearls and we sit in the courtyard of the Palace . . . as I put aside the garland, Mama gives me the thorns and I awake trembling. Enough. Then there was the bridge dilemma.

We thought about crossing the railroad bridge, but there was no place to go if a train came by. So, once again, we were on a detour. Through forest and marsh, we searched for a crossable point in the big stream. Without much trouble, we found it and made our way back to the tracks. The moon was setting, it was pitch dark. There was no time to linger. We had to make it to Libau before dawn.

Not fifty yards down the track, a guard house door opened and a watchman with a rifle stepped out.

"Why are you walking here?" he barked.

"Our car stalled near Gavieze station," Zelig answered in Latvian, "and we had no choice but to walk to Dubeni at this late hour. Want a cigarette?"

"Well just keep going along the tracks," the watchman wheezed through the smoke. "You'll see signs warning trespassers with arrest, but never mind. There's no one else between here and Dubeni station."

The journey from the watchman's shack to Libau seemed endless. Still with revenge on your mind and courage in your heart, you felt lighter on your feet. The thought of outwitting your tormentors carried you along with renewed energy, a second wind as they say. After crossing the meandering Ālande stream, we could see the lights of Libau. We soon went up on the road. Evading one checkpoint and then another, we finally entered Libau north of the canal that joins Lake Libau to the Baltic Sea. It was 5 AM.

Even in this predawn hour, people were on their way to work. From this point all you could rely on was *chutzpa* and luck. We adjusted our caps, lit our cigarettes, and calmly shuffled along, three laborers audibly having a conversation in Latvian about our pestering wives and unruly children. We arrived at the canal and had to cross the bridge to old Libau. Latvian police stood watch on both ends. We crossed with the others, without incident.

"Where are we going now?" I asked. I had already told Zelig, but not Aaron. The fewer who knew our destination, the better for those already there.

"I have a place to go to, but the conditions there are quite difficult," Aaron responded.

"If you wish, both of you can come with me," I calmly proffered.

All agreed. Off we went down Grosse Street, then Helenen and Julianen, and finally we arrived at the rear entrance of Sedols' building on Cathlolic Street. It was nearly 6 AM. We quickly headed upstairs, and Zelig knocked on Robert's door as Aaron and I hid in the hallway bathroom. After a moment or two the door opened.

"Mr. Kalish told me you were in need of shop workers," Zelig blurted out to Robert.

"Are you the only one here about a job? Robert inquired.

"No, there are two others, as well," Zelig replied.

"I think it is best if I talk to all three of you together. So call the others and come in and we will talk about the work."

And so he did, and we did, and the closed door greeting was very warm and somewhat festive. The first thing we requested was water.

"Johanna, give them something to eat, they must be starving," Robert bellowed as he continued to shake our hands and embrace each of us. "Eat, I will be back shortly." We devoured the bread, tea, and bowls of skabputra, the barley porridge with curdled milk and sour cream. Johanna gazed at us in silence as we recounted our journey from Paplaka: twenty miles in the black of night through forest and marsh, and alongside the railroad.

In fifteen minutes or so Robert returned: "From now on, you remain here with us!" Each of us was handed a pistol with bullets. One by one he took us down to the cellar and told us to hide behind the coal bins. Once again, he disappeared. Moments later he called us out of the shadows. We emerged bewildered. We could hear his voice but he was nowhere to be seen. As we cautiously moved into another part of the cellar, as if like mushrooms after a spring rain, five men and three women sprang up before us. It was, at first, unnerving.

David Zivcon, almost unrecognizable with his long hair and stubble, approached slowly. We stared at one another in silence for several moments, and then David and I embraced for what seemed like minutes. Still, there was silence. Behind David stood four unshaven men who bore a vague resemblance to Michael Skutelsky, Misha Libauer, Shmerl Skutelsky, and Yosl Mandelstamm. A bit off to the side were David's wife, Henni, and

Michael's wife, Hilde. Also, Riva Zivcon, the greatest surprise of all. Aaron, Zelig and I embraced and kissed each of the others in turn. The moment was simultaneously cordial and disquieting.

"So, where do you suppose we emerged from?" David challenged.

Seven months after the Libau Ghetto was laid bare, and these were David's first words to us! The three of us began a half-hearted search that expectedly proved futile. Exhausted, we hardly welcomed David's smug self-satisfaction. After a bit, he quit the game and led us to a workbench. Beneath the bench, in a darkened corner, was a sliding panel that led into the hiding place. It was an opening in the fifty centimeter thick false wall made with the "holy" synagogue bricks.

David directed the others to perform the drill of disappearing in seconds. I shall never forget this spectacle, this feral exercise. Like the rats with whom we share subterranean Libau, they went down on all fours and lithely slid through the hole into our cave. The panel moved into place and all trace of Adam's seed was no more. They were on the dark side of the moon.

Aaron, Kalman and Zelig in the cellar cave   David peers from the hidden cave entrance

In moments, the door slid open again. Aaron, Zelig, and I were beckoned to join the rest. Our last energy saw us through the hole. Twenty miles in twelve hours, darkness, evasion, and brazen silliness—all of it claimed our minds and bodies. With hardly a glance at our new home, we collapsed on floor bedding and slept for hours. Tight sleep, dreamless sleep, the sweet sleep of laboring men.

We awoke in the early afternoon. We washed up using a small basin nearby. Henni gave us shorts and shirts to change into, and we had some bread and coffee, and calming drags on several cigarettes. Patiently, everyone listened as we went on about our journey to Sedols' cellar and the imagined fate of our dear comrades in Paplaka.

After awhile my mind left the conversation. I was overcome with the thought of little Bubi Itrof crouched in a corner of the storeroom, confused and frightened. A small boy, his usually buoyant smile gone, surely in the talons of German necrophiles. Afternoon drifted into evening . . . all was still a fog. By midnight we were asleep again on the floor. When one is aching, John Donne is precisely correct . . . sleep *is* pain's easiest salve!

14 Kauf Street, home of Sedols   Stairway from Sedols' flat to front door and basement   Stairwell exit to rear courtyard

The next day was April's last. Shmerl roused us at 9 AM. We washed, dressed, and ate. For the first time, we looked about the cave with curiosity. It was Shmerl's assignment to unfurl the entire arrangement to the newcomers.

A stairway leads from nearby the Sedols' third floor flat directly to the cellar. It is a solid staircase of stone steps sided by a somewhat decorative iron banister topped with a wide wooden handrailing. Arriving at the ground floor, one comes to a landing. To the left is an open passage, and then down a few steps to a plain door that is a portal to the rear courtyard. To the right, one first encounters the front entrance on Kauf Street, and further on entry to the rickety wooden steps that descend to the locked cellar door.

The cellar door opens into the workroom we call the "front room." If one walks straight on, turning neither left nor right, one reaches another enclosed area. We call this the "back room." Here one finds the furnace for heat and hot water, as well as the water pump. Also, there is to one side a sink and a smallish tub we use for baths. If one walks left from the cellar entrance, to the far wall of the front room, one encounters the wall of holy bricks that camouflages our sanctuary. Against this wall is a rather substantial workbench, under which is hidden the secret door.

Our cave is divided into two rooms with only an archway between them. One enters first into the larger room which houses the eight men. A large portrait of Comrade Stalin peers down from a wall opposite the sliding door. David drew this picture with graphite on a board primed with white paint. It is a fine copy, full faced with the unmistakable moustache. The picture is a reminder: We are gathered here to effect our selfless duty to plot and someday execute a communal goal of liberation, revenge, and social justice. The chains are broken and we are free to bear arms; the pistols sit on numbered shelves to the right of Stalin's portrait, just below the shelf labeled ammunition. We will *not* be taken alive!

The second, smaller room is for the women. In here are three improvised beds, and a small lavatory carved out of an underground passageway. Also, there is a pantry stocked with enough food to last for some time should Robert's supply be cut off for awhile, and a water reservoir. Flip a coin and there you have it . . . the run of our fate. Best be prepared.

The "men's room" has ample space for us to sleep on the floor. There we also have a table and chairs, stools really, all with rubber leg-tips to avoid noise. On the walls hang several maps where the fronts are marked each day in quiet joy. As the bakers bake above us, you tread softly and speak in whispers. You shit in a shovel and throw it in the furnace, and listen to the home-made radio with a headset. You pee quietly, and move the chessmen with stealth.

Naye nestn, alte feygl (New nests, old birds)!

David, the electrician, said let there be light and it was everywhere. He also wired a signal-lamp from Sedols' flat to the cellar. One long signal means turn on the pump motor, a second long one means turn it off. Two short flashes signal that Robert is leaving the building, and three command us to disappear from the front room into our cave for a "stranger" is coming to the cellar. Five flashes mean that Robert is coming to the cellar alone or with a "friend." Many flashes in frantic succession signal extreme danger, and we must retrieve our pistols and stand ready.

All that I have just now told you about our cave was in place that last day in April. How clever were those who preceded Aaron, Zelig and me. Shmerl enjoyed giving us the grand tour and everyone seemed rather optimistic, even cheerful. Robert was elated when Aaron told him where to find the gold he had buried, and promised to bring schnapps tomorrow to toast brotherhood. That night I was mostly sleepless with relentless thoughts of Paplaka and Riga.

PART TWO

Jewish history and world history
grind me between them like two grindstones,
sometimes to a powder . . . .

Yehuda Amichai, "I Wasn't One of the Six Million"

MAY 1944

Morning brought the first of May and Marshal Stalin's radio *emes* (truth) for this International Labor Day: The brave Soviet soldiers shall fight on until all of Europe is liberated from the fascist dogs . . . . The Nazis are wounded animals retreating to their lair in Germany, and it is there that they will dangle from a rope.

As promised, Robert brought the schnapps that afternoon. We toasted the day, Comrade Stalin, and each other. With Aaron and Zelig, I raised my glass to David . . .

> It is our oath, David, our prayer:
> From this day, we are joined in life and death.
> Even should our fate be great torment,
> Nothing shall keep us apart.
> We are joined in great purpose,
> To exact sweeping revenge!
> And if one of us should falter,
> For lack of loyalty or courage,
> We shall blot out his name
> As though he were Amalek!

David's response was long silent embraces. Everyone then stood and Robert led us in singing the *Internationale*. I concluded our celebration by singing *Di Shvue* (The Oath), the anthem of the Jewish Labor Bund . . .

> Brothers and sisters in labor and strife,
> All of us are scattered thither and yon.
> Organize, Organize, the flag is set,
> Furiously fluttering, red with blood . . .
> An oath, an oath, of life and death!
> *A shvue, a shvue, oyf lebn un toyt!*
>
> Heaven and earth will know well,
> The starry host shall attest,
> An oath of blood, an oath of tears,
> We swear, we swear, we swear!
> *Mir shvern, mir shvern, mir shvern!*
> *Mir Shvern a trayhayt on grenetsn tsum bund!*
> We swear endless loyalty to the Bund!

David and Robert were startled, the others were bemused. There is solidarity in thoughts of revenge. But there are also fault lines among us: communist, social democrat, Zionist, and religious. Unity suppresses division, but not always.

Aaron, Zelig, and I lived, worked, and schemed together in Paplaka for sixteen months. We knew each other well when we arrived in the cellar, our habits, our moods, our eccentricities. Aaron is quiet, unassuming, skillful and deliberate. He is caring, very caring, sometimes too caring. Zelig is a tough-guy, mindful of loyalty, determined, often willful. He is a hardened romantic, a Jewish nationalist devoted to Jabotinsky and Betar. What can I disclose about myself that is not self-serving? I am a teacher of languages and literature, mathematics and chess. I am a poet. I am fussy, sometimes headstrong, and impatient with foolishness. I am a mass of contradictions: a Bundist who goes to the synagogue, a Zionist who never left Libau, a plug and a socket. In a bit more than a year, the three of us integrated our souls, learned to value one another's strengths and ignore weaknesses. When we arrived in the cellar, we had to begin this process all over again with eight others. We knew everyone, some very well, but living together in danger, in a hot cellar, is another matter.

Our first impressions of the others were mostly, not entirely, accurate. Perhaps it is better to say incomplete. Shmerl is regardful and obliging, always seeking to make our lives as pleasant as possible—preparing the potatoes, making coffee, fretting over all manner of daily needs. Misha, a jeweler precise to a fault, is always ready to do his share. Yosl, with his ever-present smile, is our resident comedian. Even in the worst of times, Yosl has a masterful wit, and you laugh even while crying: *"In mitndrinen schvangert di bobe!"* (In the midst of all this, the grandmother is pregnant!). We have endless discussions about "if" . . . if this, if that, if he, if she. On and on and on and then Yosl ends it: *"Ven di bobe volt gehat a puts, volt zi geven a zaide!"* (If your grandmother had a penis, she would be your grandfather!).

As for David and Michael, they are the foundation of our group, the dauntless spirit of resolution, to borrow from Shakespeare. David is sparing of words, his actions speak for him. It was David who made the cave livable before we arrived and continues to do so. He is a maestro. He can just about do it all. If he doesn't have the proper tool, he makes it. Michael is the complement of David—taciturn, energetic, resolute, and fearless. He quickly earns respect and admiration.

Henni is David's wife, Hilde is Michael's, and Riva is a widowed mother. These ladies are women first and last. They cook, clean, wash, and mend. And they talk and talk and talk. Endlessly they talk, sometimes out of the right side of their mouth, sometimes the left side, and sometimes the center. These ladies are women first and last.

On the evening of our third day in the cellar, Robert set off to dig up Aaron's treasure. It was hidden in the yard of the house at 7 Josef Street. Since Robert needed small, sturdy tools that he could carry without arousing suspicion, David forged a pointy, iron rod to probe the earth with, and a small iron spade to dig with. Robert went off in the dark of night, made blacker by blustery wind and pouring rain. The weather could not have been more perfect for Robert's mission. Still there was concern.

"I think Robert is taking an undo risk tonight," I remarked.

"There is no choice," David responded. "Money is being spent and soon there will be nothing left . . . . Supplying eleven Jews with food is difficult."

"Still, there must be some other way of getting money that is less risky," I shot back.

"If he's caught, it will be a disaster for all of us, even Johanna and the girls," added Zelig. "*Narishkeit* (foolishness) . . . . It's that simple!"

"Have faith," interjects Michael, breaking a long silence. "He will return with or without Aaron's gold . . . . Nothing will happen to him. Robert has experienced danger far greater than digging a hole in the mud in a downpour. He is clever . . . and careful."

Pacific words on their face, certainly. Still, everyone was tense. Sleep was foreclosed.

Just after midnight Hilde saw the signal-lamp flash five times: "Kalman, Sedols is coming!" I jumped up, crawled through the hole into the front room and there he was, wet and muddy from head to toe. With nonchalance and laughter, he pulled a large dirt-encrusted bottle from under his coat. "What might I have here?" chortled the nimble-footed smuggler.

Robert slowly made himself comfortable at the front room table as all the others gathered around. In great detail, he recounted his search and the effort of digging with a small spade meant for a window-box garden. He was filled with pride.

When all were captured by the suspense, and with great aplomb, Robert opened the wide-mouthed bottle. One-by-one he unwrapped the wads of cotton and removed the watches, forty in all. Then he skillfully maneuvered a small tin box through the bottle mouth. Inside were several gold rings and other smaller jewelry, as well as a few gold coins. Misha, the nearsighted jeweler, removed his spectacles and closely assessed each item. This bottle had been buried for more than two years. Still, everything was relatively well-kept, even the watches were mostly functional. Aaron has never spoken about the circumstances surrounding the bottle burial except to say that the contents belonged to his brother Leo.

In the cellar cave, the group inspects the unearthed watches and rings

Though it was nearly 3 AM by the time Misha finished up, Johanna brought manna and we celebrated newly begotten treasure. Zelig and I were happy to be wrong, and the others quite relieved that we were. We cooked potatoes and finished the schnapps that remained from our May Day merriment. Yosl, as usual, cheered everyone with a sardonic twist on a celebrated Talmudic saying: "*Oif drei zachen shtait di velt . . . oif gelt, oif gelt, un oif gelt* [The world stands on three things . . . on money, on money, and on money]." With the tink-tink of glasses, the May Day schnapps disappeared.

After awhile, someone, none can remember just who, suggested that each of us select a watch to commemorate our stay in the cellar. This was not easy. To start with, all were a bit *farshnoshket* (drunk). Then there was the matter of who had the temerity to choose first, and if you choose first do you select the best one and leave the second-rate for your comrades. All this was so bourgeois, but we managed. And then it was decided that since the watches were strapless, straps would be fashioned in the afternoon, black for the men and red with white trim for the women. At the first sign of daybreak, just ahead of the arriving bakers overhead, we crawled back into our cave to sleep until noon.

Our life in the hot little cave has its steady routine. We awake about 9 AM. Soon after breakfast we do the laundry and clean the floors. The ladies are in charge, but the men help as well. Laundry is done often because most of us came to the cellar with little more than the clothes on our back. Our *shmattes* (ragged clothing) quickly become dirty from sleeping on the ground and crawling back and forth through the cave hole. After the laundry, the women carefully mend everyone's *shmattes*, or they restyle the *shmattes*, making new from old. The men make or repair the *klikatinas*, the clog-like sandals we all wear. Shmerl often takes charge of preparing dinners, and later the evening baths we take on a scheduled rotation.

Afternoons, and evenings before sleep, are usually spent in the front room to gain some relief from the oppressive heat of the ovens. Afternoons are mostly occupied with chores for Sedols, or with reading, writing, conversing, and playing chess. In the evening, after dinner, we take care of communal business. First, always first, is the matter of security. We often review our rules, but mostly we remind ourselves about the volume of our voices, for every careless noise can be heard by the bakers above or in the courtyard. Shortly after I arrived with Aaron and Zelig, we all decided that when we are in the front room one of us must stand guard with a pistol. It was our decision that if a stranger should enter the cellar, despite our signal-system, he will not leave alive. A schedule of guard duty was prepared and we have followed it ever since.

Also in the evening, Robert usually appears. He brings food, cigarettes, and news. In that first week in the cellar I pressed him for news about Paplaka and Riga. Robert has always to tread carefully. Eager news mongering can raise suspicion. Along with his rather routine reckoning of risky trips to the market to fill his big suitcase with food, Robert often brought more immediately disturbing news such as the *Aktions* in Riga or the burning of Jewish bodies dug up from the killing-pits near the Libau lighthouse. The inner demons of these fascists are relentless.

* * *

That first Sunday in May, at Misha Libauer's suggestion, we began compiling a list of German and Latvian SD who we knew had killed Jews these past three years. Not only these, but local police, Jewish traitors, and our dear neighbors who blithely took ownership of Jewish belongings they had admired for years. By that Sunday evening we recorded forty-seven with current residences and deeds attached, and today we have many more. Even so, when I am dismally sober, I cynically conclude that this exercise is like selling a bearskin while the bear frolics free in the forest, and the hunters are locked in the lodge. Nonetheless, our psychic nourishment is hope, and the prospect of revenge, or shall we say *just vengeance* . . . .

>Time was, I was lashed as a dog . . .
>Three grim years,
>Heavy-laden grief daily
>Recompense.
>
>Time was, I was lashed as a dog . . .
>Ne'er a stride free
>Of my captor's howl
>To heel.
>
>Abreast the dour *duce*—
>I scarcely saw his teeth—
>I Jew-bilated circuitous
>Fetching dog dances.
>
>Heart burned and bled,
>Lash-throttled without end,
>I endured near suffocation
>To prophecy measure for measure.
>
>In time, kill-crazy animals
>Will doubtless know
>Every bullet for the other Jew
>Is found within my chest.

* * *

>Denned in a lair,
>Eleven intrepid Jews reveal
>Torturous heart wounds only
>Mendable by revenge:

"No longer stray dogs
Bridled by chump chains,
We are marked lions,
Comrades, lying in wait.

"Hands now emancipated,
Lungs broadly inspired,
Prepare hand-me-down shackles
For bestial necrophiles.

"Dream comrades of broken bars,
Of den-walls melting,
Of erstwhile bloodsuckers
Wrought in irons.

"Undaunted . . . unflinching,
Audacious before death,
Pledge to Comrade Stalin
Our sacrifice in his honor!"

Wednesday, the 10th of May, a day of contrasts, revealed to me the spectrum of uneven life in the cave. We awoke at 10:30 and alighted directly to the front room. It is close inside the cave, the air more foul-smelling with each passing day. The heat of the ovens, the absence of even a slight breeze, the clanging of bakery motors in the early morning, a recipe for fitful sleep when we can sleep at all. We schlepped about the cellar, from shit-shovel to wash basin to table. Not until noon did we eat breakfast. There was little conversation.

As we finished our tea, Robert arrived unusually early with jam and tobacco. Self-appointed, Misha snatched the whole lot and put it away for later allotment. Misha is very precise, well-ordered, methodical, one could almost say compulsive. It is to our benefit. Since I have been here, Misha has been cutting up bread every day and drying it out. This "suchares" (dried bread) he calls our iron ration, what shall sustain us should we come up short. Along with tobacco and some other foodstuffs, the iron ration is carefully hidden from the rest of us. The myopic goldsmith is even farsighted enough to hide away extra batteries and radio supplies.

Robert didn't say much. Just enough to insist that we make some alterations in our home. Drawers for the workbench that hides our cave entrance, and a change in the wash basin. David constructed a new wash basin with a hose that leads directly into the drain and muffles the noise of running water. Misha and I installed the drawers. Robert remained with us so that the noise of our work did not seem out of place. When we were done, he left.

In the evening, the ladies surprised us with a celebration of *Lag B'Omer*, the springtime "Scholars' Feast." In ancient times, an *omer* (measure) of barley was taken to the Temple in Jerusalem on the second day of Passover. Thus began the counting of 49 days, seven weeks, the traditional duration from the Egyptian exodus until the Israelites received the Law at Mount Sinai. The 50th day is *Shavuos*, the Feast of Weeks, and in ancient Israel the Feast of the Wheat Harvest. *Lag B'Omer* is the 33rd day of counting the *omer*, the two letters of *Lag*, *lamed* and *gimel*, being numerically equal to 33. It is the 18th day of the Hebrew month of Iyyar. So did the ladies learn from the Jewish calendar I hung on the wall, not terribly far from Comrade Stalin.

The Nazis have been in Libau for almost three years. There are maybe two dozen Jews hidden here and there in our once beautiful city. The Nazis are satiric, but not cleverly satiric. They don't print Jewish calendars with each new year. So where, you reasonably ask, did I find a current Jewish calendar? I didn't! Starting with our last printed calendar for 1940-41, each year I have calculated and handdrawn a new one, including the 1943-44 calendar that adorned our wall last May and the 1944-45 calendar that hangs there now. I think I am fairly accurate, but I am certain there are small errors. Surely, you will honor my intention.

What a Scholars' Feast it was. A festive meal filled the table. At each place-setting rested a small paper bag, personalized with a handwritten aphorism outside and a special pastry inside. With the little *schnapps* we had, we toasted our survival. For just a few hours our sad memories ceased and concerns for the future seemed silly.

"So tell us, Kalman, how did you work out the *luach* (Jewish calendar)?" Michael wondered aloud.

"Years ago, just before entering the Army, I became curious about the religious calendar and how it's made to conform to the secular calendar. So

I searched the bookshops for a volume I might understand. I never thought I'd fine one but I did. It was Ernst Mahler's *Handbuch der juedischen Chronologie*. It is a small book. I managed to keep it with me until I ran from Paplaka. It's strange, but the *luach* is a candle in the dark, the faint heartbeat of our people. Tied to the moon and sun, the *luach* is, in essence, mystical. It is a cipher."

"*Oy, mit Kalman di tsung iz der feder fun hartz* (Ah, with Kalman the tongue is the pen of the heart)," declared David in a concluding toast.

After dinner, nearly everyone remained in the front room. David listened to the BBC. Others of us read or talked. Suddenly, the alarm light flashed in paroxysmal panic In less than a minute everything was plucked from the table and carried with us as we disappeared into the cave.

Stone-faced and resolute we took up our predesigned positions. Six of us remained in the men's area, pistols in hand. Misha distributed the bullets. David, Michael, and I sat just in front of the entrance hatch, and Misha, Yosl, and Shmerl stood a few feet behind. The women went to their area with Aaron and Zelig. There was intense silence, not even a breath could be heard. The stillness was broken by the noise of the purposely unoiled hinges of the cellar door. The clopping of cheap soles went this way and that. After a few eternal moments, the hinges squealed once more. Had others arrived or did the first leave? We didn't know.

Ten, fifteen, thirty minutes, and nothing but tomblike silence. Where was Robert? We became certain of an ongoing house search upstairs. There was no escape. We had yet to dig the underground tunnel to a nearby yard. Recollection and anticipation filled our every moment. An hour of moments. An hour and a half. Then, without prior signal, a knock at the hatch. We hadn't heard the hinge. Were they there all this time waiting for a cough, a sneeze, a breath above a whisper?

"Open the hatch . . . . It's me, Robert."

Did we dare assume he was alone? If he is, why had he not signaled before coming?

"Come on, open the hatch! It's me, Robert!"

David slid the cave door aside and three pistols stared Robert in the face.

"On the ragged edge this evening, are you," Robert sneered as he crawled through the hole.

"Why no signal, just now?" I asked. "And what was that earlier signal about?"

"You need to be more careful with your talking and singing and celebrating," Robert responded, sullen-faced. "We need to set up an alarm on the stairway in case I must come with someone else and there is no time to signal beforehand."

David's idea was to install a light in the usually dark cellar stairway that when switched on would also switch off the lights in the cellar, an arrival signal. When Robert would enter the cellar and switch on the light, those in the cave would come on as well. On leaving, he would turn off the cellar light and the stairway light would go on, a departure signal.

Robert sat with us and talked about this and that while David and Michael completed the electrical work. After thirty minutes, the new stairway lamp was ready. Robert left and we were asleep by 4:30. We never did get an explanation of the after-dinner fright. As I said before, it was a day of contrasts. A day not unlike most days since.

* * *

May was near over and troubles mounted. Up at 8:00, I took my pistol and went to the front room for guard duty. I quietly opened both windows. For the first time in awhile, I could breathe fresh spring air. Two weeks ago, with Zelig and Aaron, I bricked over the small cave window between the pantry and the women's beds. Subtle food odors had attracted keen-nosed dogs, and we feared sounds might betray us to the bakers or others as well. So security sealed the fate of our whisps of outside air. Now the cave is tropical, and you notice your breathing.

Before long, others awoke and joined me in the front room. The women continued to sleep until nearly mid-day, as did David. Till now, they claim that being in the cellar for so many months causes nocturnal insomnia and they must sleep in the daytime. I argue constantly with them about this. If they would just go to sleep at 11 PM instead of 3AM they would be able to sleep and wake normally. Aside from a poor habit, their nocturnal goings-on are also dangerous. There are night bakers working above us, and I fear they can hear everything. As time goes by, some of us are less and less careful. I plead over and over for stricter discipline. "*Hoch mir nisht kein chinak*," they say to me. [Stop banging on my pot!] But they are wrong about this. The majority supports me on this.

Then there was and is the matter of working in Sedols' flat. That evening, Robert insisted that David and Michael install a loudspeaker in the kitchen of his flat. To do this, they had to drill a hole through a wall in the bakers' flat while they toiled downstairs. I viewed this as entirely unessential, and worse, damned risky! I made my case to all three. "How does the benefit outweigh the great risk to the lives of 11 fugitives and the Sedols family?" I argued. Robert began to have doubts, but David, in a very thoughtless and irresponsible flash of anger, clutched Michael's arm and both started up the cellar steps to Robert's flat. Even more startling was that the women were as witless as David and Michael. In a burst of pique, I exploded: "You are here nearly 8 months and you feel too free, not because you are secure or even brave, but because you have the habit of carelessness!" David, Michael and their wives were furious. I didn't apologize . . . it was true.

After two hours, David and Michael returned to the cellar. All went well. We all retired to the cave at midnight, but David and the women continued to mock discipline and remained outside until 1 AM. They wanted another hour of fresh air. This bothered me greatly. If one really appreciates the very great danger of exposure and betrayal, one must be prepared to endure weeks and months without entering the front room. If one truly believes in the important duty of revenge, one must be willing to sacrifice all.

The next morning, the last of May, I awoke at 8:30. Pistol in hand, I again went to the front room for guard duty. The lamp alarm flashed once. I turned on the pump motor. I opened both windows and sat down to read. After a foul-smelling night in the hot airless cave, the cool breeze was refreshing. Still my eyes burned and words moved about the page. I was seized by melancholy.

I had been in the cellar nearly a month. Each night, when the oven heat kept me awake, thoughts of Riga and Paplaka raced through my mind. It had been many many weeks since I received news of my sisters, my mother. I envisioned my comrades in Paplaka having to get into trucks, the panic that reigned there, little Bubi Itrof. About all, I imagined the worst.

These thoughts persist in countless sleepless nights. Yet how can I abandon them? Sure, I am now free of the beasts, of the sadists, but I am moored underground . . . impotent.

JUNE 1944

We listened to the BBC and Moscow Radio night and day, without letup. We searched for clues within the prattle, hints in the depth of the unspoken, concealed thoughts in syntax, even prognostic changes in cadence. When would the end begin, we wondered. The all-out Russian offensive in the East, the Anglo-American invasion in the West. We made so many calculations, and argued over their merits. Our lives depended on it.

June 6, 2 PM . . . David threw off the headphones and leaped from his chair: "The Allies have landed in Normandy. The invasion has begun!" Shortly after midnight, the American and British airborne, parachute troops, landed behind Hitler's much-vaunted Atlantic Wall, near the village of Ste.-Mere-Eglise. Thousands of warships, landing craft, planes, and nearly 200,000 Allied troops brought destruction to the Germans. For days on end we did little else but listen to the broadcasts. We hardly slept. We were exhausted and enraptured. Less than three weeks later the Russians breached the German lines at Vitebsk, signaling the start of the Eastern offensive. The future was still shrouded, a gauze before your mind's eye, but it was not too soon to plan your life outside the cellar.

One evening I opened the discussion of our future obligations to memory and revenge. I was already nearly certain of which comrades would be suited to join me, and whose worldview conflicted with mine. Still, anyone willing to embark on the journey with me was and is welcome.

"If all goes well, we'll soon leave this cellar. But let's be honest, we'll be crushed in spirit. Our severed souls will leave some of us numb. Just now we are shipwrecked kinfolk battling waves that threaten to swallow us. We swim in place, our heads barely above the water, dully mindful of those already consumed by the cold sea. We are worn almost bare, but our hope keeps us afloat. The last of our strength will carry us to shore and to solid ground beneath our trembling legs. It's only then that we'll truly grasp what has happened these last several years, what we have lost in the roiling cauldron. Many of us will be overwhelmed with grief, and then intense anger. This first reaction will set us on the wrong path, a path to extremes, an irrational path to outrages, *a shandeh far di goyim* (a disgrace before the gentiles)! To avoid this, we must be prepared, we must have a plan.

"First we must seek out the other hidden Jews of Libau. There are but a few of us. We must pool our resources for the well-being of all in mind, body, and spirit. Then a committee of the Libau survivors must be formed to establish contact with surviving Jews of the provinces, of Riga, of all of Latvia. From all of us, we will create a central committee which will register with the Russian authorities. With their help, we'll contact our brothers and sisters in Lithuania and Poland, and elsewhere. The misery of those who escaped the Angel of Death will be very great. Only a collective can salvage whatever remains. Only a collective can gather the evidence to justify revenge."

"How quickly you forget, Kalman, how quickly you forget," interrupted Zelig. "For a year before the Germans came, Russians persecuted us. Mass arrest of Zionists, not only my comrades in Betar, but the socialists as well. They arrested the Bundists, religious Jews, the writers, the bankers, the shopkeepers. They turned us all into dependents on the dole. Remember what happened to our schools?"

"But Zelke," I responded, "they're now the enemy of our enemies. In '40, '41, many Jews held important positions in Soviet Latvia. Your sister's husband, Hirsh Mark, was chief of the Bank of Libau."

"That isn't relevant!" Zelig shot back. "Besides, where did that get us in the end? Nowhere. Worse. Sure working-class Jews were integrated into the Soviet administrative apparatus . . . . This wasn't without great cost. As the *goyim* were being persecuted by the Russians, one could sense an increasing hostility toward Jews, even toward the Jews suffering the same as *goyim*. The job of the German *mamzerim* (bastards) was that much easier. You think we should go down this path again. I have great doubt."

"The Latvian nation must *also* be repaid according to its behavior," I answered. "What a treacherous and bloodthirsty lot! Who were the main *khapers* (snatchers) during the *Acktions* of '41 and '42? Who were the drunken shooters at the lighthouse and elsewhere? Who are in David's pictures of Skede, kicking dead Jews into the ditch? All Latvians! They so distinguished themselves that Jews are sent from all over Europe to Latvia to suffer their gruesome brutality. Latvia is a Jewish graveyard. It deserves a reward not much smaller than the Germans. But how do we do this?"

In a loud, seething whisper, David reacted: "Sure we can't trust Latvians who were arrested as Communists and were released. Sure they pledged to spy for the Germans. Sure many of them are those drunken shooters. Communists . . . anti-Communists. There are many *good* Latvians, even Communists, like Robert and Johanna. When we leave here, when we are back among the Latvians, the *goyim* as you call them, we will have a new struggle. It will go far beyond revenge. It will be a class struggle, one in which there is no room for the petty-bourgeois Bundist and religionist notions of a national culture that divides Jews from the others. There is only room for proletarian solidarity.

"Anti-Semitism is not social, it's political and economic. It's a fascist-capitalist trick to divert the anger of destitute workers and peasants in the direction of the Jews. After these grim and heartrending last few years, all will surely know it's not the Jews who are the enemy of the working people. The enemies are the fascists and the capitalists. Among the Jews there are working people, they are the majority. They're our brothers and sisters, who, like the *goyim*, are oppressed by capital. We're all comrades in the struggle for socialism. Among the Jews there are also kulaks, exploiters and capitalists, as there are among the *goyim*. They stir up distrust and hatred between workers of different faiths and nations. They don't work but stay in power by the strength of capital and the disunity of workers.

"That's why we must live as a collective, a collective to which we assign all that we possess and to which we pledge many years to carrying out our duties. And what are those duties? Seeing that each and every surviving Jew stands strong, and shoulder-to-shoulder with their proletarian comrades among the Latvians. And further, provide the Russians with evidence and a report on the German and Latvian sadists."

Zelig, Misha, and some others were not too pleased with David's salvaged Leninism. I tried to take a middle position, somewhat outside of communist orthodoxy.

"In my view," I interceded, "it'll be easier to carry out our duties as a collective. Still, this kind of collective must be based on moral obligation, not on coercion. We do this out of conviction, and the route to that conviction is less important than the conviction itself. The conviction is our moral obligation to those murdered, to seek justice and preserve memory.

"We're sitting here in the cellar, we know that the hour of our liberation nears. We so much want to actively struggle against our enemy. But how? For us, nothing remains except to do our work in secret, and when the moment is right, appear with our work as witnesses before the world."

"Ah, witnesses yes," declared Misha. "Not communist witnesses, not universal witnesses, but Jewish witnesses. Who are those thousands upon thousands who lie in mass Latvian graves, at Skēde, the lighthouse, elsewhere? Jews! We are not just a religious group, we are a distinct culture. Our wives and children, mothers and fathers, brothers and sisters, were slaughtered because they were part of the family, the Jewish family. To hell with politics and economics and class struggle and Stalin. I'm interested in justice. Not justice for proletarian comrades, but justice for the Jewish people . . . as a people!"

We went on like this until 4 AM, with no resolution.

The days that followed possessed an uneventful sameness, sometimes welcome, sometimes not. The noose from the east, west and south was closing ever more tightly around the German neck. I began clipping important stories from the local newspapers and magazines which will later serve as evidence. The propaganda from Moscow Radio became more interesting. I recall a story about the *Fraueneinsatz* (Women's Deployment) in Germany.

A woman in Neuhausen lost both her sons on the eastern front. Her husband had been severely injured by Allied bombing and was bed-ridden. She was desperate, bereft of any help or resources to deal with her fate. Unexpectedly, without notice, the authorities appeared at her doorstep and demanded she register with the *Fraueneinsatz*. Wanting to avoid trouble with the Gestapo, this woman complied. Within hours after they left, she set fire to her home and left to drown herself in the river. The next day, her body was found along the riverbank—ready for the *Fraueneinsatz*. Of course, if this once proud woman had bothered to read the footnotes to the Nazi social contract, she would have noticed that even *within* the master race there exists slavery in some form or other.

It was in June that we began our study groups. I study Latvian and Russian with Misha and Yosl, and Hebrew with Riva. David is teaching many of us electricity, and David, Michael and I study mathematics together. We have taught each other much. Moreover, study is an escape from bondage, or at least the appearance of bondage. As when I am writing, it creates a new reality.

It was also in June that we began to dig an escape tunnel to the yard. We took turns in the afternoon. First Zelig, Shmerl, Michael and David, then myself, Misha, Yosl and Aaron, each group for three hours. The work was daring, lying stretched out on the ground, doing gymnastics with the shovel. Since we had to be very quiet, the digging progressed slowly. Robert was unhappy.

Robert seemed to be more and more angry, agitated, and anxious as the month went on. First it was the slow pace of the digging, then it was the bicycle we had not assembled quickly enough, and then there were simple problems which seemed to blind Robert of simple solutions, like the wood by the window.

One day the bakers were demanding that Robert remove the wood piled in front of our bricked-up cave window. Why? They throw down hot coals from the bakery window and they feared the wood would catch fire. The purpose of the wood was to hide the fact that the window was now a wall. Robert was beside himself. We calmed him with an obvious alternative, a large wooden box filled with sand. We built the box and the next day it replaced the scraps of wood. Since Aaron doesn't look Jewish, he helped Robert carry the box to the yard and fill it with sand. Naturally, a building resident appeared in the yard and Aaron became Mr. Kalnins, Robert's new helper. In less than an hour they were both back in the cellar, Robert with a smile and Aaron a bit numb.

I would not want to imply that all matters were trivial. The baker from whom Robert bought his bread mentioned to Dr. Emilija Cena that since Robert bought such great quantities, he almost certainly was feeding underground fugitives, perhaps even Jews or communists. Dr. Cena, a friend of Robert's, passed on the gossip. Robert was quite upset, and together we planned alternative, less obvious, ways of procuring food for eleven criminals.

And then there was the heat and smoke. One afternoon we had decided to burn all the garbage and other useless junk that had accumulated in the cave. Zelig and Shmerl put it all in the furnace. Before long, but too late, we realized the draft was closed. The cellar filled with smoke, and then billowed into the yard. Tenants gathered in the yard. We could hear them ask Robert's daughter where her father was. On an errand, she told them. We feared someone might call the fire department. Quickly David made his way to the furnace and opened the draft. The smoke soon cleared. But this was not the end. Soon the temperature rose to nearly 90°F. When Robert returned, the tenants wanted to know why he would turn on the heat in the middle of the summer, making it unbearable to stay in their flats. He apologized and mumbled something about the need to get rid of garbage that might attract the rats. When he came down to the cellar, he was furious. We offered no excuse for our stupidity. Still, you almost welcomed little crises such as these, they fractured tedium.

By mid-June, sleep had become increasingly difficult. The heat in our cave was unbearable. Within minutes your whole body was drenched in sweat. You couldn't cover up with a blanket, and, lying uncovered, you were bitten by flies. Sleep arrived when exhaustion overtook discomfort. This nightly dance left you weary and depleted in the morning.

Also, in mid-June, the BBC announced that 4000 Jews had been gassed in Birkenau and 3000 more awaited gassing in a few days. I was fat with rage, made worse by the sobriety of impotence. The murderers walk about freely and I live the life of a mole. Once again, at David's urging, I raised the moral imperative of revenge, unmerciful revenge, and the non-negotiable need for a committed collective.

"We can't do this as individuals," I began. "Communal Jewish interests must trump personal ones. Every available resource, ours and others', must be placed at the disposal of the collective for communal purposes. We shall elect a troika to guide us in carrying out the plans agreed upon by the whole collective, including the use of communal resources in our war against the tormentors. Even after liberation, we'll meet here in the cellar, and no one will be permitted to amble about Libau alone, and without a pistol.

"We must be very careful, comrades. We have few friends, we can trust even fewer. Relations with Latvians are forbidden. For an exception, the collective must be notified and it must determine if the person concerned has murder on his hands. His deeds since '41 must be weighed with precision."

Unlike prior declarations, there were no objections. I was uncomfortable then and I am now. Agreement is always made more binding by disagreement. I am suspicious, and suspicion begets suspicion. What loneliness!

The penultimate day of June marked two months of my stay in the cellar. By then I had begun to master monotony. I wrote, listened to the radio, studied languages, and did chores. That evening we organized a checkers tournament, and played until past 2 AM.

The next morning, the last of June, I wrote while David and Misha were over at the workbench fashioning chess pieces in a cellar variant of the Staunton design. Later that morning, I began a novel by Maurice Dekobra, "The Madonna of Sleeping Cars." Some years before, I had seen the movie adaptation of this story. It was a silent French film. Claudia France portrayed Lady Diana, an heiress of royalty, a rather reckless widow who travels the world in search of mischief. The movie plot was highly improbable, even frivolous, but I had greater expectations of the book. I was rewarded.

The news at 2PM was uninteresting, so David, Michael and I studied mathematics for awhile. We had previously agreed to study geometry because it seemed most practical. That day we began our investigation of parallelograms, a topic critical to constructing things large and small, say a chest or a house. Hours later, as we neared conclusion of the day's study, I introduced David and Michael to a Fibonacci sequence trick.

Fibonacci was an Italian mathematician in early 13th century Pisa. He developed number sequences to solve practical problems such as those a farmer might encounter, like the fecundity of his herd. The most well-known sequence is: 1 1 2 3 5 8 13 21 34 55 89 144 233 . . . . The next number in the sequence is arrived at by simply adding together the prior two: 144+233=377. This sequence, of course, is infinite. I told my study partners to pick any number in the sequence, and I would instantly give them the sum of that number and all that preceded it. David selected 21, I said 54. Michael said 89, I said 232. They caught on quickly.

JULY 1944

Saturday, 1 July, *meshuge Shabbes*! Early in the morning, 1:30 AM early, Robert roused us from our fly-bitten sleep. We all tumbled into the front room, abruptly anxious and uncertain. Immediately, Robert asked Zelig, Riva, and Aaron to go back into the cave.

"I'm bringing down my bride, and she only knows about 8 of you," Robert declared as he left.

Riva, Henni, Robert, Tony, and Hilde

We were troubled. Was Robert drunk? He did not appear so. Had he suffered head trauma? After all, Johanna knew all 11 of us. From the outset, she has been essential to our safe passage to freedom. Was this a joke, a trick? Was this more serious? Was Robert being forced to sacrifice 8 to save 3 and his family? Perhaps he chose Riva because she is a mother, and Zelig and Aaron because they are generally less bothersome than the others? Ten, fifteen minutes of intramural speculation, and then Robert returned.

"Everyone, this is Antonija Zvirgzdina. You may call her Tony."

"Nice to meet all of you. It's amazing that you can all live down here . . . here, in Libau . . . and it's so hot, and no one suspects, and you all look so well . . . . Robert is a wonderful man, don't you think?" Tony was very jumpy.

"You can trust Tony, she is my new bride."

New bride! It was a disturbingly impudent moniker for his *freg-nisht-tse* (don't ask). A bit of a frontal dare, it was: defiance, disrespect, impertinence, and rashness all wrapped in *chutzpah*. What about Johanna and the girls? Tony seemed trustworthy, but why did we need to know about her? And what was her need to know about us?

I won't say it was altogether unpleasant to meet Tony. We hadn't seen a stranger in 2 months. And for some, Tony was nice to look at . . . . *sheyne ponim, sheyne tukhes . . . . in mitndrinen, sheyne moyshe ve-arendlekh* (pretty face, nice ass . . . in between, great tits)! Still, it was provocative to bring her to the cellar, and surely Robert had to know this. I didn't draw near, not even to shake her hand. Neither did the others, except for Shmerl who fondled Tony's feet to measure her for a pair of shoes. Yosl promised they would be ready in a few days. Within an hour of Robert's startling arrival, he and Tony were gone.

"Shoes! She needed to know about us so Shmerl and Yosl could make her a pair of new shoes! He risks eleven hunted Jews, his wife, his beautiful daughters . . . for a *knish* (pussy)!" I was almost beside myself.

"There must be more to this than we know," countered David.

"But, David, you know, as we all do, that chance is the reason eleven hapless souls are in this cellar tonight. Risk is the bedrock of chance, but not careless risk."

"What are you talking about, Kalman?

"You know what I'm talking about, David. I'm talking about being sensible. None of us have an aversion to risk, if we did we would probably be dead. But one needs to weigh the risk against the gain. All of us should have an aversion to uncertainty, to ignorant risk. For Robert to reveal our existence to Tony is pure ignorance. He has no idea who Tony will be tomorrow, what interests will dictate her prudence, what contingencies will demarcate her loyalties. She's one large uncertainty. Let's be honest, many in our group act in ways that increase our risk of exposure. Still, *besser mitn taivel vos m'ken eider mitn taivel vos m'ken im nit* (better the devil you know than the devil you don't). As Shakespeare's Hamlet tells us, uncertainty 'makes us rather bear those ills we have than fly to others that we know not of.' Who *is* this *tchotchke* called Tony!?"

Not another word was said, just heads shaking east and west or north and south. We crawled back into the cave, slept till noon, and spent the remainder of the day reading, writing and playing chess. In the evening we listened to the daily report from Marshal Stalin. The German armies were fleeing in panic into the forests, into the hands of the partisans. Stalin is a genius. The Soviet Army is almost supernatural, like marvels in a fairy tale.

July nights in the cave were torture. The heat was stupefying, surely over 120 degrees directly under the hot bakery oven. Lying without blankets, you were regularly bitten by flies. One morning in early July, I awoke with a swelling on the left side of my chest. It was red, hot, irritated, and painful. My skin felt tight and looked as though it was stretched over a drum. I was ill and dizzy from the pulsing pain. By the next morning it was larger.

I showed my swelling to David. He was certain it was an infected fly bite and immediately cleansed the area with alcohol and applied a bandage with Ichthyol ointment. Ichthyol is an old Austrian remedy, basically sulfonated shale oil that is miscible with glycerin and made into a drawing salve. It kills the bacteria and lessens the redness and heat. By the next morning, my swelling had a fistula.

I was prone all day with a chamomile compress and a hot water bottle on my chest, changed regularly by David and Michael. I was in terrible pain, as if a knife twisted in my chest. Yosl tried to distract me with our usual game of chess, David and Michael with conversation and mind puzzles. In the early evening, the large boil burst. Into the early morning, every couple of hours, David changed my Ichthyol bandages which slowly filled with pus. David, Michael and Yosl continued this routine over the next several days and my chest wound healed. They were truly good friends.

At about the time my infection was healing, a BBC broadcast appealed to the people of Hungary, Czechoslovakia, and eastern Germany to do their utmost to assist the Jews to escape and hide. The international railway workers were urged to sabotage the transport of Hungarian Jews to Poland, where they were being murdered. British officials promised that everyone who helps the Jews will be honored as an ally in the war against Hitler's minions. That evening I told Robert about the BBC appeal.

"*I* took you on without being asked," Robert responded. "I didn't wait for you to come to me, I went to find you. I didn't crave your money or your possessions. I wanted to save you because David is my dear comrade, and because I'm simply willing to take heavy risks for the cause."

"You know, Robert, Aaron and I had other places to hide, with other Latvians," Zelig interjected.

"Who are these other Latvians?" Robert asked.

"I can't say . . . not now."

"Don't you trust me?"

"I swore on my honor I would tell no one."

"Well, if that's how things are, fine. For you, I have told lies. For you, I have broken my word of honor. For you, I play with fire everywhere. And you don't trust me?" Robert was more crushed than roiled.

"If you trust him with your life, you can surely trust him with your word of honor," I reproached Zelig. Everyone agreed with me, but Zelig was unmoved. Robert turned to go upstairs, and then he turned back.

"I want to say something quite serious to all of you. I know that the time of Latvian liberation will soon be here. How and what will happen, I don't know. I only know that you want to take revenge on the murderers, and you have a right, even an obligation, to do so. I have one request—that no more innocents suffer. Should innocent Latvians come to you, don't slam the door in their faces. Help them, don't allow yourselves to become like those who wouldn't help you. Remember, I helped you only because you were innocent . . . innocent comrades."

"Robert," I reacted "we Jews have never sought to eliminate another group of people. It would be unthinkable. In our eyes, every person has a right to live, as long as he hasn't taken the life of an innocent person—then he must be punished. We will never pursue innocent people. I would say that the main concern of innocent Latvians should be with other Latvians, the ones who are quite willing to bury you in order to ingratiate themselves with the Germans, and maybe soon with the Soviets. The opportunists. Remember Ducmanis, our comrade, an enthusiastic Stalinist. Remember how he betrayed me to the SD. Soon he will be an enthusiastic Stalinist again."

Robert said nothing in response. He walked over to the pump, inspected it carelessly, pushing this and that. Earlier in the day, David took it apart several times to replace worn parts. It took 4 hours to get it running again. Robert turned from the pump to leave, and then he stopped.

"I don't want to be paid. All I ask is that you help my wife and children, and maybe a little something to help fix my leg."

"Robert," I responded, "we don't even think about paying you a specific sum, what you have done for us can't be repaid with money. Everyone of us will help Johanna and the girls as long as we are able. We simply feel a love for them and a moral duty to support them in any way we can. No less you!"

"Goodnight, comrades," Robert softly said as he ascended the cellar stairs. We continued to sit in the front room, most of us more reflective than reflexive.

Before long the alarm-signal flashed several times and then went off. Swifter than an arrow, Yosl grabbed the coffee and extinguished the gas flame. With almost military precision, everything suspicious was removed from the front room table, the lights were turned off, and we disappeared inside. The hidden hatch was secured, the blue alarm-lamp lit, and we stood at the ready, pistols in hand, envisioning our defense.

We could hear heavy shoes on the stairway, then talking. Soon there seemed to be a knock on the hatch, or was it the police tapping the walls to find a hollow space. We waited. Then there was more knocking. Assuming it was Robert forcing yet another practice drill, David and Michael moved to open the hatch. I stopped them. There is to be no opening before Robert's voice declares the password, *Vienpadsmit* (eleven). After half an hour it was quiet again. We all went to bed for what remained of the unbearably hot night. It would have been a relief if we could have left the cave before morning.

Till now there are several episodes of this sort every month. Sometimes it is one or more persons rousting about, sometimes it is someone tearing at the coal-hatch in the boiler room, presumably to gain entry. Who are these people . . . police, neighbors, bakers, Jews on the run, desperate Latvians, some of these, all of these, none of these, Robert? This is just one of our games in an otherwise monotonous, one might say grim-gray, imprisonment. The others are ignorant speculation about moving map pins, a human behavior game I call *shmucks*-in-prison, and the equally fascinating, though more pleasurable, chess.

By July, the unity among us was beginning to fray. Maybe it was the heat, perhaps the tedium, certainly the absence of privacy. All of us were becoming a bit edgy, some more so than others, especially the women, most often Henni. One evening Michael entered the cave to listen to the news and Henni was ironing. Instead of calmly requesting that he wait until she was through, she began to scream and call him "dog." When Michael reminded her that a calm request is more effective, she snapped back: "Ask you!? You with your murderous eyes. I wash your dirty underwear. Do you wash mine!?"

Another evening, we were all in our beds when Henni came in and saw that hers was a bit rumpled. She immediately became unhinged.

"Who sat on my bed . . . how disgusting!"

"Robert was in here earlier, and he sat on it," I answered.

"Which of you dogs sat on my bed?"

"Robert did," I reiterated.

"There's no need to get so excited," Misha interjected. "Afterall, you yourself often step on our ground beds with your shoes. What's the harm if Robert *sat* on yours?"

"You dog . . . You liar . . . *Pishn zolstu mit grine verem* (you should piss green worms)!"

All three women are very hard-working. Three times a day they wash the cellar floors, tidy and clean the cave, even in the extraordinary heat of summer. Thanks to them there are no vermin to be seen here. Also, they wash and mend our laundry, darn our socks, and cook lunch for us nearly every day. For all this, you have not the slightest complaint. Indeed, you greatly admire their diligence and devotion.

However, they have no idea what is required to adapt to furtive confinement, to limit oneself, to be prudent, and they do not tolerate being instructed. They seem to behave as though they are in a hotel. From morning to night, their part of the cave is walled off by a curtain of sorts. Behind the veil they wash and splash in a tub of water like ducks. Why, you cannot imagine. Riva is the *agent provocateur* of this rather odd sport. You understand that it originates from boredom, but the noise is part of a larger pattern of recklessness.

The men cannot enter the "ladies' room" for nearly the entire day, even presence in any other part of the cave is almost an imposition. This is a big part of the tension and conflict between the men and the women. Indeed, it is precisely in such circumstances that you can accurately judge the character of a person. Henni is particularly excitable, often out of control, and careless with language, helter-skelter sarcasm and insults. She is difficult to calm, and she cares little about the danger such raging outbursts may be for all of us. Henni is pathologically angry. Unfriendly, sullen, she looks askance at almost everyone and everything. Never a "good morning," she has her nose in the air. When she is friendly on rare occasion, it doesn't seem genuine.

The most even-tempered and composed of the three women is Hilde. I have yet to see her angry or accusatory. She does her work calmly and quietly. This behavior does not go unpunished. The other two, especially Henni, often ignore Hilde for no apparent reason. She doesn't make a great fuss, she just sets it aside with dignity. What does trouble me about Hilde is the extent of her devotion to Michael. Their relationship is a puzzle to me. Whenever, I gently explore this with her, the response is evasive and filled with double meanings. Surely I am biased and meddlesome. Why not? Michael is an old, dear friend, and his murdered first wife was close to my mother. Everyone finds their felicity in their own way. I need to butt out.

One July evening, Robert asked me to compose a code of behavior for all to sign. I told him this would not work, but that I would call everyone together and try to reach an understanding about our common interests.

"I call everyone together tonight because while hundreds of thousands of *Yiden* are being murdered, we are breathing free in this cellar and fighting about *narishkeit* (foolishness)! Comrades, it is *a shandeh far di goyim* (our shame before the gentiles)!

"Each of us struts around like we are special. Hoo-ha, *an eigener fartz shtinkt nit azoy vi a fremder* (our own farts don't stink like everybody else's). Well . . . they *do*!

"*Yeder mentsh hat zein eigeneh pekl* (everyone has his own pack of burdens to carry)! We need to think about that. We need to honor that. We need to be sensitive to one another. We need to recall the golden rule: *A vort un a fartz ken men nit tzuriknemen* (neither a word nor a fart can be taken back)!

"Let me finish my tirade with a story, a story told 200 years ago by the philosopher Rousseau. A small group of men went to hunt a deer, a prize that would provide each of them with meat for a week. Everyone knew that he had to remain faithfully at his post, for no individual was strong enough to subdue the deer. As it happened, a rabbit appeared within reach of one of them, and off he went without thought. Having caught his rabbit, which provided food for but two days (and hunger for five), he cared little about having caused his comrades to be without any. Well, the next time they went out to hunt a deer, each man thought the hell with the others and he caught a rabbit. Before long they were all hungry, indeed too hungry to even catch a rabbit.

"So, comrades, we either hold together or we will perish separately! This is as certain as day follows night, and night day."

I wish I could say that my harangue brought sobriety to all of my comrades, it didn't. Sure, Misha made peace with Michael. They shook hands and buried a grudge that dated back before the war. Otherwise, mostly the *narishkeit* continues, and worse, we have Robert and his shoe-needy *tchotchke* adding to the mess. And so, deadlock and tit-for-tat too often prevail. *This* is the game I call *shmucks*-in-prison!

I would rather play another game, chess. Chess is conflict in miniature, civilized conflict, harmless conflict. Chess is not about risk, chance, or probability. It is about controlled conflict between rational but suspicious actors. Chess is about possibilities and camouflaged intentions. Coffeehouse chess is about that and more—seduction, mock encouragement, gibes, and puns. Coffeehouse chess is for kibitzers. Before the war, I was a coffeehouse chess player.

In the late afternoons, after teaching and tutoring, I would head to one coffeehouse or another in search of a game, a kind of slender cigarette-smoking gypsy in search of weaker players, patzers. Coffeehouse chess rests on one's cleverness in setting subtle traps. Such traps are baited with a seemingly critical pawn no patzer can resist seizing. For such opponents, greed is reflexive. As in real life, short-term gain is most often mindlessly irresistible. I was master of offering the innocent pawn and feigning blunder. After 3 years on the run, the game I now play is a ghost of the past. Still, the pleasure, if not the skill, remains.

Chess, of course, is circumscribed by its rules. Clever iterative combinations of these simple rules quickly force this closed reality to emerge complex. It is about battle, siege, takeover, and death. Not unlike the last three years. Perhaps, this is the origin of our near obsession with the game. Day after day you witness how ingenuity and patience always checkmate the enemy. Sometimes you envisage a future world of categorical goodness: how many ways can you place all sixteen white pieces on a chessboard so that each piece protects only one other piece; how many ways can you be your neighbor's keeper?

Just now our neighbors have disappeared, only bystanders and scoundrels remain. In mid-July we all hoped to learn the fate of friends and family in Riga and Paplaka. On a pretense, Robert went to see Margrieta Pietchis, a Latvian, who lived with her teenage son (Georg) and daughter (Miriam). Her husband, Lev Schulman, is a Jew and worked with me at Paplaka. Last we knew, Margrieta had also continued to correspond with her former neighbor, Benno Mindel, who, after suffering the murders of his wife and children in July of '41, was deported to Riga to work on the *Reichsbahn* (railway). What Robert happened upon at Margrieta's flat was disgraceful.

"She has entirely forgotten Lev. Parties take place there every day, funfests of drinking with the SD. Even Miriam—can't be more than 14—has a lover. Obviously, Margrieta is not to be trusted."

"Can we approach anyone else?" I inquired.

"After Margrieta, I went to Leontija Dribin's flat, also a Latvian. She lives there with her two young sons. Her husband, Gutman, was also deported to Riga. This was also disappointing. She's also forgotten her husband . . . . She's hoping to marry a driver for the Women's Prison. I have the impression that all the Latvian women who had Jewish husbands are now very much alike in this way."

"But, what about Eliza Israelson?" I responded. "She's remained true to her husband, Ber, and even raises their three children in the Jewish spirit."

"I hadn't thought of her. Johanna knows her fairly well, and speaks with her at the market almost every morning. Lately she walks with a limp and has some sort of bandage on her leg. Maybe I can ask her?"

The group spoke against this idea. It was too risky. We would just have to wait until our liberation. Grim, our mood was grim. Still, that evening we were cheered a bit by the news on Moscow Yiddish Radio. With Stalin's blessing, two colonies were established for Jewish children who have lost their parents. A million rubles had been collected among the workers. The founders promised Stalin that the children will be raised in the generous spirit of Communism.

As the month spun out, we continued to burrow our underground escape tunnel. With the water pump motor running, we could work all afternoon and not be heard. The digging was more uncomfortable than it was difficult, having to work in such a confined space. At one point we encountered a rock weighing more than 50 pounds. We thought to lift it out of the hole with a rope, but even this was awkward. Zelke said he could do it alone. We all doubted it, so he bet each of us one cigarette. In he went and after 5 minutes, with enormous exertion, he brought out the stone. It was quite a *tour de force*! To be sure, he earned those cigarettes.

As the last fortnight of July began, the Red Army was moving relentlessly ahead. They had advanced to within 10 miles of East Prussia and had penetrated 8 miles into Latvia. Vilis Lācis, a leader of Latvian communists, announced on Moscow Radio that Latvia would be liberated in days. The German army all but collapsed on the Eastern Front and the mood in Libau was tense, even among the Germans. Robert saw an SD-man, apparently Baumgartner, riding his bicycle in the park one afternoon. As he passed three German sailors, one threw a stick and the bicycle tumbled over with Baumgartner beneath it. He reached for his pistol, but the sailors lunged at him, beat him mercilessly with sticks, and left him for dead (may he never rest in peace). July was the third anniversary of the first mass murders in Libau, and unmerciful revenge was a welcome balm.

July 20, 1944 was proceeding as predictably dull as all that preceded it. Yosl and Shmerl had their hands full making several pairs of shoes and boots for *tchotchke* Tony. She is proving quite persnickety, and Robert bounces hither and thither to please her. A few of us were salting *Strömlinge* (Baltic herrings) for emergency reserve. David was listening to Moscow Radio. As the afternoon drew to a close, he became quite excited.

"Assassination attempt on Hitler in the *Führerhauptquartier*, his headquarters in East Prussia . . . three generals severely wounded, eight lightly . . . Hitler survived with minor injuries . . . the Army is in revolt in Berlin!"

"Wonderful! The Germans are killing each other. Maybe they will forget about the Jews!" responded Misha.

David dialed to the BBC for more news of this blessed event, but there was nothing. German radio was silent. Finally, shortly after 6:30 *Deutschlandsender*, a radio station heard all across Europe, announced that there had been a failed attempt to kill Hitler. Then silence again. Shortly after 9, *Deutschlandsender* announced that the *Fuhrer* would speak to the German people later in the evening. This message was broadcast every few minutes for almost four hours. Finally, just before 1 AM, Hitler's hoarse voice exploded into the close air of the hot cave:

"My fellow Germans!"

"I speak to you today so that first you will hear my voice and know that I am unhurt and well, and second that you should learn of a crime without precedent in German history.

"A very small clique of ambitious, irresponsible and, certainly, senseless and ignorant officers concocted a plot to do away with me and the staff of the High Command of the Wehrmacht.

"The bomb planted by Colonel Count Stauffenberg exploded six feet to the right of me. It seriously wounded several of my true and loyal comrades, one of whom has died. I am entirely unhurt, other than some minor scratches, bruises and burns. I regard this miracle as a confirmation of the task imposed upon me by God . . .

"This circle of usurpers is very small and has nothing in common with the spirit of the German Wehrmacht and, all the more, none with the German people. They are a gang of criminals which will be destroyed without mercy . . .

"We shall settle accounts with them in the manner to which we National Socialists are accustomed."

For days after the broadcast, unrest in Germany continued. *Deutschlandsender*, BBC, and Moscow Radio all told of Himmler carrying out mass murders in Germany of those disloyal, or perceived disloyal. Hitler managed to suppress the revolt, but surely not the underlying motivation.

As the month concluded, motorized Red Army units stood 60 miles from Riga, the Riga-Dvinsk railway was destroyed, and Dvinsk fell shortly afterwards. The noose was tightening on the Germans. Lublin, Minsk and Vilna had also fallen, and not only that. General Vassilii Rakovskii and General Ivan Danilovich Chernyakhovsky, the celebrated Marshals of the Red Army, the very ones who directed the lethal attacks at Minsk and Vilna, and who were poised at the gates of East Prussia, are Jews! *Ganaiden un gehenem ken men baideh hoben oif der velt* (heaven and hell can both be had in this world)! A Jewish general could not imagine greater gratification than, with his own cunning and his own army, destroying the fascist murderers and enslavers of all peoples, especially his own. Surely Hitler must know that these generals are Jews, and this must burn his *kishkes* (innards).

Moscow Radio tells all. We never miss the reporting of Ilya Ehrenberg, a Jew born in Kiev. I first came upon this wonderful storyteller when I read his satire of injustice, hypocrisy and pretension, *The Stormy Life of Lazik Roitschwantz*. Lazik is a born loser, a *shlimazl*. He is an artisan whose only desire is to earn a living. When liberated from Czarist anti-Semitism, he is accused by Soviet bureaucrats of being a petty bourgeois. Escaping to the West, he is jailed as a Bolshevik agent. When he finally lands in Palestine, he dies of malnutrition. Lazik is universal, and in every age. Abraham ibn Ezra, the 12th century Spanish-Jewish poet, wrote of him in "Luckless":

> The heavenly sphere, the constellations
> Departed from their path
> Upon my birth;
> And should my business
> Be in candles,
> The sun would never set
> Before I breathe my last.

Ehrenberg is also an impassioned journalist, best known for his reports in *Izvestia* on the Spanish Civil War. Now he broadcasts the truth not told by others.[7] For two weeks, he traveled the front with General Chernyakhovsky to take a measure of the crimes and murders of the "heroic" German army. On the towns' streets he spoke with many who marveled at the Red Army, including a Jewish Gymnasium student who asked: "How is it possible? Not long ago, you were still in Minsk, and now you are already in Vilna?" Ehrenberg recounted other stories about his visit to the front, two of which will stay with me always.

Wherever the Germans had been, they ruthlessly murdered Jews and Russians. In Vilna they murdered 80,000 Jews in the last three years. The liquidation of the Vilna Ghetto did not happen without a ferocious battle. With limited arms, the Jews heroically resisted to the last. Under the leadership of Itzig Wittenberg, a Jewish Communist from Berlin, 500

Jewish fighters fled to the forest and joined the Partisans in the struggle to liberate Vilna. With the Red Army, the Jewish resistance triumphantly, if bittersweetly, returned to *Yerushalayim de Lita*, the "Jerusalem of Lithuania," Vilna. Nearly 6000 survivors from the forests and elsewhere collected in the city, some even went to pray in the Choral Synagogue (*Khorshul*) on Zavalna Street. July 12, 1944—the new Purim.

Another story told by Ehrenberg was about another Itzig, this one the son of Avram, a simple farmer in the back country of Kiev. It is a story of unimaginable evil, of joyful fascist neighbors. One morning, Avram sent Itzig and a few farmhands to work in the field. They were viciously set upon by gentile goons. The farmhands slipped away, and Itzig was murdered. Crushed by this senseless outrage, Avram fell into a deep depression. Before long he received a visit from the governor of the district, a petty bourgeois anti-Semite. Avram asked for justice, and the *khazer* (pig) responded: "You're an old man, you have no son, and you no longer need a farm." In days he was homeless, tossed aside like an old shoe. But then the Red Army came to this once placid village, and the *khazer* and his minions became tree pendants. Avram got his justice, if not his son. Long live Comrade Stalin—but not too close.

* * *

Wednesday, July 26. Johanna was upset.

"Robert is being careless and reckless again. This morning he had a bitter quarrel with Mrs. Strauts, the building owner. She won't tolerate his disrespect and defiance of her authority. She even forced the issue with a bit of blackmail—'You cook a big pot of food every day. Who is it for? Do I detect a guilty conscience?'—On and on she went. This is trouble."

"For certain," I responded, "but the foremost trouble is Robert's need of celebrity, to boast everywhere, to chance being exposed by strangers in new shoes. We are imperiled and we need to seriously consider leaving here, though I don't know where to."

The others were silent. Johanna left in tears.

Thursday, July 27. Robert was agitated. Mrs. Strauts called him on the phone. She had something she wanted to say to him, face-to-face. We thought this is it, this is the end. Robert returned an hour later, seemingly unnerved.

"Everyone to the front room, hurry! This is a very serious matter . . . . Tonight you may expect liberation."

"So, now you speak in euphemisms?" I asked. "What you really mean is that Strauts has informed on you, the police will soon arrive, and we'll turn to naught."

"Kalman, you're so pessimistic . . . always the worst case is before your eyes . . . . In town there's enormous anxiety. The police are unstrung and running about the streets. They say Russian paratroops have descended nearby, the front has crumbled, and the Red Army will surely be in Libau by nightfall . . . ."

"This is nonsense, nothing but irrational panic," David interrupted. "Sure the Russians are skilled and swift, but they don't make miracles. They're only in Dvinsk!"

"What theater!" I added. "The Latvians are seeing ghosts, the ghosts of murdered neighbors who weigh more heavily on their consciences with each Russian advance into Latvia. The great heroes who have murdered old men, women, and children are suddenly becoming unbalanced. The ground shifts beneath their feet, and panic replaces bravery." Sheer, *joie de vivre* in the cellar!

Friday, July 28. Apprehension was spreading.

"A new panic has erupted in town," Johanna reported. "They say Mitau has fallen, and the Russians are rapidly closing in on Libau. Mines are being placed everywhere, at bridges, in factories. Clearly, the Germans are preparing to leave."

"Perhaps so?" David responded.

Saturday, July 29. We prepared shoes for ourselves, the sole luggage should we have to flee. The evening was introduced by air raid sirens. Anxiously, we waited for the bombs, Russian greetings we called them. Only silence. Not even a struggling intruder.

Sunday, July 30. Tisha B'av. On this day the First and Second Temples were destroyed, and the Jews were expelled from Spain. Disaster after disaster. Should we have been surprised that liberation did not come this day, nor the next, nor the day after that . . .

AUGUST 1944

The month began with ever greater heat, and more aggressive flies. I took myself to the front room where a bit of air still circulated. At the open window, I could hear old Mrs. Rosenbach's rant. Every day, all day, she went on like a perpetually wound gramophone. With a deep baritone, clearly heard, she broadcasts the town news from her second floor flat.

"Hundreds of political prisoners have escaped from Saldus. How, you ask. Well I will tell you . . . and think about this. A Latvian officer, yes, *a Latvian officer,* let them break loose, and he gave them pistols. What an abomination! I can't stay here another day. I'm going to Germany. When the Russians show up, our lives will be over . . . even if they don't kill us. The wealthy ones in town registered for passage to Germany last Saturday, and now they are waving goodbye from the top decks. The rest of us must sit and wait!"

Mrs. Rosenbach declaimed endlessly. Her beating drum had little inside but air, so occasionally, she turned to rattling chains.

"The Russians are near Riga. Why aren't the men given weapons to fight them? Surely we all know countless, brave men who are eager to battle the Russians. Let them into the taverns, they can get themselves roaring drunk and chase away the Russians. Then those bastards won't come here . . . . It's those *putsch* plotters who wanted to overthrow the German government, and now they let the Russians into Latvia."

What logic. von Stauffenberg and his comrades failed to kill Hitler, and instead they had given the keys to Latvia to the Russian Army. If only there were enough armed, drunken Latvians, they could turn back the tide. Could one be more ignorant. A few days later, though, she beat a different drum.

"What good fortune that I didn't go to Germany. Everyone has been stranded in Kretinga [Lithuania], and they are starving . . . 2 ounces of bread a day! They took everything from them, and only allowed them 2 changes of clothing and 2 bedsheets . . . . Twenty—six train cars were travelling, wall to wall with refugees from Rezekne, and German and Latvian soldiers with ammunition, and everything was blown to pieces—*beigas, pagalam* (the end, dead)!"

What a pity, I thought, *only* 26 full train cars from Rēzekne. Rēzekne, where three years ago 5000 Jews were marched out of town, made to dig a large pit, and machine-gunned . . . all in one day! What a disgrace, I thought, *only* 26 full train cars.

Between Rosenbach's outbursts, Robert brought us news that a great many Jews have arrived in Libau.

"I have been sniffing around. I can't be too curious. I think they are from Dondangen, maybe 1200, men and women, skeletons all. They hurled themselves on the garbage heap, hoping to find scraps to ease their hunger. A struggle erupted between the SD guards and some Latvians who wanted to throw the Jews some food. A woman who accepted a roll was shot on the spot, and others were smashed in the head with rifle butts. I don't really know what is happening to them. For now, I think, they're being sent to the plywood factory."

The mood in Libau had otherwise calmed down considerably. German leaflets claimed that the Russians had been driven out of Mitau and Tukums, and when the German reinforcements soon arrive they would be gone from all of Latvia. This leaky life raft was all the Libauers had, and they tenaciously clung to it.

"You see," crowed Tony, "the Germans can still work wonders. One can travel to Riga again, and the sappers have gone to fix the bridge in Mitau." By then Tony was a regular late night visitor. She would disappear into the cave with Robert while we all sat out front and Shmerl fixed her shoes, or whatever. By 2 AM she was gone and we were off to sleep, quite nonplussed by Tony's declarations and Robert's careless infatuation.

Robert continued to snoop about the plywood factory. We had talked of devising plans to help some of the Jews escape, and we needed to know what their situation was and how strong the guard was.

"Some folks across the way from the factory told me five truckloads of Jews were driven away, where to is unknown. Some thought maybe to a boat to Germany. When I sauntered by the yard, I recognized a few Libau Jews, some whose name I knew, like Ida Kassel and that young fellow Chaim Kriger. With a kind of sign language, Chaim told me they haven't eaten in four days and they sleep out in the open field of the factory yard. I know some Jews have been shot trying to escape."

Robert estimated that 60 of the Jews were from Libau. I didn't know how he came to that number. Still, I thought perhaps my siblings were among them, suffering heat and hunger. If there were more of us, we might have orchestrated an escape. But with six pistols and a large SD guard, our only option was to do nothing. If we trusted the Latvians, we would have sought out the Partisans, and together we could have done something. This was not to be. Robert himself is more fearful of his closest Latvian friends than we are, except for Tony. Cave-dweller opportunities are few . . . .

* * *

Moscow Radio, Monday, 7 August 1944. A Latvian journalist traveled from Dvinsk [Latvia] to Kovno [Kaunas, Lithuania] to report on the fate of the Jews. In Kovno, there were still 7000 Jews at the dawn of July. Before the Russian Army entered on the first day of August, most were murdered. First, the children and old folks were taken away, and then the ghetto was set ablaze. Almost everyone who remained was burned alive. Those who escaped were provided a truck by the Russians, and they drove around searching for those Jews who had previously fled to the Partisans. Altogether, 500 Jews managed to save themselves. Then the Russians went to the ghetto. All that remained was a pile of ashes and a lone old Jew sitting with his hands covering his tears, the charred bodies of his wife and children at his feet.[8]

* * *

Since July I have been unable to sleep through the night. There is the heat and the flies, but mostly there are the dreams. As soon as I fall asleep, I am tormented by hideous nightmares of my family.

One night, I saw my youngest sister, Ida, running over to me. She is wheezing and struggles to insist that I hurry to Lt. Frank, Chief of the Libau *Schutzpolizei*: "Beg him to free me, tomorrow is the last day!" I run to an open field and beg him not to shoot my sister. "What? Shoot?" answers Frank. "For saying this word, all is lost for you and your sister. Only a woman's gold watch can save you . . ." I wake up, shaking.

Another night, I am together again with my mother. We are hiding in a place unfamiliar to me. Then I see my sister-in-law, Rosa, through the window, walking toward us with the *Überjude* [chief Jew] of the SD who was shot in Skede in December 1941. I point him out to my mother. Rosa turns away from us, but *Überjude* continues toward us with his twisted, otherworldly face. I am afraid and crouch down to hide beneath the window, but the window grows to the floor and *Überjude* relentlessly comes at me.

"You are dead . . . go away!" I scream, and I start to kick at the window. *Überjude* wants inside and he bangs at the window with wild ferocity. His face is spectral. I wake up screaming, exhausted and drenched in sweat.

Such dreams torment me nearly every night. I don't fear intruders or confronting the police in our cave, or even death itself. I fear the dreams, the nightmares of being powerless to protect my family.

* * *

Moscow Radio, Thursday, 10 August 1944. A Russian journalist broadcasted a report on Lublin [Poland] and the Majdanek concentration camp. There were hundreds of thousands of slaves from all nations: Jews, Russians, Belgians, Dutch, Czechs, even German deserters and Chinese. The Germans fled from the Soviet Army in such haste, they had scant time to destroy this necropolis, not even the gas chambers.

The journalist detailed a horror even my dreams could not devise. The gas chambers were 400 square feet. Naked men, women, and children were herded inside, 250 at a time, so crammed it was impossible to fall over. The sadists stood outside and peered through portals specially placed to allow satisfaction of their blood thirst. Indeed, naked bodies writhing brought some to ejaculatory climax, even drunks.

Each group was exposed to the Zyklon B gas for 10 minutes, not enough to kill but enough to render a victim unconscious. Then they were dragged from the chamber and burned alive, one layer of bodies, one layer of wood, and so on. The commandant of the camp made certain that he attended the burnings. "I love the smell of roasted flesh," he would declare with his head held aloft.

The journalist finished his report with a most remarkable story. He met two engineers in the camp, a Russian and a Pole, who had survived the ordeal. They told him that merely weeks ago, just before liberation by the Red Army, a Jew approached them and pointed his finger at another.

"Look over there. That old Jew collapsing under the heavy boards he is dragging, that is the socialist Léon Blum, the premier of France."

"You're crazy. Blum is probably in America." The Russian insisted.

"Go, ask him yourself, if you think I'm lying."

"Is it true, you are Léon Blum?" asked the Pole.

"Yes," he whispered, "it is I, Léon Blum, the premier of France."

"Why didn't you save yourself? Surely you had *proteksia* (connections), a way out." the Pole responded.

"I suppose I did, but I was not interested in saving myself. I wanted to experience the same fate as my comrades." Blum took his boards and continued along.

Several weeks later, days before liberation, the Russian and the Pole again encountered the Jew who had fingered Léon Blum.

"Where has Léon Blum gone to," the Russian asked.

"Where I will be before long," the Jew responded, pointing his finger this time toward the sky, tears escaping the corners of his eyes.

Léon Blum, the great Jewish statesman, was murdered on 7 August 1944.[9] In his memory, the allies are marching on Paris.

Moscow Radio, Saturday, 12 August 1944. The Russian journalist was reporting again from Majdanek, a report more horrible than the last. He noted that, even if they had gassed and burned night and day, they would not have been able to gas the hundreds of thousands who they eliminated in such a short time. So, these animals resorted to other incomprehensibly savage acts, the kind that could only emerge from the deranged German mind.

A 4 year-old child was thrown to the ground, naked. The child screamed "Mama, Mama," but she had already been burned half-alive. Ever more enraged, almost in a reverie, he placed one foot on the child's head and the other on the legs, and pulled the arms until they ripped free of the body. He threw them to the ground, calmly looked at the child, took out his pistol, and fired. Laughing, he spun around and walked away.

Two other Germans confronted a prisoner who displeased them. One drew his pistol and announced, "I have come to shoot you." Accepting his fate, the prisoner snapped to rigidity to await his mercy bullet. The Germans laughed.

"I don't know where to shoot you. What do you prefer?" one asked. As he fired into the air, the other one pounded the prisoner's head with a club, sending him to the ground. When he stumbled to his feet, the first German informed him: "You know, I have shot you. You are dead. You are now in what *Saujuden* (Jewish pigs) call the World to Come, but even here you are not free of us. We are everywhere . . ."

Once 18,000 Jews, men, women and children, were herded to their grave, large pits dug by other prisoners. With precision, the first group stood before the abyss. Several bursts of machine gun fire and the people fell over the edge. Though many were groaning and whimpering, a second group went through the drill and toppled upon the still-living. This was repeated until the pit was full. Then the next group had to top off the pit with soil, and proceed to the next pit to receive their execution. Before long, the efficiency of this *modus operandi* improved greatly. The Germans are nothing if not masters of methodology. Indeed, Majdanek will forever remain a symbol of German culture.

* * *

By mid-August, the mood in town had calmed considerably. Seemingly pointless air raid alarms mimicked the boy who cried wolf. The streetcars were running again, and each morning German soldiers would march through town singing. All this normalcy was denial before the gathering storm. Symptomatically, every evening, Tony unfurled the flag, convinced that the Germans were preparing to carry out decisive and wondrous battles.

A reasonable person would ask "who is Tony," or better yet, "who is Robert." What is this all about? Why is a Communist *shtupen* (fucking) a booster of the Fritzen? Not simply *shtupen*, but *shtupen* in a cave of hidden Jews! Evening after evening, Robert behaves like an adolescent, a dog in a circus, a clown. Tony is so impressed she cackles for more. Robert exchanges more and more of our precious British pounds into reichsmarks. There is always a pitiful excuse: "I want to send tomatoes and cucumbers to my girls in the countryside." We know he is spending all the money on Tony, but we can say nothing. When they arrive at the cave each evening, I ask Robert a question in rhetorical silence, *"Vos geystu mitn cholemoyed in hant?"* (Why are you going around with your dick in your hand—a patsy, a *shmuk?*)

Meanwhile, in late August, Johanna unexpectedly returned from her family village, Asīte. She had been there most of the summer with the girls. There the atmosphere is calmer, no air raid sirens, no Tony. She had become impatient with her village and yearned for Libau.

When Johanna arrived, she headed straight for the cellar. We were happy to see her. Minutes later, Robert entered and was quite shocked. He flashed Johanna an angry glance, curtly said "Hello," and sat down without saying another word. His silence for the next hour was simply ugly. After that, he stood up and left, not a word. Clearly he was unhappy with the likelihood that his escapades with Tony would be less freewheeling. Johanna was heartsick. We assured her this was all temporary insanity, and after the war all would change. Just now . . . . Johanna drove back to Asīte and her daughters.

The last two weeks of August proved unusually unpleasant for David and me, over and above the attempted break-ins and the Robert-Tony matter. David had an inflamed hand and I a horrid toothache.

David's hand was bitten by a fly. The knuckles swelled and two lumps appeared between them and the wrist. David was certain he had blood-poisoning, but I disagreed. I saw no red lines moving up his arm. I placed compresses with aluminum acetate that Robert bought at the pharmacy. David's hand swelled further, it was red hot. It was too risky for David to go to a doctor, even sympathetic and trustworthy Dr. Sandberg. We decided to try the Ichthyol compresses David used on my chest last month, and gave David *shnapps* to dull his senses and the pain. Days later, it had only grown worse. I told David if there was no end to this, we would have to cut off the hand ourselves. I must have frightened the hand, for the next morning the swelling lessened and the redness lightened.

As David's hand healed, I awoke one morning with a roaring toothache, a pain so intense that I thought my head would explode. I lost a filling in my molar tooth and I suppose it was severely infected. David told me to rinse with very strong saltwater, as hot as I could take it. And so I did. The pain eased for about an hour and then it was worse than before. So David decided it would be best to put Cardiazol [10] on the gum surrounding the molar. I don't know what it is, but it didn't help. The toothache went on for days, nothing helped. Finally, David took one of his tools and pulled it out. What a relief it was.

Latvian newspapers were full of fearful stories about the Russians: They are robbing and murdering in Tukum; eighty year-old ladies are being raped on the streets and their gold teeth yanked from their mouths. Such nonsense always preceded a call for Latvians to join the battle against the Red Army. What *chutzpah* these stories, after three years of plunder, torment and murder. I wish these stories were true. The Latvians have earned such punishment. To do otherwise to such traitors, such criminals and the bitches who bore them, is itself a crime!

And look at this story in *Tēvija* [Fatherland] that appeared on Tuesday, 29 August after 7 Jews were betrayed by their *landsman* (fellow citizens):

> "**Jewish Bandits Liquidated.** The Commander of the Security Police and SD in Latvia announces: On 25 August a Jewish bandit group was liquidated after hiding in a flat at 15 Bade Street in Riga. The Jews, armed with pistols, opened fire on police units from their hiding place. One Latvian policeman was fatally wounded. Two Jews were shot dead by the police, and the others sought refuge in nearby buildings. Immediately additional Latvian police and SS-patrols were positioned in the area. Every building was searched from basement to attic. All Jewish bandits were discovered and arrested. Also arrested was the Latvian janitor, Anna Polis, who had hidden the Jews and provided them with food. She too will get the deserved punishment"

The parallel of this story to our own did not go unnoticed. We were depressed for days about this story. The tragedy of betrayal was compounded by the nearness of liberation. I keep these articles because I look forward to freedom and the chance to hear what these Latvian scum will say then. I pray we shall be liberated in time to celebrate the October Revolution.

SEPTEMBER 1944

The month began with *Yahrzeit* (memorial) for my oldest brother who died in Riga in 1939, *alav hasholom* (may he rest in peace). Days later Eisenhower arrived in Paris. Every day announcements appear in the newspaper reminding men and women 14 and older that they must go dig trenches. As a janitor, Robert is excused. We continued our routine: night guard duty, chess, reading, and I wrote. Waiting for the offensive to start here, the days seemed endless, interrupted only by the sirens of hope and danger.

The atrocities continued. Robert told us a story Tony recounted to him of her cousin, a Mrs. Voinovich. Her husband deserted the Latvian Army, was caught, and was imprisoned in the Salispils concentration camp[11]. With the aid of some prison guards, Mrs. Voinovich managed to remain in communication with her husband. On 26 July, at 2 AM, she went to the forest near the camp to await a guard with whom she exchanged notes, her husband's for hers. As she hid in her usual spot, suddenly Latvian police and Germans appeared, herding a large group of Jews to a clearing nearby. The Jews were forced to dig up dozens of bodies, most likely Jewish bodies, lay them out on a makeshift table, extract gold teeth, and then toss them back in the ditch. In the end, they doused the bodies with a liquid and set them ablaze. The "cemetery worker" Jews were then marched away just as they had arrived. Mrs. Voinovich was lying on the ground five hours watching a very white cloud of smoke rise higher and higher. Only by chance was she able to withdraw undetected. Mrs. Voinovich had no idea of the marching Jews' fate. We, of course, knew the end of this ghastly episode. We asked Robert to spare us of any further stories of this sort, at least for awhile.

Sunday, September 17, 1944. At 10:30 AM, the sirens wail. At first we thought this was yet another "cry wolf" exercise. But, we were soon startled by the sound of heavy bombardment. Several bombs shook the cellar when they landed nearby. We quickly prepared for the worst, pistols and shovels at the ready, walking shoes laced and tied, small sacks packed for travel. Though the bombing continued for some time, everyone was calm.

By noon it stopped, but at 6 PM it began again, a fierce barrage that lasted an hour. Then at 9 PM the sirens howled once more, but the sky was silent. Moments later, Tony arrived with Robert, particularly buoyant. She cradled several large cartridges she claimed came from downed Russian planes in the Libau countryside. In a breathless tone, she told us of a Russian pilot who cut free of his parachute and disappeared into the forest. Tony seemed so aroused by all this, as she and Robert repaired to the cave.

In the meanwhile, that night began Rosh Hashana, the new year 5705. We listened to Rabbi Salzburger deliver a short blessing from London: "Our God and God of our fathers, we acknowledge Thee and thank Thee for having kept us alive, and having sustained us to this day.... Standing between a past which is gone and a future not yet born, we declare with the deepest yearning, *Leshana Tova Tikosevu*, may we all be inscribed for a good year."

Merely a few years ago, Rabbi Salzburger spoke from his pulpit in Frankfurt, a pulpit adorned with flowers and burning candles. It was *yontif* (holiday)! Today the candles are extinguished, the synagogue is in ruins, and nearly all his congregants are dead—murdered by their neighbors. Indeed the measure of Doctor Salzburger, of any of us, is that we can still say *Leshana Tova Tikosevu*. This is not a miracle, it is a victory.

Monday, September 18, 1944. The first day of Rosh Hashana and all was quiet. You marked the day in your heart, each in your place, according to how you felt. My thoughts were with my family in Riga, or wherever they may be now. This was the first Rosh Hashana I was completely alone, my mother was elsewhere. On this day you read of Hannah, whose example teaches us that the future of the Jews is largely in the hands of the Jewish mother. I thought deeply about her prayer:

> God is all-knowing,
> And before Him there is an accounting.
> The bows of the mighty shall break,
> While the weak are girded with strength.
> The sated ones shall work for their bread,
> While the hungry are freely sated.
> Barren women shall bear seven,
> While she with much shall go wanting.
> The Lord gives life and takes it away;
> Lowering us in the grave to raise us later.

> The Lord impoverishes and makes wealth;
> He brings low and He elevates.
> He raises the destitute from the dust,
> And delivers the needy from trash-heaps,
> To sit beside princes
> Upon a throne of glory.
> The pillars of the earth are the Lord's
> And our world's foundation.[12]

When midnight arrived, all was still. I had guard duty with David.

Tuesday, September 19, 1944. The second day of Rosh Hashana. Fierce battles had begun again on the Eastern Front. Marshal Stalin announced that the breach near Riga was 80 miles wide and 30 miles deep, and that an invasion had begun from the northern border with Estonia. I found it difficult to concentrate on *yontif* for very long. Still, I had recurrent flashes of Jeremiah's assurance: "Refrain from whining, away with your tears, for God promises you shall be rewarded for your deeds, and they shall return from the clutches of the evening; there is hope for your future."[13]

Food is so important to *yontif,* to celebration of the new year. But it was and is now impossible. Access to food grows more difficult each day. Our main food is bread and potatoes. Some days one of the two is missing or even both. I fear becoming a Hamsun hero . . .

Some days later, a few days ago, Robert's appearance in the cellar was occasion for indescribable joy. He is free, and fate has smiled on us all.

In mid-September, Robert received a summons to appear before the draft commission on 22 September. They are increasingly desperate, cripples and sick people are rarely excused. Robert's chances seemed meager. Imagining what life without Robert would be like, alone in the cave, no contact with the outside world, was more than disorienting. We discussed our response to such a contingency, but none of it made sense.

"David, could you help me put a bandage on my leg?" Robert asked, as he took a small bottle of concentrated acetic acid from his jacket pocket.

Robert and David went off to a far corner of the front room. Robert rolled up his left trouser leg, and David was caught off balance. There, beneath the skin of Robert's lower leg, was a mass of bulging purple, ropy, veins.

"That's why I haven't been taken into the Army 'til now. But the Nazis are desperate. They don't care that my legs ache and sting and swell every day. Now they take everybody, no matter what. Maybe they won't send me to the front, but life elsewhere isn't exactly sweet either. I need to open up those old wounds, make those ulcers like I had a few years ago."

David remained silent. Before the war, Robert suffered painful and swollen legs. Often the skin seemed to fall apart and he developed ulcers that healed with difficulty. Robert had managed to get this malady under control in recent years, and he suffered much less. Yet, now, he wanted to use acid to open the old sores. Why? For the sake of 11 Jews hiding in his cellar? Because he feared death? Because, as a Communist, he recoiled at aiding the Nazis? For the sake of his little girls? For Tony? Perhaps, all of these?

"David, let's get on with it," Robert barked with some impatience. David did as Robert asked, and the acrid smell of the acid wafted through the cellar and into the cave behind the holy brick wall. It was the smell of salvation.

Robert was salvaged, as were we. After days of treatment, he was a limping invalid with deep wounds beneath the leg bandage. The pain was real and intense. Robert was excused from army service.

This past Saturday, a day after Robert's dispensation, Johanna dropped in for a visit, another break from Asīte. At first Robert barely looked at her. When Robert did speak, he asked when she was going back. When Johanna replied "a few days," Robert bristled and left. Johanna collapsed in tears. This situation is now entirely untenable. We understand both of them, we are unable to help either. Johanna keeps Robert from spending time with Tony, and Johanna is the object of Robert's bad behavior.

Later that evening, Robert insisted that Henny and Riva go up to his flat to bake bread. I am strongly opposed to such risky behavior. Better we eat dried bread than chance being exposed. I argued strenuously, but Robert insisted and the others agreed with him. Off they went. After half an hour, we heard crying and screaming upstairs. We couldn't imagine what had happened. David and I took our pistols and started up the cellar steps, but stopped on hearing Johanna's voice. She was the one crying, and her words told us Robert had hit her.

Then hours passed in silence. At 5:30 AM there was a signal. They were returning to the cellar. Just then we heard the bakers padding the stairs leading to the third floor flats. We were terrified that Riva and Henni would be caught. We waited. Ten minutes, twenty minutes, thirty minutes. Finally they arrived, deadly pale. They nearly encountered the bakers several times and had to run back to Robert's flat to hide. They were steps and seconds from exposure. I was enraged. We can't allow this risk taking to go on. David agreed, and then the others. We vowed that no one may go upstairs in future.

The next morning Johanna came to say goodbye. She was quite despondent.

"We all need to endure this madness," I commiserated with her. "How can we speak with Robert about this now? He is unreasonable. Soon, though, things will change."

"You know you can depend on us," David interjected, "we are on your side. Johanna, I think it's best that you and the girls stay in Asīte, and not come back before we come to get you."

Henni, Hilde, and Riva stared in silence, a cold stare, or perhaps simply a disinterested stare . . .

PART THREE

Far from growing familiar with my prison
    I beheld it every moment with new horror . . .
Thoughts to which the mind had grown immune
    Soon sickened me against me, turned me
in among me stranger than before, my quarantine a panic
    room bricked in, a tightening around me
in increments only animals know . . . .

Timothy Donnelly, "Poem Beginning with
A Sentence From *The Monk*"

We have now come full circle: **present tense, tense present.** Yom Kippur, 27 September 1944, and you await arrival of the future. The late afternoon sun casts its unique shadow. This is particularly portentous on Yom Kippur, for soon the *shofar* will sound and signal our sealed fates, and the end of the fast. Still, you must go slow and make room to consider Jonah, who, like us, was cast into the belly of the beast:

> The waters closed upon me,
> The deep engulfed me.
> Weeds wound about my head.
> I sank to the base of mountains;
> The bars of the earth shut forever.
> Yet, You brought my life up from the pit
> O Lord my God![14]

As Jonah, you are forced to master the future with sad smiles, to overcome the past by swallowing it, to turn our story inside out. But you struggle. Man is wicked, not least because of indifference, and God is unreliable. For us, justice and anger lead to vengeance and retribution. For God, you are reminded in Jonah, to *rachmones*, to compassion. The vile survive and the good perish. What a mystery this Divine *rachmones* . . . . It is nightfall and there is no sound of the *shofar*, only the elemental sound of rain.

* * *

The last days of September pass with little news from the Front. This afternoon, German radio reports that in Palestine a Jewish brigade has been assembled to battle the German army and occupy the German nation. They view this development with vituperative outrage. We raise glasses filled with our remaining *schnapps*.

This evening Robert insists that Riva come to his flat, it needs cleaning. Everyone is silent. I tell him leaving the cellar is too risky and, as a group, we have decided against it. Robert explodes and tells me to shut up. I calmly repeat what we decided. He curses me and storms out of the cellar. A few hours later he is back, this time with flowers for Riva. September 28 is her birthday and he wishes her all the best.[15] He seats himself, puffs up a bit, and says nothing further until he leaves. We celebrate Riva's birthday.

The next evening Robert arrives with Tony. It is her birthday. David presents her with a small token of our best wishes, a *tchotchke* for a *tchotchke* (a plaything for a plaything). We know that Robert expects this of us. He is still angry with me. I really don't care. Better his anger than Riva in the hands of the SD.

When Robert and Tony leave, David and I take up night guard duty. Before long we hear pounding outside. Perhaps the bakers are pounding their dough, we speculate. Just then Hilde bolts from the cave ghost-faced, eyes bulging. She is shaking and mute for several seconds before she tells us what's wrong.

"Some people are breaking the back hatch with crowbars . . . they are shining flashlights. Probably the police are here. I think one of them has already broken in!"

"We're lost . . . they're already inside!" screams Henni, who followed Hilde, even more excited, clutching her head.

David and I quickly load our pistols. David runs inside. I stay in the front room with the ladies. They are overwrought, I remain calm.

It makes no sense. Why should the police come through that tiny cave hatch. They can come in by simply smashing the cellar door. It must be the bakers making that racket.

David quickly comes out of the cave and tells us that the bakers are hunting rats. The rats scurry into the cave through a small opening in the hatch, and the bakers are pounding it with crowbars. They seem to be losing interest. Ah, once again, serendipity prevails. But, even a rat is a potential informant . . .

OCTOBER 1944

The month begins soberly. It has been a year since David, Michael, Henni and Hilde arrived in Sedol's cellar. They came for 2 months, assuming liberation by the Red Army was near. Using the *schnapps* Tony brought us, a thank you for our friendship, I mark the occasion with a toast, using the words of the other Robert—Burns that is . . .

> The best-laid schemes o' mice an' men
> Gang aft agley,
> An' lea'e us naught but grief an' pain
> For promis'd joy!

Still, we are hopeful. The air raid sirens wail, the bombs fall, and the anti-aircraft flak lights up the night sky. Perhaps the final push will soon begin, and we will know freedom again.

The days drag on. More than routine, they are tiresome, even irksome. Robert is still in a foul mood over challenges to his authority. We take turns indulging him with all manner of praise and gratefulness. He's irritated, but he needs to put his pique on the shelf. Perhaps he has and he is merely manipulating attention.

Our food supply is more uncertain, not unreliable but tight. Misha volunteers to Robert that a gentile friend, Mrs. Henning, is holding several watches for him. He prepares a note asking that she give them to Robert. Though Mrs. Henning is a friend of longstanding, this is still a bit risky. There is little choice.

Robert returns with the watches and more, items Misha had completely forgotten about. Soon Misha begins to balk and only agrees to sell a few watches. Misha has his reasons: "this was a present from my wife, this one my father gave my mother, this one you are only allowed to touch," and on and on. I can see the anger in everyone's eyes. Each of us has offered up for sale everything of value we possessed. Misha is the last to take his turn and he is being difficult.

"Misha, truly I'm surprised," I plead. "You are a comrade. We have all sacrificed our objects of memory for the good of all. No excuse can justify your refusal."

"If I say no, it's no!" Misha barks, fully revealing the kernel of his character.

Days later, Misha sends Robert back to Mrs. Henning for other jewelry. Robert returns empty-handed. Mrs. Henning has sailed for Germany, Misha's jewels and all. Misha is not unhappy.

"So Misha, with what shall I buy food . . . my good looks?" Robert sneeringly intones. "Maybe I should sell my daughters into slavery so you might have some soup and a bit of bread." Misha turns his back on Robert, and the rest. To keep the peace, we set this sordid episode aside. What can you say to someone who values things over life? He has an advantage. We will not let him starve. It is not our way.

Jews can still be seen in Libau. When Robert went to Mrs. Henning he saw Jews on Ulich Street, and again on Raina Street. Supposedly, they are from Westphalia, but he knew nothing else. This is how the Jews wander about from city to city, driven until the last bit of vitality is sucked out of them.

On the second Monday of the month tumult and disarray prevails. The *Arbeitsamt* (Employment Office) has been shuttered. All day we hear tanks and trucks rumbling through town. Latvians flee wherever they can, at least those with blood on their hands. The others remain in place. The building custodians have been reassigned to the German Wehrmacht. Only 7 remain, one being Robert. Even trench-digging is no longer being done.

With nightfall, the air raids begin. Bombs fall and our building shakes violently. We hear intense air battles. Everyone retreats to the cave. It seems safer there. I have guard duty and stay up front with Michael and Zelig. The blasts are titanic and tear open the cellar windows. It feels as though every bomb is falling next to our house. David emerges from the cave and asks Michael to come inside because Hilde is frightened. Zelig and I calmly remain on guard in the front room.

The bombs fall until 10 PM. Robert returns from the building owner's flat, and reports that the wire factory, train station, and Naval Port have all been hit. In town, folks are talking of how well the Russian pilots are hitting their targets. No private homes have been struck. Late at night, Riva goes upstairs with Robert. Why, I don't know.

Tuesday, 10 October 1944. *Simchas Torah*. A holy day of transition. The Torah—God's word, the legends of the Jews—concludes and begins anew. How fitting just now, our metamorphosis from slavery to freedom. Air raids continue in the daylight. For the first time since our arrival, the bakers upstairs are not working. Bombs again fall on factories and the Port. Robert comes to the cellar to report the word on the street: from 6 PM to midnight the city will be evacuated, possibly to set mines or blow it up. We remain calm, stay in place, and prepare. I recall Joshua's admonition to the Israelites, the passage read on Simchas Torah: "Prepare yourselves provisions, for in days you will cross the Jordan . . . . Strengthen yourself and persevere. Do not fear nor lose resolve, for God is with you wherever you may go." The battle for Libau has begun and you must be up to the task of survival.

The turmoil continues, and Robert is out and about each day this week taking the temperature of the town. On Wednesday he chances upon Trofim, the Russian "simpleton" who works at the SD, David's friend and savior of Shmerl, Yosl, and Misha. Trofim tells Robert the SD will turn tail that evening. He wants to make himself scarce, and asks for Robert's help. Robert agrees to take him in, but he is yet to show up. This evening, Libau Radio, in German, makes a stunning announcement: *"Der Jude Kirchenstein ist von Moskau als Oberkommissar für Lettland bestimmt geworden* (the Jew Kirchenstein was appointed by Moscow as Chief Commissar of Latvia). We all roar with laughter. Kirchenstein is not a Jew at all, he is a known anti-Semite. A German name, a communist . . . certainly he *must be* a Jew! The Nazi propaganda continues even as they prepare to flee.

All about town there are military police with dogs. In the harbor, 200 ships stand ready to evacuate the entire civilian population of Libau. If this happens, all will be fair game for Russian bombs, even neighborhood bakeries. Still, we are quite calm in the midst of troubles. Food is harder to come by and our diet is mostly black bread and bitter coffee. David, Michael, Zelig, Aaron, and Yosl have had diarrhea for days now, and I, Misha, and Shmerl have toothaches. We all manage, buoyed by the Red Army advance and our oncoming freedom.

Robert is not calm at all. He is certain the house will be blown apart any moment. He argues with everyone about the daily news, on the radio and in town. This annoys me without end.

"I don't care what the town babble is. If there is going to be evacuation and demolition, we must coolheadedly decide what we are going to do."

"The mine setters must be shot!" Robert explodes.

"You may be right," I concur, "but we will have to judge the circumstances.... What if the house burns because of a Russian bomb or some other unforeseen reason?... The boiler blows up... We will need a new place to hide."

"I have been thinking about this," Robert answered. "I have three places for you, but you will have to divide into groups of three or four."

This will not be easy. As much as we may bristle at one another from time to time, we are also quite attached. Yet, we have come this far and we cannot lose our bearing to sentimentality. We agree on three groups, each with one woman and two pistols. Group 1: David, Henni, Yosl. Group 2: Michael, Hilde, Zelig, Aaron. Group 3: Shmerl, Misha, Riva, myself. The groups are not without a clear logic to them.

"Riga has fallen!" David shouts as he jumps to his feet. "Marshal Stalin proclaims the capture of Riga!"

Our joy is ineffable.... But, then, what of the Jews? Who knows if any still live? My sisters, my dear mother, my brother... Have they lived to see the liberation? I don't want to think about this any longer. I can't change a thing. Their fate has already been decided. I will know it soon enough.

The last day of the week passes quietly. Then, about 7 PM, there is an air raid. Bombs fall, heavy flak fire in response. The cellar windows shake and spring open. We all remain calm. I sit at the table and write.

Week three of October and chaos mounts. American radio announces that the Baltics are completely liberated. German radio declares the Russians in retreat. Wishful thinking takes no side. Libau is not liberated and the Red Army only advances. There is endless talk of civilian evacuation, the same civilians who have begun to steal from the Germans. Everyone on the street is carrying parcels. Vecvagars, the chief of the bakery above us, gave Robert 25 packages of yeast to hide, along with some news.

"Even with the yeast I gave you, we will only have enough to operate 2 more days . . . Listen, last week two German officers and a woman visited the bakery. I asked them what they wanted and they insisted they were just looking for a room to use as a bunker. But I heard the woman say to them as they left that it would be good to blast here."

"This makes sense," Robert responded, "because if the building collapses it would block the narrow street to the market, making house-to-house combat more difficult for the Soviet soldiers."

"So what can we do?"

"Even with the city full of SD from Riga and elsewhere, we have to stockpile grenades and pistols, and together we won't let them demolish the building."

"The bakers will be with you on this . . . One more thing, Robert. You know I have not been sympathetic to the Fritzen, and in my job I have come to know many secrets about our own countrymen. I suspect these Latvian collaborators want to lynch me before the Soviets arrive."

"Don't worry," Robert assures Vecvagars, "just ask and I will hide you and your family. The only ones swinging will be the collaborators, the fascists."

Each day Vecvagars steals more from the Germans. Not only yeast, but sacks of flour as well. With our muscle, Robert hides the contraband in the cellar. The bakers' continue to bake. We are certain there will be no surprise blasts or German takeovers, the rumors notwithstanding. Robert brings us many.

Bekona Eksports (Bacon Export) has been confiscated by the Germans and the workers sent by ship to Germany. They say the bakery will soon be next. You will have to leave the cellar." A large business and a little bakery, hardly equals. We disregard this.

"The military police are patrolling Libau with dogs, inspecting basements and attics, looking for deserters. What if they come here?" This seems more plausible so we make a new hatch cover and keep it well-rubbed with kerosene to mask the human scent. We also fashion a metal plate to reinforce the strength of the hatch, though this makes it a bit unwieldy.

The bombing continues almost daily, but Robert confirms that the principle target is the harbor. Every day scores of corpses wash up on the

Libau beaches from the bombed ships. Burial? They are placed in paper sacks and dumped in a common pit. *Az me grubt a grub far yenem, falt men alain arein*! If you dig a ditch for someone else, you fall in it yourself!

Tony remains a frequent visitor to the cellar. By now, of course, she is well-acquainted with all eleven of us. She brings gifts, information, and a bizarre faith in the prowess of the German military. On Monday, Tony gives us various medications entrusted to her by her Jewish dentist, Alexander Rischman, who was murdered at the lighthouse in July '41. She also brings us garments from the abandoned men's clothing factory. The owner, Stulpe, left for Germany and the merchandise was liberated by the townspeople.

Later in the week, Tony relays news. Near Rucava, 26 Jews were working in the forest, guarded by Latvians. When the Red Army attacked, 20 of them escaped to the Russians. The Latvians captured and executed the other six. Tony also tells us that the Naval Harbor is heavily damaged, and days ago a munitions train was destroyed. Surprisingly, 350 trucks from Riga sit like carnival ducks in the Naval Harbor, awaiting an order to move out.

"Where to, Germany?" asked David.

"No, back to Riga, of course," Tony answers.

"That makes no sense. The Russians control Riga."

"No problem, the wait will be short. Before long Riga will be recaptured and the trucks will drive back."

Tony's good sense has gone on a trip, and is a constant source of amusement for us. Indeed, in Libau fantasies are pandemic, being regularly concocted as uplift for nervous Latvians with guilty consciences. We and they are counting the moments until the Russian attack on Libau, we with hope, they with dread.

The Latvian newspapers *Tēvija* and *Kurzemes Vārds*, which Robert brings us almost daily, have spent 3 years serving up anti-Semitism and German propaganda. Now they are published together as a single page, merely 3 times a week. The victory articles have been replaced by eulogies for the Latvia they must leave behind, the Latvia that could have been, the Latvia that is broken . . . . Lamentations, lamentations, lamentations!

But where were the softhearted when thousands of women and children were murdered, and their beloved land bathed in Jewish blood? Then they were great patriots, heroic followers of Hitlerism. Well, true evil is the absence of empathy, and far too many of our neighbors are truly evil. They will soon meet the same fate as we Jews. The Red Army is near!

This morning I was sitting in the front room with Michael and Misha and suddenly the alarm-lamp flashed. Quickly we turned off the gas, hid the hot coffee and disappeared into the cave. Time passed and we heard nothing. Apparently, a baker had come to hide some contraband in the space beneath the cellar stairs and triggered the alarm when he turned on the light. There seems to be more of these scares lately. Just yesterday someone made 3 rhythmic knocks on the cellar door. There was a period of tense silence and nothing came of it.

I have overnight guard duty with David. Misha sits with us. They play chess. I read Maxim Gorki stories. He was a Leninist who always defended the Jews. These days I often recall his story *Pogrom*, a veiled tale of the Kishinev massacre of 1903. But now I am reading simple stories of human foible.

Saturday, 21 October 1944. Robert is quite sullen. He sits with us all day in mopish silence. We think he may have confided too much in Vecvagars, king of the upstairs bakers, and now he regrets it. Vecvagars, who gave Robert flour and yeast to hide and whom Robert trusted, has disappeared.

It is evening. We suddenly hear a dog barking outside the bricked-up cave window. Soon after, there is another barking dog on another side of the cellar. We are certain Vecvagars is the target of a search. Still, we place rags soaked in kerosene against the hatch and wait. Fifteen minutes pass and the dogs are gone. Another fifteen and some of us leave the cave. David and I search for Moscow Yiddish Radio to hear some news about Riga, but the station no longer seems to be on the air.

These last days of October are now entirely dominated by bombardment and panic in the streets. Heavy flak is aloft day and night. Bombs fall near and far. It's 6 PM, and an extraordinary intense air raid has begun. Bombs explode with shorter and shorter intervals of quiet. Artillery shells buzz and sputter past our house, detonating more distantly with such force our whole cellar shakes. The cellar windows spring open. Wave upon wave. It feels as though the explosions are getting closer. We are calm and ready to leave if need be. Two hours pass before the all-clear is sounded. Robert ventures outside, through the courtyard and onto Catholic Street. He quickly returns to inform us that the harbor is in flames.

Shortly after sunrise, Robert walks about Libau to look upon last night's destruction: "Bombs exploded on Kirchen, Espen, Ludwig, Bade and Bruder Streets. The whole quarter near the harbor has burned down. At Goldman's on Wiesen Street, the whole building has been reduced to rubble. Many ordinary folks have been killed. In a cellar near the bridge, two Jews from Westphalia were also killed." Robert retreats to a corner in despair. I think he merely seeks attention.

This afternoon, Robert wordlessly bolts from the cellar. Several hours later he returns with the ominous announcement printed in *Kurzemes Vārd / Tēvija*: "All residents of Libau are forbidden to leave their homes after 6 PM. Violators will be dealt with severely, and risk being summarily shot." This triggers even greater panic in town. All are certain the plan is to ship every Libauer to Germany. Most don't want to leave. For us it is even worse. We need to make new calculations.

Robert's spirits tumble lower than this morning. Tony's husband is a fireman and he plans to be off with the Germans for Germany just days from now. He expects Tony to be with him, but she wants to separate from him. How will her husband act? Does he know about Robert? Will he bring the police? In Johanna's absence, Tony visits with Robert in his flat. Now he wants to hide her in the cellar. Tony is nearly frantic with indecision.

Terrible bombardment begins again this evening. Robert brings his bed to the cellar. He fears for his safety. There is shooting in the streets and residents are set upon in their homes. A *khapene* (snatching) is anticipated in Libau on Saturday. Even now, whoever is caught on the street is dragged onto ships bound for Germany.

. . . Two days have passed uneventfully. I sit up front this afternoon and write. Michael and Yosl are playing chess. The rest are dozing. The *pax* Libau is shattered, without warning, by dreadful explosions near our house. The whole cellar quakes, almost a rolling bounce. We are all dressed and ready to flee from the frying pan into the fire. What other choice do we have? Our frayed nerves are taut.

Bombardment ends in 30 minutes. Robert leaves to assess the damage. Hours later he returns, just in time to hear Goebbels' uncharacteristically subdued rant on *Deutschlandsender*:

"We shall never surrender, we shall see victory . . . Our enemies seek world domination, but we will not be under the thumb of that Jew Morgenthau or Englishmen . . . The Führer has never had as much hope for victory as now."

Disenchanted, Goebbels hardly seems to believe his own words. What a blissful thought before sleep . . .

Saturday is here, Tony is here, but the *khapene* is not. Last night Tony slept with Robert in the cellar. We are not certain of the meaning of this. Has she abandoned her husband? Is he already bound for Germany? Was she simply trying to evade the *khapene*? We don't ask.

Robert takes his morning walk, Tony stays behind. He returns with the portentous finding that the Germans are mounting anti-aircraft batteries on the Rosenplatz and in several other central Libau locations. This menacing development has increased the panic in town. The *khapene* worries are forgotten. Word on the street today is, should the Germans fire flak from central Libau, the Russians will tear apart all of our beautiful city, citizens included. If this is so, our situation is dire, we have no way out.

Riva is distracted and distraught with worry about Adinka who is hiding just a few blocks away. Robert has gone to see Adinka's protector from time to time, and Mrs. Shimelphenig has provided pictures of Adinka for Riva. But, it has been more than a month since Robert's last visit and the heavy bombing has Riva on edge.

It is 11 PM. All of us are in the cave, but Henni and a few others. Suddenly, Henni enters the cave shaking. Grabbing her ghostly pale face with both hands, she whispers, "A patrol is inside!" The others follow Henni into the cave and we close the hatch. Though a bit muffled, we can hear several people screaming, "*Macht mal auf hier!*" (Open up here!) They walk about upstairs for half an hour and then they leave. Who are they looking for? Could it still be Vecvagars?

I have night guard duty with David. Robert and Tony sleep in their corner . . . .

Sunday was a day of rest. There were no air raids. This morning, however, there is a massive bombardment, but it lasts only 30 minutes. The immense panic today is German made. The *khapane* has begun. People are being seized in the streets. Entire neighborhoods are being surrounded, and families are taken from their homes. Many are fleeing to attics, cellars, and other hiding places. Whoever falls into SD hands is immediately sent away on a ship to Germany. Families are often torn apart, children left behind, alone. All of Libau is burning with rage. Absent the murders, all this is not unlike the Jewish *khapenes*. God, forgive me, I take pleasure in the pain of my neighbors.

Riva is even more distraught over Adinka's safety. She begs Robert to visit Mrs. Shimelphenig. Robert agrees. He returns with the news that Otilija and Adinka left for the countryside on Saturday. He promises to get her the address.

"I don't believe it," Riva cried. "I'm sure she took my beautiful Adinka to Germany."

"Riva, this can't be," I assured her. "It is totally illogical. A person with a clear conscience, a good person like Mrs. Shimelphenig, would not flee from Courland, where the war will soon end, to Germany, where the bombs now fall and war is just beginning."

Riva is inconsolable . . .

NOVEMBER 1944

> For what wears out the life of mortal men?
> 'Tis that from change to change their being rolls;
> 'Tis that repeated shocks, again, again,
> Exhaust the energy of strongest souls
> And numb the elastic powers.

So said Matthew Arnold, the brilliant British poet of the last century. After more than three years of staring down evil, you are indeed numb. Randomness, chaos, uncertainty, and chance contrive your fate. You live in that place of torment between what you know and what is beyond your knowing. The winds of accident blow stronger each day.

> . . . *You redeemed us from Egypt, HASHEM our God, and liberated us from the house of bondage. In famine, You nourished us and in plenty You sustained us. From sword You saved us; from plague You let us escape; and from severe and enduring diseases You spared us. Until now Your mercy has helped*

us, and Your kindness has not forsaken us. Do not abandon us, HASHEM our God, forever . . .

* * *

Robert returns to the cellar this afternoon, the first day of November, with the precise address of Mrs. Shimelphenig and Adinka in the countryside beyond Libau. Riva is bursting with happiness, almost ravished by it. Who is not moved by this?

Libau Radio broadcasts an announcement: "We seek to protect all citizens of Libau from bombs. Thus, all civilian residents of Libau *must* voluntarily evacuate. Whoever does not evacuate by the 6th, will be removed by force. Only those who are essential to the war effort may remain. Such persons possess a red pass."

Robert has a white pass, he is more anxious than ever. For Robert, the red pass precludes the cruise to Germany, for us it makes slavery and death far less likely. Robert is determined to obtain the red pass.

In town, the panic increases with each hour. The Germans and their Latvian collaborators are terrorizing the residents as if they were Jews. Persons without guilt desperately want to remain in Libau. They stay in their homes to avoid "voluntary" deportation. Rumor has it that on the 9th, the police will patrol with dogs to ferret out unauthorized persons who remain. We are confident they will not find us.

Deutschlandsender broadcasts propaganda that becomes more absurd each day, if not obscene. Hitler youth now impersonate "relocated" Dutch or Norwegian youngsters:

"So tell me," queries the interviewer, "has it been long that you have been working at this trench digging?"

"Where did you get that idea?" answers the Dutch girl. "We women don't work with spades at all. We are only here to cook for the men, and to encourage them."

"Now that's nice," responds the interviewer.

"And how old are you?" he asks the boy.

"I'm 15 years old. I'm Dutch. I know what I owe the German nation. In Holland, they are fighting to liberate my fatherland, and here I am standing for Germany.

"And how long do you have to work here?"

"Oh, it really doesn't matter. I'm not leaving here until we are victorious."

"So tell me, how are things here as far as rationing is concerned? Please, be open and honest about this."

"Oh great. We have enough to eat here."

Such transparent, amateurish propaganda. Hardly worthy of a master like Goebbels. Germany is collapsing.

Friday evening, the hot and cold water pipes in the bakery come apart at the joints and water inundates our cave. Relentlessly, we bail out the water with buckets and wipe with mops, but the water continues to rain down. Robert has not, as yet, been able to fix the pipes or redirect the water. It is too risky for David or others of us to go up to the bakery to help. Meanwhile, we can no longer sleep on the floor. We stand all night. We are exhausted.

Sunday, 5 November 1944, Tony's indecision comes to a close. She completely inserts herself in the cellar. She fears that she will be snatched if she sleeps at home. She and Robert are trying to relocate her mother and 8 year old son to the countryside. Tony sleeps with Robert in a far corner of the front room. Robert has partitioned the space with a curtain. I have night guard-duty with David. My mind's voice admonishes, "Robert, *mit ein hintn zitst men nit oif tsvei ferd*! (You can't sit on two horses with one butt!) This can only be ruinous for everyone . . . You, Tony, Johanna, your daughters, and the eleven who count on your good sense to keep them alive." Even if I were to say all this aloud, Robert would not hear me. He is too angry-drunk with infatuation.

Morning light and Robert is off again in search of the elusive "red pass." He has been knocking on every door for nearly a week. Today he strikes gold. Robert is provided with a red pass for himself as "bakery mechanic" and a red pass for Tony that is blank. This is a great relief for all of us.

Tuesday, 7 November 1944, the 27th anniversary of the Great October Revolution (26 October on the Czarist calendar), the arrival of Lenin and the Bolsheviks in Petersburg, afterwards Petrograd, now Leningrad. Marshal Stalin halts all fighting in honor of the day and exhorts his soldiers to tear apart the Germans with ever greater rage. We celebrate as members of the proletariat, day and night bailing out cave water!

The panic in Libau continues. The residents are being seized on the streets and carted off to waiting ships. People are trying to hide wherever they can. Libau radio announces several times a day that everyone must cooperate with the evacuation, it is in their best interest. Now everyone is praying for the Russians to arrive quickly. *Kurzemes Vārd / Tēvija* writes: "Those who hide are being irresponsible. Ships with 1000 places are leaving almost empty. The Soviets are deporting everyone to Siberia. Germany is certainly preferable to Siberia." Such propaganda is now hollow.

Robert tells us that all of Möven Street is being forced to evacuate. The intention is to clear Libau from the harbor to the market, including Kauf Street where we sit, just blocks from the market. We tell each other that now that the bakery is fully operating again, our building will be spared searches and bombs. What foolishness!

Friday, 10 November 1944. It has been nearly a week since we've been able to sleep properly. Water from the bakery has been relentless. David has thought of a solution. With Misha and Shmerl, he erects a gutter-like sluiceway across an entire cave-wall and the water now flows directly in pails which we empty regularly. With the flow of water slowing a bit and our sluiceway solution, tonight we are able to relieve our exhaustion with real sleep, at least for awhile.

Misha and Yosl have night guard duty. At 3 AM, someone beats at the cellar door, and they run to the cave and alert the rest. We secure the hatch and take our customary positions with loaded pistols. An hour or so goes by and Robert signals us it is safe to emerge from hiding. The same scene repeats at 7:30 AM. Robert makes yet another curtain call. It seems the general unrest is reaching out to our cellar door. Lately, several times a day there is knocking and banging, and we must scurry to the cave. Robert tells us it is just the bakers hoping to steal from him. We don't believe it. Outsiders are playing a game of jitters. Perhaps someone is searching for Tony. She no longer ventures outside, she is as hidden as we are. Surely this is why Robert brings boards and 8 x 10 beams to reinforce the cellar . . .

These last three days have witnessed mounting tension, just as I predicted. Robert is grim-faced, imperious, angry, and dangerous. He frequently goes into hysterics, making a racket that surely can be heard beyond the cellar walls.

"You need to calm yourself, Robert," I implore.

"I don't care. I want to yell so the whole house hears. Let the police come. Let it cost me my head, and your heads as well," Robert rages.

What little respect I had left for Robert after his adultery and other risky behaviors, is now nearly gone. Our survival depends solely on his mood, and he is too often out of control.

Sunday evening Robert insists that we begin reinforcing the cellar. I make the point that we could prepare the beams, but banging on a late Sunday evening is particularly dangerous. Others agree.

"Shut your fucking mouths! I don't give a damn about your opinions. I only listen to David," Robert bellows. David, unfortunately, says little and is carelessly lax himself. The cellar wars have begun.

Very early Monday morning many hands rap at the cellar door. We all scramble to position. We could hear Robert talking to two men. They had fled Asīte and were asked to bring greetings from Johanna. They also inform Robert that Johanna and the girls have gone to the forest to live in an underground potato storage until the Russians arrive. Robert thanks them for coming and they are off. Robert and Tony are bitchy the remainder of the day. This is rather *chutzpadik* (nervy) of two people who waste so much of our money on trifles.

We continue our work on the supports. Michael and I prepare the beams. David and the others put them in place. The work is exhausting and we need breaks and sustenance. The others eat bread with lard, I eat dried bread. At one break, Robert chances upon me and Michael eating a bit of meat and he grabs it from our hands. "Have you no common sense," he rants. We have no idea what he means, but we remain closed mouth.

New wood bunks: Shmerl, Yosl and Kalman

As the job nears conclusion, Zelig asks Aaron for a cigarette. Just then Robert happens by.

"Why aren't you working?" Robert barks.

"I'm just taking a break for a moment," Zelig answers.

"A break . . . there are no breaks 'til the job is done."

"Ah, the ball-buster speaks . . . . How easy it is for you to order others to work here, to make the cellar safe for your whore."

Robert explodes. When he takes a pistol to threaten Zelig, I and the other men surround him. He backs off the stupid threat, only after we are obliged to endure his rude rant. Zelig is right, but it's pointless to argue with Robert. The way he acts, his impolite tongue, it is obvious he thinks less of us. Still, we must suffer Robert's behavior for the sake of future freedom. To be frank, I forgive him every day because his one deed—rescuing us—outweighs all else.

Wednesday, 15 November 1944. The cellar supports are finished and we all feel more secure about surviving bombardment. With the extra wood, we erect plank cots for ourselves, sort of bunks. Most of our cave space on the ground and above is now for sleeping. We also build a folding table that can be stored at night.

In the afternoon, Shmerl and I clean the boiler room. We shovel the coal, mop the water, and stack the boards and planks. This is several hours of work.

In the evening, Robert reveals that last night the police searched our building when they heard our banging. They found nothing. Surely, they weren't terribly diligent. How could they have missed the cellar as the source of the noise? Now Robert decides that banging is forbidden in the evening. Apparently, one of the new tenants upstairs is a *kurveh* (whore) and the police stop by each night to partake of her favors. We are lucky . . . Robert's carelessness could have been our end.

Before we bed down, I distribute the blankets and the few linens we have.

"So, I think I have the right to ask Zelig and Aaron for my blanket," declares Yosl.

"Why?" I innocently inquire.

"Because the blanket belongs to me, I brought it."

"If this is your reason, then certainly you can have it. There is no discussion if it is yours." Yosl takes the blanket, puts it on his plank, and proceeds to the front room where I can hear him talking to Michael.

"Kalman is angry that I took back my blanket. Who else was I supposed to take it from? Shmerl? Misha?"

Yes, this is the new Yosl, the changed Yosl. Time and tension have deformed his character. A kibitzer, jokester, teaser, has now become a yente, troublemaker, rumormonger. Just this morning he told Zelig: "Robert is angry with you because the others have bad-mouthed you." Later he told Robert: "Zelig is angry with you because the others have cast a slur on you." This behavior is corrosive.

This backbiting continues in the morning. For reasons that are altogether indiscernible, Michael is terribly upset about absolutely nothing. He insists that the others have been talking about me, saying that I put on airs. I am not surprised. It's quite possible that what they say of me is not without cause. While others busy themselves with *narrishkeit* (trivialities), I pay them no mind. I avoid idle gossip. I do the work I am responsible for; I do my share. But then I mostly sit and write or read. I think their biggest gripe, however, is probably that I won't grovel or be pushed around by anyone, even Robert. I extend myself for him like the others but he doesn't appreciate it. Maybe to him we are Jews, not people, and so he can treat us in any manner his mood dictates. Well, he is wrong, very wrong.

I will always be grateful to Robert for the good deed of hiding us. I will repay him in everyway I can, but not with my integrity, nor with my Jewish pride that even the Germans couldn't crack. They beat me and called me *Saujude* (Jewish pig), but I am more proud than ever.

Late in the evening, David and Robert announce that they are going to inspect the underground storage room in the yard. We don't believe them. We rather think that they are going up to Dr. Straumanis' flat. He left for military service, and Robert has been looting things, small items he stores in the cellar.

In an hour they return and our suspicion is soon confirmed. An automatic circuit breaker, an ultraviolet lamp, all items of little value. Looting only diminishes us as people. This greatly annoys me. What irresponsibility, to risk the lot of us for a petty crime!

The next morning Robert bounds upstairs and is shocked. Dr. Straumanis has returned from the front. Robert runs down to the cellar with the news. He orders us to put the loot in the cave. Of course, Straumanis doesn't suspect Robert, and Robert calculates that once Straumanis leaves he can resume his thievery.

I am especially tired in the afternoon and decide it's best to sleep. Before long, or so it seems, Zelig is shaking me awake. There is panic on his face: "Some of our mates have poisoned themselves with gas!" We scramble to the front room. Misha is stumbling from one table to the next, about to collapse. Zelig and I grab him and stand him just beneath the open window. Zelig supports Misha, and I hasten to Robert's curtained corner. There, near the bed, lie Shmerl and Riva, motionless. David and the others are trying to revive them. I take Shmerl in my arms and carry him closer to the open window. I lay him on the ground, slide a pillow beneath his back, and blow stale air in his mouth. I feel drained of energy.

After awhile, Shmerl begins to groan very loudly, and then a forlorn scream. With the window open, this is dangerous, so I hold his mouth shut off and on. Soon he vomits and feels better. I look over toward the bed and Riva has regained consciousness as well. Robert suddenly appears and is altogether bemused by the tumult.

Minutes later Yosl, Michael, Aaron, and David complain of throbbing headaches, and then can barely stand on their feet. Moments on, Hilde, Henni, and Tony become ill in the same way. Our cellar looks like a pauper's hospital ward. Robert is off in search of a cause. It turns out that a gas pipe has cracked and everyone but Zelig and me was poisoned. Robert is making repairs while our comrades recover.

Almost everyone decides to spend the remainder of the day in bed. Yosl and Riva stay in the front. Yosl goes into the boiler room to wash his clothes, and Riva stays in the front room to watch the signal lamp. Suddenly there are several knocks at the cellar door. Riva panics and, without alerting Yosl, runs into the cave. We can't close the hatch with Yosl outside. We wait 10, 15 anxious minutes, and there's no tapping. David and I go out to get Yosl. These erratic door-taps are increasingly wearisome.

Saturday, 18 November 1944. Robert and Tony announce their decision. They are settling with us, permanently and fully until liberation.

No more diddling in the upstairs flat. They have a corner of their own in the front room, and that's it. Robert insists we build a new bed, cupboards with shelves, and a closet for Tony's clothes. Day and night we hammer and hack. Each whack is a danger, but Robert doesn't care. The police and their *kurveh* be damned!

I have night guard duty. I sit just outside the hatch. Robert and Tony are in their new bed at the far end of the front room. The sounds of screwing are unmistakable. Rhythmic slurps and squeaks. With moans, groans, and deflations, they selfishly shred our social contract. There is no privacy in the cellar, curtain or no curtain. David and Henni, Michael and Hilde, married couples both, have forsworn marital relations for the duration of our hiding. Not out of embarrassment. But because others of us have been torn from our spouses and lovers, and being in earshot of orgasm is cruel. Robert knows this, but he and Tony have rekindled aroused adolescence.

Morning arrives. The signal lamp flashes three times and fingers tap on the door, in a way prearranged to indicate that Robert was entering. But Robert is sleeping in the cellar! I assume it is Johanna, and walk toward the door. Then the lamp flashes a fourth time and remains lit. I wake Robert and whisper what has happened. Tony is quite upset that Johanna might surprise her. I have no patience for this silliness and I disappear into the cave and close the hatch.

Robert dresses quickly and, after depositing Tony in the cave, leaves the cellar. In moments the alarm lamp lights, normally our signal to turn on the water pump. David urges me to do it, but I point out that Robert could not have arrived in his upstairs flat so quickly. Tony echoes David, but again I refuse. Robert returns to the cellar in about 20 minutes and I tell him about the signal.

"When I got to my flat, Skara was there. I guess I forgot to lock up yesterday. I suppose Skara hit the lamp button, probably just curious. You remember Arvīds Skara, the librarian. He lives nearby. He's a bit nosy, but I think he's a good person."

"Still," I respond, "if we turned on the motor while you were talking with him, he would've asked who was downstairs."

"Wouldn't he want to come down here and see for himself, this nosy guy?" adds David.

"Probably . . . we have to be more careful now," Robert agrees. "Even with the signal lamp and all, things seem less secure. Someone must know my signal to you."

In town there is talk that all of Libau must evacuate by 2 December. There have been no air raids in many days, an eerie quiet.

Tuesday, 21 November 1944. Johanna and the girls have returned from the countryside village of Asīte. They arrive first to the cellar. It is afternoon. Tony is out and about now that the bombing has taken a holiday. This good fortune prevents a horrid confrontation.

"Look how big the kitten has grown," Henni remarks of Johanna, looking at the other two women as she speaks.

"It isn't good now, so why are you here?" Hilde cross-questions.

Just as Riva turns her back on Johanna, without a word, Robert enters the cellar, sees Johanna, and becomes misshapen.

"Out of here . . . out of here . . . out of here, now!"

"What's the matter with you? Don't you care about your family, me . . . or at least your daughters?" Johanna weeps.

"How many times and how many ways do I have to tell you I don't want you here? Are you stupid? I don't want you here. Go home!"

"You don't understand," Johanna sobs, clutching the girls. "These last months have been nothing but struggle. For weeks we hid in the potato cellar from the Germans. And then they caught us and they hauled us to Libau and they ordered us to board a ship . . . . I will kill myself first!"

"To hell with you!" Robert screams as he flees the cellar.

David takes Johanna aside and calms her with softness and reason. He signals to others of us and we join the conversation. The eight men promise to stand by her and the girls. We pledge to provide for them in any way possible after the liberation. With some solace, Johanna takes Indra and Irida to their third floor flat.

For awhile there is silence in the cellar. Then the women chide David and the rest of us for taking sides. Henni and Riva argue that Robert is right and true. I get into a huge quarrel with Riva over this. The others slowly enter the fray and in a flash the gender war is joined. An unwieldy sea of feelings overtakes the levee of civility. I walk away.

Friday, 24 November 1944. There have been air raid sirens on and off the past few days, but we strain to imagine explosions. Tony and Johanna have not yet seen one another. Robert is upset for other reasons. Men from Dr. Straumanis' unit stop by to fetch his microscope and ultraviolet lamp. The problem, both have been sold. Robert tells the soldiers they were stolen soon after Dr. Straumanis left for Danzig about a week or so ago. I hope they believe him or there will be a house search and this could be trouble.

This evening BBC announces that today, in Palestine, the 70th birthday of Professor Chaim Weizmann is being celebrated with a rousing chorus of public affection, and a promise by Roosevelt and Churchill of free immigration for Jews from Europe to Palestine.[16]

The concluding days of November pass with sameness. Robert nurses a toothache with the help of the ladies and David's hot chamomile compresses. Still, he ventures into town with his red pass, very often detained for inspection. Robert reports that the Westphalian Jews remain in Libau. We are astonished. There are sirens from time to time, but all but one announced raid is sterile. The daily door-knocking continues, as does the carelessness.

One early morning, I was startled awake by unfamiliar voices. From my bunk, I caught sight of a fully open cave hatch. For a moment or so I did not move. With the half eye of jolted arousal, I perceived that all the others were asleep in the cave. Who was the night guard and why was the hatch open? I slowly slithered to the floor and peered through the opening. Just a few feet away was the green coat of a policeman. I feared we had been discovered.

While Robert continued to speak with the police, I turned off the blue night light. Then I carefully roused the others so sleep sounds wouldn't reveal our presence, if it had not done so already. Zelig and I moved back toward the opening so we could close the hatch when it wouldn't be noticed. Minutes later, the conversation moved to the other side of the front room and we slid the hatch into place. There was a lock step exhalation.

In time, the voices were gone. Robert signaled us to open the hatch. It seems Robert had overslept and, in the haze of awakening, he allowed outsiders to enter the cellar without first telling us to close the hatch. Such carelessness will yet summon our demise.

DECEMBER 1944

Last night there was an *"Aktion"* in already tense Libau, a manhunt they prefer to call it. Nearly 1500 frightened civilians were herded from workplace or home and placed on a ship to Germany. All women between 16 and 38 will be forcibly evacuated tomorrow, and the remaining men by the 5th. Of course, sailing to Germany is for protection. What good deeds the Nazis do for their Latvian cousins.

It is 10AM. Most are asleep. Yosl and I, out front for awhile, disappear into the cave when Robert's little girls come to the cellar. Henni, the seamstress, remains up front. She is known to Indra and Irida as Aunt Julia. Her task this morning is to take measurements for new winter coats.

"Good morning Aunt Julia," the girls coo in unison.

"Good morning Indra. Good morning Irida. Are you ready to start making new coats today?" Henni responds.

"Yes I am," each says in turn.

"Well, Irida, you first. Step up on this box and I will measure you for size."

"Papa—show us—where do you sleep?" Indra queries while Irida is being measured.

"On the table," Robert answers.

"No, no, you have a bed here. Show us where it is."

Robert has a problem. The bed is behind the fabric wall and Tony is still in it! Robert throws off the scent with candy.

Panic in town increases moment by moment. Rumor mongers insist that 20,000 men will be evacuated. At last count, there *were* only 20,000 males in all of Libau, including infants and toddlers. Of course, the females will evacuate as well.

Evacuation is also our problem. We propose that it is only right that Johanna and the girls come to the cellar and hide with us. Of course, then Tony would be obliged to act as another hunted Jew. She refuses and threatens to return to her estranged husband. Robert will have none of this and threatens to leave with Tony.

"I'm not bound to any of you. I'll go my way and Johanna can take care of you. I don't care. I care about Tony and that's it!" Robert is incensed.

And then there are the girls, Indra is seven and Irida is four. To hide with small children is very dangerous. Still, Johanna has taken great risks for us and we owe her the same. Henni fiercely disagrees.

"There, you see now, when Riva wanted to bring Adinka here, everyone opposed it, and a vote was taken, and it was decided . . . NO!"

"You're wrong. We never took a vote. Robert was against hiding a child and made the decision himself," I respond.

"How do you know this? You weren't *here!*" Henni shouts back.

What irony. Johanna welcomes us unconditionally, risks her life for us, and now there is no room for her with us. We argue about this all day. Being irresolute is not an option. There is no way to put two cats in one bag. David and Robert decide on a plan. Johanna and the girls will take refuge in Dunika, 16 miles south of Libau, with friends.

At 11:30 PM Robert brings Johanna to the cellar. She is calm and, as always, very friendly. David presents the proposed solution.

"We so much want you to hide with us, but we are so afraid that the children will behave as normal children and give us away."

"Yes, David, I know I can't hide here. You're right, Indra and Irida will run about and squeal, and our hiding place will be revealed. I've no choice but to evacuate to Germany with the girls. Whatever happens, happens."

"There is another way, Johanna. You can take refuge with friends. Robert has arranged for someone to take all of you by boat across Lake Libau to Dunika. You'll be safe there. The Fritzen will be gone soon enough."

Johanna agrees. I am silenced by shame, and so are the others. Only Henni speaks a few words. Her ersatz concern is a *shandeh* (disgrace).

Johanna had scarcely left the cellar, when Tony emerges from hiding, triumphant. She had been lying on the bed behind the fabric wall, listening to everything. She and Robert do a jig. We all watch in silence. The vision of Hagar corners my thoughts . . .

> *Cast out the bondwoman and her son, for he shall not be heir with my son, Isaac . . . And Abraham arose early and gathered bread and water, and put them on the shoulders of Hagar and Ishmael, and they departed and strayed in the wilderness of Beersheba.*

The casting out of Johanna and the girls was the tipping point for Riva. She has completely lost her nerves. She is impetuously disquieted by the most minor of problems, collapsing into uncontrollable sobbing. She has a profound sadness, and lacks interest in everything but the cloth scraps she uses to make and remake a ragdoll. We all have cabin fever, but Riva is lost in an emotional wasteland. How can we help her?

Wednesday, 6 December 1944. Johanna and the girls have not departed. Perhaps because of the endless wind and rain. Lately we are more obsessed with the barometer than with liberation.

Tony brings two bottles of *schnapps* to celebrate her *Namenstag* (name day), the anniversary of her baptism. We toast the occasion quietly. Robert urges me to say something pompously florid. I resist because Johanna is always in my thoughts. I fear expressing my true feelings. To be brief, vague, and generic, I choose verse:

> "A pity I must be brief
> About all that's in my heart.
> But, still, I must proclaim best wishes
> On this, your *Namenstag*.
>
> Fate lashes us together
> Forever, with friendship's ties.
> Long live Tony, long live Robert
> We all understand why."

"You see, only doggerel would do, and doggerel it is. A toast to doggerel and cellarized *dolce vita!*"

After everyone goes to sleep, I remain for night guard duty. Robert emerges from his curtained nook, sits beside me, and asks my opinion of Tony.

"No comparison with my wife, eh Kalman?"

"I know exactly how indebted we are to Tony. She knows everything about us and reveals nothing, she even supports us in her own small way. Still, the respect and reverence we have for Johanna has not and will not diminish in our eyes. I have only praise for Johanna. Your relationship with Johanna is your personal matter, it has no influence on our judgment of her."

"I understand," he mutters on his way back to bed.

The next morning, Robert brings us a most curious notice published in *Kurzemes Vārds / Tēvija*: "Due to the reopening of the schools in Libau, all children up to age 14 are required to register no later than 16 December."

Is this a trap to draw the remaining civilians out of hiding? What is the logic of evacuating the parents without the children? Would they be that cruel to their erstwhile apologists, even champions? Perhaps the evacuation is over.

A school doesn't open for merely a few days. Could this mean the fighting is over? The Germans will simply abandon Libau? Maybe so. A few days ago, Tony brought us rumors that the *Wehrmacht* (army) will leave Libau by 15 December. Only the navy will remain. This certainly would fit with the school announcement in *Tēvija*. What a riddle this all is.

On top of enigma, is Robert's triangle. Tony and Johanna are at opposite ends of the base and Robert is at the apex. We have struggled to maintain its equilaterality, but it becomes increasingly scalene.

"Tony's mother knows that she's sleeping in our cellar," Robert announces, "and she's threatening to tell Tony's husband. Now Tony wants to leave. I'm going with her. I don't want to stay here anymore. Let Johanna take care of you. You like her better than Tony, anyhow."

"We know what we owe Tony," I respond impatiently, "and we appreciate her risks and all, but this is not a reason to bear a grudge against Johanna. How can decent people betray someone who has saved their lives? Tell me."

"Be reasonable, Robert," David interjects.

"My decision is my decision," Robert insists, "I'm through with all of this. Finished!"

Hours later, Robert returns with Johanna and recounts his decision, only by now he is aware that Johanna knows all about Tony. What sharpens the nastiness is Tony lying hidden behind the curtain wall listening to the whole argument.

"I know all about that bitch you sleep with. Is this how you want your children to think of you—a whoremonger."

"Things happen . . . she has a child also" Robert responds.

"Well, get rid of the thing, if you don't want the thing's husband to set upon you like a fox on a squirrel."

"If you do that, I'll just disappear and you'll put all our friends in danger. Is that what you want?" This back and forth beats the air for an hour. Ultimately, Johanna's catharsis is palpably palliative.

"Enough of this, Robert. Let's compromise on this, then. You leave me alone, I'll leave you alone. You took on the obligation of hiding our comrades—*remember, our comrades*—and you need to see it to liberation. Do this and you can diddle all day and I won't say a word."

Robert agrees. Johanna's seeming capitulation surprises him, but not us. We know she had our interests at heart from the outset. Johanna leaves with a warm good evening to all of us. Moments later Tony emerges from her warren livid. We ignore her.

Tonight is the first night of *Chanukah*. We have been preparing *Chanukah* candles for the past two months. Misha blesses the first:

> *Boruch Atoh Adonoi Eloheinu Melech Ho-olom Asher*
> *Kideshonu Bemitzvosov Vetzivonu Lehadlik Ner*
> *Shel Chanukah* (Blessed are You, Lord our God, King
> Of the universe, Who has sanctified us by Your commandments,
> And has commanded us to kindle the lights of Chanukah)
> . . . *Sheoso Nisim La-avoseinu Bayomim Hoheim*
> *Biz'man Hazeh* (. . . Who wrought miracles for our
> Fathers in past days, at this season)
> . . . *Shehecheyonu Vekiyimonu Vehigionu Lizman*
> *Hazeh* (. . . Who has kept us alive, and has sustained
> Us, and enabled us to reach this season)

I present the *D'var Torah* (homily): "On Chanukah, brave Jewish Partisans, the Maccabees, waged an unrelenting battle to defeat the idolaters and oppressors. Tonight we kindle the first of eight lights to remind us that with God's assistance we can overcome all obstacles. As the *Siddur* (prayer book) tells us, on Chanukah the mighty were delivered into the hands of the weak, the many into the hands of the few, and the wicked into the hands of the righteous. The Chanukah lights give evidence that we must not be discouraged by the turmoil, for even a tiny light dispels much darkness. May we merit justice and revenge, and may it come speedily in our days. Amen."

Chanukah, Day 1. In the lunar Hebrew calendar, Chanukah is from 25 Kislev to 2 Tevet. This year it corresponds to 8 days beginning on 11

December. Each day may be our last or our first or neither. Forgive me for saying so, God, but these days fatuous fortuity governs our fate.

Life with Tony is ever more tense. Her mother and son want to leave for Germany, and she insists that Tony return to her husband so they can all depart together. The threat hangs over Tony that her mother will reveal the cellar romance to Tony's husband. I suspect Tony has told her mother far more than she should have. We shall see.

Tonight we light two candles on the menorah. This time three years ago, the *Aktions* began. In merely days, thousands of family, friends, lovers, and neighbors were murdered in the dunes at Skede. Michael's wife, Hava; Zelig's uncle and aunt, Julius and Muscha; my dear friends Shmuel Khasdan, Voldemar Dolin and Moishe Rapoport; my mate Moishe Hirschhorn. I light the Chanukah candles and then recount Shmuel's words of farewell:

"Kalman, tonight is Chanukah. I wish for you that the Jewish fire always burns in your heart, that it affords you courage to fulfill all your plans . . . Let this fire burn bright until you have exacted revenge for every murdered Jew.

"Kalman, I still wish to light Chanukah candles. If I do manage this, it will also be my *Yahrzeit* (memorial) candle that I will be lighting with my own hand. And if you light Chanukah candles in the years to come, light another candle for those of us who reside within the sands of Skēde."

I light a *Yahrzeit* candle and we recite *Kaddish Yatom*, the mourner's benediction: "May His great Name grow exalted and sanctified in the world that He created to plan . . . May His great name be blessed forever and ever . . . He who makes peace in Heaven, may He make peace for us, and for all Israel. Amen."

Chanukah, Day 2. Last evening, Robert convinced Tony's mother that it would be best to move, together with Tony and her son, into an empty flat in our building. In this way, Tony makes a clean, if unofficial, break with her husband, and her mother is assured of some comfort and security. For the moment, anyway, the tension seems deflated. We work all day sawing wood and cleaning the boiler room.

Chanukah is about freedom. In the evening, after lighting three candles, I think about the meaning of freedom, particularly now, in the midst of the 20th century, in a Europe that has gone mad. I remember a

BBC broadcast years ago about Roosevelt's idea of four freedoms: Freedom from fear, freedom from want, freedom of speech, and freedom of worship. These are what the Maccabees fought for. They are a means to an end, a humane world, but they are too plain-speaking, too neat, too bare-bald. I need to search for first principles.

Chanukah, Day 3. Johanna's brother, who recently managed to buy his way out of prison, now wants to join us in the cellar to avoid conscription. Johanna apparently promised to hide him here. At Tony's instigation, Robert is certain Johanna told her brother everything of our arrangement. Knowing Johanna's commitment to us, I and the others refuse to believe this.

At nightfall, we light four candles. I resume my thoughts about freedom. I think essentially it is a matter of liberation from the social and cultural and political pales that obstruct our full human potential. Set over against this notion, though, is the need to have limits, without which there would be chaos. Limits are effected by laws, but by whose law, whose authority. A first principle can't be susceptible to the tyranny of the majority. I have no solution.

Chanukah, Day 4. Articles in *Kurzemes Vārds / Tēvija* continue to reflect the desperation of the Germans and their Latvian collaborators. Today Jānis Niedra, the Latvian SD chief of the evacuation committee, defends himself, claiming there was a misunderstanding about the Libau evacuation: "Residents of Kurzeme province are not and never were required to evacuate, only refugees from other provinces." This lie is exposed in another article that rails at those in Libau who refuse to go to Germany, professing that Latvia is their homeland, that they wish to live and die here. The article refers to these folks as Communists and provocateurs. Tellingly, *Tēvija* avoids the obvious. Most Libauers have come to their senses. Greeting the Russians is far more preferable than their demise in Germany, at least for those without blood on their hands.

After we kindle five candles, I come upon a rather different way of understanding freedom. It occurred to me that freedom, at its base, was a dialectical conundrum, with a ready solution. Freedom is immunity from the power of another; the antithesis of this is that you cannot reasonably assume a right of unlimited self-gratification. Thus, freedom is limited. How do you reconcile this dialectic? Allegiance to and reverence for God. We often pray: "Please, God, make us not needful of human largess or favor, but only of Your Hand that is full, open, holy, and generous, that we not feel remorseful or be humiliated forever and ever." Yes, freedom is living outside anyone else's dominion, but not outside God's Dominion, your obligation to God's moral law, and your duty to emulate God's limitless justice and compassion. This is difficult and that is why most of us live somewhere on the arc between saint and sinner.

Chanukah, Day 5. Noon. Soviet bombers are attacking the harbor and the inner city. They meet with opposition and an enormous air battle ensues. Flak fires incessantly. Bombs explode so near, the whole cellar is shaking. We ready ourselves to flee. In an hour the bombing ends and Robert departs the cellar to assess the destruction. The harbor is in flames and many houses are destroyed or damaged.

The bombing resumes at 4:50 PM. It is more intense than anything we have experienced till now. The sky is a stew of flak, machine gun fire, and dog fights. All but Zelig sit in the cave. Zelig has guard duty in the front room. About 5:20 there is an immense explosion that undulates the entire floor beneath us. You can feel an intense air pressure wave as the cellar pitches from side to side. All are certain the whole house is crashing down upon our heads. A tempest of sand and debris encompass us. As the whirlwind wanes, we realize the cellar is intact, and most things are in place.

Bombs detonate nonstop, many of them close by. Two hours into the raid, 6:50 PM, there are two titanic explosions. Everything around us pendulates and crashes to the floor. As protection against the air pressure wave, we press our ears closed and open our mouths. Zelig dives through the cave hatch as if an arrow.

"Everything's collapsed up front," Zelig screams.

"Where is Robert?" David shouts.

"Went upstairs maybe 30 seconds before the explosion . . . I can't say what happened to him," Zelig responds.

Our cave is nearly undamaged, but the front room is a mess. Doors have been torn loose from their jambs, hinges and all. Windows are now empty holes. We stand here almost as though we are in the street. Quickly we cover all the portals with blankets. We turn on the undamaged lamps and the chaos is illuminated. Finally Robert arrives, limping.

"The air wave threw me down all the stairs . . . a bruised knee, that's all," Robert assures us.

"What about Johanna and the girls? . . . and Tony?" David asks.

"No real damage upstairs. Tony, everyone's fine," Robert responds.

"What happened outside," Hilde gasps.

"The bomb exploded about 30 feet from us, another just across Catholic Street," Robert explains. Our good fortune will forever be remembered.

We immediately set to work restoring order and security. David, Zelig and Yosl make new doors, Aaron and I windows, and the others reorganize the cellar. After awhile, Riva looks away from the ragdoll and calls out from the cave that there are German SD in the yard announcing that everyone must come along for rescue work. We all disappear into the cave and reinforce the hatch. Soon we hear the bakers being hauled away. Minutes later, we resume our work up front.

From time to time, from the ruins across the way, you hear the cries and screams of children and women. The sins of the fathers visit upon the children. Three years ago, just exactly now, harrowing wails from Jewish children and women rose from the pits at Skede. Senseless, all senseless!

Late in the evening, the cellar is finally restored to order. Misha leads us in lighting six candles.

Chanukah, Day 6. The bombs fell for a bit over an hour this morning. Robert reports that the harbor is ablaze again, and that four ships sank. Everyone is impatient for the Russian offensive, and our liberation. David and Michael are being careless again. The lathe runs without letup, making unnecessary chess pieces. They file and bang 'til the early morning hours. Needlessly they endanger the rest of us. Even when we light the seven candles, they bang away. Obsession grips their mind.

Chanukah, Day 7. Today the skies are quiet, but our food supply has become desperate. We have no bread, only black coffee. Adding to our distress, Robert tells us that Skara, who now lives in our building, passed on information he gathered from Klava, the policemen's whore. They told her that "amazing things" are happening rather regularly in our building. They plan to do a long and thorough search this week. What can we do but clean our pistols, light the remaining eight Chanukah candles, and celebrate with a fine dinner of black coffee.

Chanukah, Day 8. The BBC reports a massive offensive by the Germans into Belgium and Luxembourg.[17] The others are discouraged, but I argue this is merely a desperate act that will ultimately dig their own grave.

*   *   *

Wednesday, 20 December 1944. Aaron's pain radiates every which way from his *pupik*. Touch his abdomen, and he writhes in agony. The torment is more harrowing each passing hour. He is quite nauseous but doesn't seem to have a fever. We fear it is appendicitis. It's too risky to take Aaron to Dr. Cena, the surgeon. Yet, not doing so may well be a death sentence. Aaron lies awake all night with pain. Zelig comforts him as best he can, telling tales of their youth and fantasies of their future.

Morning brings some relief, at least from the pain. But now Aaron has a fever, and liquids pass through him as water through a drain. We are more hopeful than yesterday, though not much. Robert brings us rumors that a policeman has disappeared and suspicion has fallen upon the residents of 14 Kauf Street. We remain in the cave for most of the day.

Eight policeman arrive in the courtyard displaying hand grenades and submachine guns. They begin a thorough search of the flats, and carefully inspect the papers of each occupant. The problem, of course, is that midday most occupants are at work. So they return at 6 PM to complete their investigation. They begin by smashing open the door of the flat they know well, that of Klava *der kurveh* (the whore). What a shock to find her seated at the kitchen table, naked, playing checkers with the old professor, Markus Dushavs, fully clothed.

At 10 PM the Russians return and the cellar walls quake. A bomb falls not three meters from the cave hatch. *Baruch Hashem*, it doesn't explode! The air raid lasts less than an hour. Robert reports that Günter Street and Espen Street are ablaze, and many ships have sunk in the harbor. Just beyond midnight, the police return to roust the bakers working above our cave. Aaron seems to have recovered and he sleeps through all of this.

As Christmas approaches, the estrangement between Robert and Johanna worsens, and now the imbroglio includes the neighbors. The residents of 14 Kauf Street, even the bakers, openly disdain Tony for coming between Robert and his family, and Robert for mistreating Johanna and the little girls. Arvids Skara, the librarian, now living in a flat on the third floor, has taken to harassing Robert.

"You need to chasten yourself, Robert, because your secret is no longer a secret," Skara admonishes.

"What are you saying?"

"Soon your tenants will have had enough of this, and the police will come and break down your door and discover everything!"

Robert is more resentful than ever.

Tony is more contrite. She makes a public display of inviting Robert's little girls, Indra and Irida, to afternoon tea with her and her son. The ceremony includes putting real sugar in the girls' tea but only a substitute in her son's.

"Now, who's your better mother?" Tony stupidly asks.

"None of my father's whores are my mother!" little Irida shouts back as she bolts from her chair and leads her older sister out the door. It all ends badly.

Christmas Day. There are no bombs and no bread. I have fever and flu. Misha has Aaron's disease. Riva is remaking her ragdoll. Robert spends the day with his "new family." Johanna and the girls spend the day with Johanna's sister and her family. She visits with us when she returns in the late afternoon. Apparently her brother-in-law is very suspicious of Robert's "secretive cellar."

The concluding days of December are more than unpleasant. The police continue surveillance of our building and randomly harass the tenants. Robert appears in the cellar only rarely, and our hunger grows. David and Henni continue making noise into the early morning hours. David celebrates Henni's birthday on the eve of the new year, but I ignore the frivolity.

JANUARY 1945

Happy New Year! The water pipes have burst and all the flats are flooded, the cave for a second time. Robert is agitated, on the edge. His demeanor is limited: from alarm to dread to panic. He insists that David and Michael repair the pipes in his absence. Banging, hacking and welding while we pump the water without letup. The basement sounds like a factory. The danger is unimaginable, but Robert is uncaring and sleeps a great deal. Johanna is spending more and more time with us.

After a week's work, the pipes are repaired. Now, Tony boils over. She is in a jealous rage over Johanna's visits to the cellar. She learned of these from Henni. Tony insists that Robert cease all support for Johanna and the girls. Robert passively obeys.

Days pass with no wood for Johanna and the girls. They walk about with incessant cold shivers while Robert and Tony give themselves over to heedless pleasure. The callousness of Tony! But that's not all that sickens me.

Our women stand with Tony, even helping her to concoct deep-dyed falsehoods about Johanna. When I object, Henni always responds: "When we come out of the cellar, it will be different. Each of us will go our own way." While somewhat cryptic, I take her sentiment to be, if you don't like me you are free to ignore me after liberation. So, in a devious way, she is saying, "*Kish mir in tuchis!*" (Kiss my ass.)

The situation is unbearable and Johanna has decided to confront Robert squarely. She asks the bakers to deliver a note to Robert while she waits in the cellar. The missive implores Robert not to abandon her and their daughters at this difficult time. Bitter cold and hunger, day after day. She reminds Robert that old sins have been set aside by others till now only because he has a wife and children. This may end if he continues to act without a conscience. He needs to consider this carefully.

Robert reads her message and bounds to the cellar, livid, waving her letter like a Chinese fan.

"I want a divorce! A divorce! A divorce! A divorce!" spitting out the word in all directions.

"Only God will separate us!" Johanna screamed as she stormed out.

"If that woman continues to cause trouble, I will abandon all of you," Robert seethes. "Let *her* take care of you!"

Later that evening, we talk with Johanna. She agrees to back off for our sake. We promise to share whatever we have. Food is very scarce just now. Robert brings almost nothing. We have been dividing one loaf of bread among 11 of us for a whole day. Now it will be among 14.

Friday, January 19. Radio Moscow announces that Lodz has fallen. When the glorious Red Army entered the city 900 Jewish survivors remained.[18] I am overtaken by happiness for these Jews who have been tormented for the past 6 years. We celebrate a small victory, and mourn the two hundred thousand who will never come home.

Wednesday, January 24. Lublin's Yiddish Radio is back on the air greeting Jews everywhere, as it were. It is a welcome guest in our cave. Moscow Yiddish Radio disappeared months ago. Lublin was liberated last July and it seems the Jewish community is recovering quickly. There is so much of interest to listen to, political discussions, music, plays. I am starting to feel human again even if our diet has been reduced to *suchares* (dried bread) with unsweetened tea, and Robert's malfeasance perseveres.

This evening, without provocation, Robert paces about the cellar yelling, "Not being a Jew, I will not go and cheat . . . never . . . never . . . never!" He claws beneath the debris. Yesterday, Dr. Cena's wife warned Robert that Arvids Skara is an informer. The very same Skara who celebrates with Robert and Tony, and knows of a "secret room" in the cellar. Another neighbor, Mrs. Kārklins, daily accuses Robert of hiding Jews. Johanna's sister, Emma, who likely knows all, had warned Robert that his bad behavior will soon have very nasty consequences. Then last Sunday, Robert chased Emma from the building when she came to visit with Johanna and the girls. Emma's response was so verbally vehement, even the erstwhile sailor was stunned. *Tsuris* upon *tsuris*, trouble atop despair. Robert has Tony and I have a lump in my nose, and they're killing me.

Tuesday, January 30. Today is the twelfth anniversary of Hitler's ascent to power. The Führer marks the occasion with another speech broadcast on *Deutschlandsender*:

> ".... The question is whether Germany has the will to remain intact or whether it will be destroyed.... The loss of this war will decimate the German people... Defeatism is a disease.... I have never known the word 'capitulation'.... Nothing is new about our situation. I have been in much worse. I tell you this so you will understand my single-mindedness and why nothing can wear me down. Though I may be troubled by worries and even physically shaken by them, nothing will deter me from the fight until the scales tip to our side.... And, so, I most emphatically forbid generalizations and conclusions regarding the whole situation. Only I may do this. In the future, anyone who tells anyone else that the war is lost will be treated as a traitor, with all the consequences for him and his family.... We each have a duty... We shall yet master our fate!..."

His words are overwrought, but his voice is quiet and restrained. He seems to be saying *Kaddish* for his own death.

FEBRUARY 1945

The air raids have resumed. The heroic, invincible Red Army continues its march to Berlin, liberating Latvia and Poland on the way.

Robert, Johanna, and Tony continue their not so private war. Johanna visits with us in the cellar, Tony declares her intent to leave Robert, Robert vows to follow her, and David negotiates peace. Days later this whole circus begins anew.

Starvation threatens us. Robert has lost his motivation and food prices are nearly beyond our means. More often than not we live on *suchares* and water. When we do obtain a loaf of bread, I divide it carefully, using a compass to insure precise equity.

Now and then we have a treat. Tony brings us horse feet, shoes and all, and the ladies cook "cavalry soup." One afternoon we discovered an overlooked bag of oats. The ladies prepared a fine gruel with water.

Suddenly, David noticed that our lunch was populated by worms. As hungry as the others were, the "living soup" was set aside. I was undeterred. I removed the largest worms and ate every bit in the bowl. I did the same that evening. Though the worms floated about by the hundreds, I simply imagined them as small noodles. On an empty stomach, it tastes like a delicacy!

Monday, February 12. Moscow Radio reports on a conference at Yalta that concluded yesterday. Apparently Stalin, Churchill, and Roosevelt traveled to this resort in the Crimea to plan ways to accelerate the German surrender and to forge solutions to the great problems that will arise afterward: refugees, the thirst for revenge, the need of necessities and restitution.

Hours later, Hitler responds with another tirade[19] on *Deutschlandsender:*

> ". . . . Those warmongers in Yalta must be denounced – so insulted and attacked that they will have no chance to make an offer to the German people. Under no circumstances must there be an offer . . . . I've always said: Surrender is absolutely out of the question! . . . History is not going to be repeated! . . ."

The wolf has lost his teeth, but not his inclination.

Tuesday, February 20. Today is Robert's birthday. I try to interest the others, but no one seems to care. We are all so tired, worn raw, emotionally hollow. Each has turned within, found their own cave within the cave. Riva is again remaking her ragdoll.

Tuesday, February 27. Purim. Haman, enemy of all the Jews, plotted to destroy the Jews of Persia. He cast their fate (their *pur*, their lot) with the intent to exterminate them. But the evil plot meant for the Jews was visited upon his own head. The forces of good impaled Haman, his sons, and his minions on the stake. Haman appears in every generation, and in every generation he meets the same end. Haman nearly 2500 years ago, Hitler this year. I celebrate with living noodle soup and a few squares of dried bread.

SPRING 1945

Saturday, March 10. Our hunger deepens. Our minds remain alert, but our spirit less hopeful. Today is a special *Shabbos*, *Shabbat HaChodesh*, the celebration of the Jewish calendar. On this day we read that God instructed Moses and Aaron to create a lunar calendar, and to begin it with *Nissan*, the month of springtime.

On my calendar, this beginning month starts on Thursday. This is the third calendar I have calculated. I think about the next while David repairs the bakers' cracker machine. Robert quietly sits beside him. In recent days, Robert has become as introverted and lost in thought as the rest of us.

"Listen, David," Robert murmurs, fixing his eyes upon the floor, "soon you'll all be liberated. I have no real skills. You could take me on as an apprentice, couldn't you? You do everything so well and I could learn from you."

"For your sake I would . . ." David begins to say before Robert cuts him off.

"There, you said it again. Let the others feel beholden, but you, my friend . . . this is backhanded, an insult."

"You're distorting my words, Robert, and . . ."

"Won't people say that I risked everything, even my children, so that I could personally benefit, if even you now think so?"

"You make no sense, it's twisted . . ."

"I have to go . . . get some lunch. I'll be back soon." Robert bounds upstairs, agitated.

"*Der ponim zogt ois dem sod* (The face tells the secret)," I offer to David.

"What do you mean?"

"We're all lonely, but Robert is more lonely than any of us. Why? Because Robert distrusts everyone, even his family, even Tony. David, there is no greater loneliness than wearing a blanket of distrust."

"I don't understand him, Kalman. Maybe it's all these months of deception on our behalf and then . . . What's that?"

"What's what?"

"That bang . . . I hear another one!"

"I think it's an air raid, but there's no siren."

A few more explosions that barely shake the cellar and then the street is creepy-silent.

"As I was saying, David, such suffocating distrust inevitably turns Robert's fantasies into fact. Think of all that's gone on with Johanna. And now he pays the price. As mother always says, *Di klensteh nekomeh farsamt di neshomeh* (Even a tiny revenge fouls the soul)!"

David falls silent. He resumes work on the cracker machine. I put down the calendar I was studying and sit down at the table with chessmen, intent on discovering a better response to the opening gambit Michael surprised me with last evening . . . .

Johanna and Tony enter the cellar together, without warning: "Robert is dead!"

Not thirty minutes ago, Robert had gone to his flat to prepare lunch. Tony wasn't there, so he spent a few moments sorting through the scraps of paper with this or that tenant complaint. Then it was off to the kitchen. As he gathered the makings of a simple lunch of bread, sausage, and tea, a single artillery shell fragment smashed through the window and tore Robert's body to shreds. It was a sudden and unexpected death, even a quiet one. None of the tenants knew of it until Tony returned from the market and pierced the silence with mad screams at the sight of Robert's bloody head detached from his torso.

Johanna and the girls came running. The bakers followed. All that remained of Robert were body shards, scraps of clothing, and his pocket watch. The bakers did all they could to calm the dreadful heartbreak. Later, they will gather the remains and arrange the burial. On Monday they will slide the casket on the cart and their dray horses will lumber to the cemetery.

We are stunned, overwhelmed, silent. An hour passes, two.

I try to understand our response to this awful trauma. Is it despair, is it fear, is it both? I recall the poem by Emily Dickinson: "The difference between fear and despair is like the one between the instant of a wreck and when the wreck has been." I think we are simply fear-shaken.

Some of us will want to kill the fear. How does one do this, I wonder? Become cataleptic, I suppose. Others will simply be terrorized, alternately expressing anger or resignation. I prefer to welcome fear as the sagacious professor. We are alone now. Worse, we are, each of us, lonely, shut off from the rest, apart because we have no patience for the other. Fear can move us to recapture affinity. Fear is a gate-crasher worthy of our acquaintance.

* * *

Johanna and Tony come to the cellar. They talk of the burial, of the future, of survival. There is no response. Looking full in the face of your comrades, a portal to souls, the silence is pure innocence. In silence you bind truth to yourself and to the other. Still, a silence too long felt breaks the heart. David speaks first.

"If another janitor replaces Robert, all will be lost. We have discussed this among ourselves and, Johanna, we think it best if you simply assume Robert's job as if it were day following night."

"Even so," Michael interrupts, "this will not solve our gravest problem . . . food. It's going to be very difficult for both of you, together, to find enough food for the eleven of us and your children and yourselves and Tony's mother. You need to involve a third person, another man."

Tony suggests the librarian, Arvids Skara, who also lives on the third floor. Johanna agrees; "Arvids has often spoken to Robert and me of his hatred for the Germans and what they have done."

"But several weeks ago Robert told us that Dr. Cena's wife accused Arvids of being an informer," I protest.

"So let's put Arvids to the test," David proposes. All agree.

In the evening, Johanna visits with Skara in his apartment.

"You know Arvids," Johanna hissingly whispers, "I suspect that Robert has hidden gold somewhere in the cellar, gold he used to provide Tony with the best, gold he did not use for his children."

"Why do you suspect Robert did such a thing?"

"Arvids, he went to the ghetto so often and, later, endlessly busied himself in the cellar . . . Arvids, I can trust you. Help me look. I badly need the money now."

Skara reluctantly relents after several more minutes of similar pleading. Unnoticed, Johanna signals the cave as she and Skara descend the stairs to the cellar. Our camouflaged sliding door is ajar with purpose, and David and Michael, guns in hand, are hiding in the shadow of the back room furnace. Skara paces about the cellar knocking on walls and tapping here and there on the floor with a shovel blade.

"There's nothing here! We're wasting our time!" Skara blurts.

"That's not possible. There's got to be something." Johanna protests. "Maybe Robert hid comrades here, maybe even Jews! I would always ask him why food seems to disappear from my kitchen . . . We need to look for an underground passage. I don't care what we find . . . gold, people . . . it's all the same. The SD pays well for Jews and Communists."

"Shut your mouth!" storms Skara. "Are you a fool? You should be ashamed of such thoughts! You are a mother. Is this what you tell your children? What has . . ."

"She isn't serious," David laughs as he exits the shadows with Michael.

"What is this?" Skara scowls.

"It's a test," David responds. "And now we have a favor to ask of you."

David tells Skara the real secret of the cellar, of our desperate need of food, of our courage. Skara, awed, agrees to help. The night ends well. Pacific dreams usher you safely inside an illusory banquet. Dreams are true while they last.

Morning brings news that Skara has been arrested. It seems that he busies himself with changing birthdates on the passports of young men wishing to avoid the military. Will he exchange our lives for his freedom? Perhaps hunger breeds madness, but I no longer fear clouds, The others do.

Alone, Johanna and Tony embrace the task of keeping eleven hapless souls alive. They endlessly search for food with the little we have to barter. The daily ration, 5 ounces of dried bread and weak tea. Too little to sustain us, too much to die. Each day you learn anew that no two people starve alike . . .

My grandfather and I were close during my school years, before his heart tired to death. Again and again he told me that there is a difference between then and now. Then, study was the main concern, Torah study. Plain work was merely a practical necessity. In those days, both thrived. Now, plain work is the main concern, and Torah study is not even thought of as a practical necessity. So now, neither thrives. Over the growl of hunger, I hear my grandfather often these days. His words replace food.

> You shall remember the entire road on which
> God led you these years in
> the wilderness so as to afflict you, to test you,
> to know what is in your heart . . . He afflicted
> you and let you hunger, then he fed you
> manna . . . to make you know that not by
> bread alone does man live . . . .[20]

Every morning I awake more fatigued than yesterday. Battling dizziness and little energy, I sit on the edge of my bunk and recite the morning prayer, the *Shema*. Then I crawl through the cave hole and ready my *omer* (portion) of *suchares* (dried bread) and feeble tea. The *suchares* is your manna, your "bread of the angels," your final foxhole.

For some of us, the *suchares* is miraculous. Without cooking, or baking, or any other adjusting, it attains the flavor of any conceivable food. Spend a few moments thinking of your desire and there it is. On Shabbos you imagine roast chicken and potatoes. On Passover you imagine matzah and gefilte fish. This was not, alas, flawless:

Menachem, the baker[21]:	What does it mean, "He afflicted you and let you hunger, then he fed you manna?" Was it a starvation diet!
Rabbi Jonathan:	Here are two cucumbers, one whole and the other snapped in pieces. How much does this whole one cost?
Menachem:	Two shekels.
R. Jonathan:	And how much does this broken one cost?
Menachem:	One shekel.
R. Jonathan:	Why the difference? Isn't the fate of the whole one the same as the broken one?
Menachem:	Perhaps there should be *no* difference in cost.
R. Jonathan:	Yes, there should! Just as one revels in the taste, one revels in the semblance.

The thinner I get, the fatter my feet, the more cerebral my life. I am not alarmed. I am quite sober-minded. My grandfather also taught me that the advantage of a well-developed intellect is that it preserves the life of its possessor.²² With books as scarce as borsht, Michael and I have taken to playing chess for hours, daily.

I play Talmudic chess, where cleverly controlling the center of the board matters more than occupying it. Evading hunger or playing a deep game, the strategy is one and the same: *danim efshar mi-she-i efshar* (deduce the possible from the impossible). I learned this from the *Riga Tagblatt* chess columns about a Riga *yeshiva bokher* (seminary student), Grand Master Aron Nimzovitch, *alevasholem*.

It has been 10 years since "Nimzo" died. To honor his blessed memory, Michael and I decide to play his favorite opening, Four Knights. Michael, playing Black, tries a minor variation but, essentially at the conclusion of 5 moves all four knights are in play as are both King bishops, and there is mutual King side castling:

	WHITE	BLACK		WHITE	BLACK
1	P-K4	P-K4	7	P-Q4	N x P
2	N-KB3	N-KB3	8	N x N	P x N
3	N-B3	B-Q3	9	Q x P	K-R1
4	B-N5	O-O	10	B-KN5	B x P
5	O-O	N-B3	11	K x B	K-N1
6	P-Q3	K-N1			

... At this point Black has little control of the center and its forces are trapped on the back rank. In a misguided attempt to expose the White King, Black plays 10 . . . B x P. The White King captures the Bishop and the Black King begins to panic . . .

	WHITE	BLACK		WHITE	BLACK
12	P-K5	K-R1	17	N-Q5	K-B1
13	P x N	Q x P	18	N x R	K x N
14	B x Q	P x B	19	R-K1	K-Q1
15	Q x P	K-N1	20	Q x P	P-QR3
16	Q-KB5	R-K2	21	Q-KB8	MATE

... The Black troops commit blunder upon blunder. Their field general, the Queen, is captured, and before long the King of Darkness is dead!

* * *

Tuesday, 1 May 1945. Moscow Radio brings us Comrade Stalin's morning message for yet another International Labor Day: The brave Soviet soldiers sacrifice life and limb to liberate all of Europe from the fascist dogs . . . . The Nazis sit without hope in their Berlin lair, and it is there that they will soon dangle from a rope!

Last May Day, Robert brought schnapps and we toasted the day, Comrade Stalin, and each other. With strong voice we sang the *Internationale* and *Di Shvue*, the anthem of the Jewish Labor Bund. A year later, there is no Robert and no schnapps. Barely able to speak above a whisper, we are skeletons draped in dry, scaly skin. Our feet are swollen, our gums are bleeding, and we spend most of the day trying to remember what we don't remember.

I think of King David hiding in a cave in the wilderness of En-gedi, and his prayer . . . [23]

> I cry out to God; I plead with God.
> I lament and make known my distress.
> A diminished spirit parallels my perilous path.

I have no friend; escape is not possible.
I have supplicated to You, my refuge,
My portion in the land of the living.
Please hear my cry, rescue me,
Release my soul from prison.

My calendar tells me today is also *Lag B'Omer*, another reason to celebrate, if we had the vigor. My comrades in the Bund have often made the connection between May Day and *Lag B'Omer* beyond the picnics and outings to the forest. Both celebrate the proletarian victory over persecution and exploitation, a brief respite from anxiety about tomorrow. Last year the ladies prepared a joyous feast of soup, fresh bread, and little cakes. This year my comrades sit sullen, detached, indifferent. Some have a twitch, others a tic, one paranoid delusion, another catatonic stupor. Riva has always to remake her ragdoll. Even if we were all euphoric, how does one celebrate with squares of dried bread and the tinted water we call tea?

Aaron with the radio

Evening ushers in the usual errant bombing and attempts to break into the cellar to steal away the imagined barterable treasure. We have long ceased paying attention to this folly, and we crawl back to the cave at dark. Aaron and I pass time with the radio, searching for news or lyrical music. Tonight we find Bruckner's Seventh Symphony on Radio Hamburg. The Adagio movement is magnificent with its *sehr feierlich und sehr langsam* C-sharp minor theme. It climaxes with the cymbal clash.[24] Curiously, there is no continuation with the *Scherzo* movement, just prolonged silence, then a drum roll, and then a voice:

"Our *Führer*, Adolf Hitler, fighting to the last breath against Bolshevism, fell for Germany this afternoon in his headquarters at the Reich Chancellery.[25] Yesterday the *Führer* appointed Grand Admiral Doenitz his successor. The Grand Admiral and successor of the *Führer* now speaks to the German people."

We are numb . . .

". . . It is my first task to save Germany from destruction by the advancing Bolshevik enemy. For this sole objective the military struggle continues . . . ."

Our nightmare is over. Celebration would be commonplace. Silence just now is more seemly.

* * *

Tuesday, 8 May 1945. The Germans surrender Libau and the Russians enter at nightfall. We best remain in the cave until morning. Skara, again free, tells of local fascists running madly about in search of witnesses to their crimes. And so, in the new reality you do not need Jews to kill Jews, for Jew is now the one who will put the finger on you.

Morning is more than flesh and blood can bear.

Johanna comes to the cellar with news that the Russians are in complete control. Without reserve or hesitation, I summon the others to pray with me . . .

>*Boruch Atoh Adonoi Eloheinu Melech*
>*Ho'olom Shehecheyonu Vekiyimonu*
>*Vehigionu Lizman Hazeh.*
>Blessed are You, Hashem our God, King of
>the universe, who has kept us alive, and has
>preserved us, and enabled us to reach this day.

We are alive, we are free, we are disoriented. What shall we do now? We turn to David. He guided our entry and he will our exit.

"Johanna please go to my Russian friend Trofim Torbik. I think he is still in the refuge Robert found for him a few months ago. Tell him about the cellar and all of us . . . he knows us well. Ask him to bring a Russian officer, someone to help us safely leave the cave.

Johanna bounds up the staircase. She returns in less than twenty minutes.

"Trofim was overwhelmed with happiness. He says you should not come out yet. He will be here soon with the officer."

Johanna bounds up the staircase once more. She returns before an hour with Trofim and the officer, who are greeted by skeletons holding pistols. The officer draws his and the air is closer than usual. Riva sets aside the ragdoll and defuses the tension, "Come in. Come in. Welcome. We have been waiting for you a long time."

"Everyone. Everyone. I want to present a Soviet hero, Colonel Sorokin," Trofim gushes.

"You have survived my dear comrades," Sorokin proclaims enthusiastically.

"My dear Colonel," I respond, "you must understand. We have not survived, we have endured."

As the others embrace one another, Trofim, the Colonel, I whisper to Riva, *"Lech lecha!"*[26] We ascend the staircase to alight on Kauf Street, Riva clutching the ragdoll.

Just as we come to the landing in advance of the street door, there on the steps to our left sit two young girls, Johanna's daughter Irida and another little girl in a white hat and flowered dress. It is Adinka! Riva jumps out of her skin. She falls on Adinka. She cries and hugs and kisses with warmth and passion. I leave them, unable to breathe.

I exit the building for warm sunshine, a cordial cloak upon a ravaged body. I stand but a few feet from the door, fluttering with the breeze, trembling. Passersby look askance at me, some even say "good day." I am unable to respond. Enchanted by the clouds He made to obscure the heavens, I search for the Healer of the brokenhearted . . .

Zelig emerges, puts his arm around me, and hands me the Colonel's gift of cigarettes.

"Kalman, come back inside. You need to write some things for the Colonel so that he can bring it to the new Mayor's office and you can get new papers.

"Kalman, do you hear me?

"Kalman, are you all right?

"Tell me, Zelke . . . tell me where I might I find another mother like *my* mother . . . in *all* the world!"

AFTERWORD

After knowledge extinguished the last of the beautiful
fires our worship had failed to prolong, we walked
back home through pedestrian daylight, to a residence
humbler than the one we left behind. A door without mystery,
a room without theme . . . .

Timothy Donnelly, "The New Intelligence"

Of approximately 7000 Jews who resided in Libau (Liepaja) on June 21, 1941, about 200, or less than 3%, remained alive when the city was liberated May 9, 1945. Of these, maybe two dozen were hiding within Libau, itself, eleven in the care of Robert and Johanna Sedols. For their courage and moral stature, the Sedols are permanently memorialized as "Righteous Among the Nations" at Yad Vashem, the Holocaust (Shoa) Memorial in Jerusalem.

In the years following liberation, all those hidden by the Sedols would visit Johanna Sedols and her children, Indra and Irida, for birthdays, Christmas, New Year, and other important celebrations. Most momentous, every year on the 9th of May, they would all gather at the grave of Robert Sedols to honor his bravado and tenacity. Even 50 years later, those who were still alive and living in Libau (Liepaja) embraced this tribute, this salute to an extraordinary couple.

Johanna Sedols was nearly 34 on liberation day. For the remaining 43 years of her life, she continued to live in the same flat on 14 Kauf Street (now 22 Tirgonu Street), working most of those years in a factory that manufactured paper products. A remarkable and loving mother, Johanna raised two accomplished daughters: Indra (b. 1937) was a geography teacher at the Rainis Secondary School and Irida (b. 1940) was an accountant at the Liepaja Sugar Factory.

Several days after liberation, all the cloistered Jews left the cellar and the building at 14 Kauf Street and resided for a very short time in the prewar home of David and Henni Zivcon on Ludvika Street. It was there that two Soviet officers brought their new identification papers and, in exchange, insisted that they relinquish their weapons. This foreshadowing of life under Soviet rule added unwanted stress to their collective realization that it was near certain that wives, children, mothers, siblings, and other family did not survive. Before long, they all went off to resume their lives separately. Only Riva Zivcon (David's cousin-in-law) and Adinka remained at Ludvika Street for awhile.

David and Henni Zivcon never left Libau (Liepaja). David used his considerable skills and cleverness to provide for his wife and two daughters, Ilana (an interpreter) and Miriam (a violinist). Together they took delight in their two granddaughters and two grandsons. Still, life was difficult. As Henni related in an interview 6 September 1993, "After the war our life was also not easy . . . We were constantly persecuted although we did not give any cause for that. We lived honestly and worked honestly. But some people wondered how we could have survived under such difficult conditions." This was not unusual. Soviet authorities and Latvian anti-semites long feigned suspicion that Jewish survivors must have survived because they were collaborators. David was not deterred by this contemptible defamation. He worked tenaciously to expose the murderers in Liepaja (Libau) who hid under assumed identities, and he often appeared before investigative tribunals to give eyewitness testimony. David died in June 1983 at the age of 69. Henni, age 92, lives still in Liepaja.

Kalman Linkimer was alone. As best he could determine, none of his family survived. In 1941, Linkimer lived in his mother's flat, in his own room with another man, Moishe Hirschhorn, 13 years his senior. This residence was now otherwise occupied. As observed by Aaron Vesterman and Hilde Skutelsky, as well as his close friend from Paplaka, Arkady Scheinker, Kalman was openly homosexual but not forward. This is notable because Linkimer's partner, Moishe, was murdered early on, and it was difficult, if not risky, for Kalman to seek out other gay men in the small, disquieted postwar port city of Liepaja.

Nothing keeping him in a city of hostile neighbors and hurtful memories, Linkimer moved to a flat on Jauna Street in Riga some time before 1950. This move was facilitated by Misha Libauer and Tony who lived in the same building with their son. Misha and Tony married shortly after leaving the Zivcon's home and lived in a first floor flat in Johanna Sedol's building at 14 Kauf Street. After the birth of a child, they moved for unknown reasons to Riga. It is not clear what became of Tony's first husband or her child. Misha's first wife Hanna and his 5 year-old son Avram Leib were murdered in 1943. Misha was 40 when Libau was liberated. According to Aaron Vesterman, he died young; Tony died of cancer in 1976.

Based on testimonials from Arkady Scheinker, Aaron Vesterman, Hilde Skutelsky, and others, one may draw a fairly accurate composite sketch of Kalman Linkimer, the man, before *and* after the war, one similar if not identical, to the one in the cellar.

Kalman was an intelligent and multi-talented man with great educational depth; he was religiously observant and learned in the Hebrew Bible and Talmud. Politically, he was a Labor Zionist who was closer to the socialist Bund than to Communism, an interesting position considering the Bund's opposition to Zionism. Kalman was a careful reader and deep thinker who considered all sides of an issue. In addition to being an avid chess player, he was also an excellent athlete. In his youthful days prior to the war, he was an exceptional soccer player for Maccabee Libau, alongside his friend Zelig Hirschberg. He also played competitive ping-pong into his old age. By all accounts, Kalman was a gregarious conversationalist who was engaged by one and all, educated peers as well as common folk.

Kalman worked in the lumber business in Riga, and for many years was deputy director of a plywood factory, defending the legal and financial interests of the company in so-called "Arbitrage Courts." For a short while, he supplemented his income with a fox farm in the Riga suburbs, but this left him with little time for reading, chess, and other interests, and he sold the farm. Even without the farm, he was financially comfortable.

Kalman lived a reasonably long and fulfilling life in Riga, having many close and lasting friendships. Perhaps, his major disappointment was not being able to immigrate to Israel. As with many, if not most lives, the end was not entirely pretty. One afternoon, when he was in his early 70s, he hopped off a street car and caught his overcoat in the door; he was dragged along the pavement for several meters before the car halted. As a result, Kalman suffered serious disability and, given his age, a not unexpected decline in health. On 27 January 1988, he died at home in his own bed. He was 75. He is buried in the Riga Jewish cemetery.

The loss of their wives and children, of a family life that was their joy, and with nightmarish imaginings of brutal murder, made it particularly difficult for Shmerl Skutelsky and Yosl Mandelstamm. Yet both remained in Libau (Liepaja), married again, and built new lives. Indeed, Shmerl resided in the building with the Sedols until he died in the early 1980s. Yosl lived elsewhere and has passed on as well.

After departing the Zivcon home, Zelig Hirschberg lived with Hilde and Michael Skutelsky. His mother, brother Yudel, and sister Rochel were gone. Soon, however, he learned that his older sister, Bune, had survived in Russia. Bune had been married to Hirsh Mark, the president of the Bank of Libau. When the Germans attacked, Hirsh secured a place for Bune on a train bound for Moscow. Hirsh was murdered at the lighthouse a few weeks later. Bune arrived in Moscow safely. After awhile she met and married Dr. Isaac Ausmann, a physician and Soviet Army General. After the war, they went to live in Leningrad, but like many others they fell victim to Stalin's purges and were exiled to Sverdlovsk in the Ural Mountains. There they lived until 1980s when they were "rehabilitated" and allowed to return to Leningrad. Bune and Isaac have passed on, but their daughter Irina, an accomplished pianist, now lives and performs in Israel.

Bune communicated regularly with Zelig and she was able to travel to Liepaja for his marriage to Ramsa. In March of 1955, Zelig and Ramsa became the parents of twin sons, Elias and Jakob; twenty years later the first of six grandchildren was born. For the first 15 years after liberation, Zelig and Aaron Vesterman worked together in a warehouse that stored hides, furs and wool. They enjoyed relative prosperity in those years. With the 1960s came heightened tensions with the West and economic hardship at home. Zelig did not live to see the collapse of the Soviet Union. He died in Libau on 22 December 1987; Ramsa died in 1994. Elias, an engineer, lives in Riga; Jakob, a warehouseman like his father, lives in Liepaja (Libau).

When they were concealed in a cave, many of Sedols' secreted Jews dreamed of immigration to Israel. Remarkably, at a time when immigration to Israel from the Soviet Union was nearly impossible, four of the eleven did so: Hilde and Michael Skutelsky, Aaron Vesterman, and Riva Zivcon (with Ada). Hilde and Michael Skutelsky arrived in Tel Aviv with their son, Carmel, in 1972. They enjoyed free, if ordinary, working class lives.

Michael became ill and died of kidney failure in 1985. Hilde, 92, passed away in a town south of Tel Aviv. Long in ailing health, she was always doted upon by her son, two grandchildren and two great grandchildren.

Leaving David Zivcon's home, Aaron Vesterman went to live in the flat he had shared with his brother Leo and Leo's wife. It was unoccupied and exactly how he imagined it. Only now he was alone. He did not know the fate of his brother or sister-in-law. He thought to go to the police station to ask about relatives, perhaps they had registered for papers. The police knew nothing of Aaron's brother or sister-in-law, but they did make a startling discovery. A document in their files (book cover photo) stated that on 20 June 1944 Aaron Vesterman, Kalman Linkimer and Zelig Hirschberg were arrested and "taken away," a euphemism for executed. This arrest and murder would have been 2 months after their escape from Paplaka. Surely this document was a cover for the failure to capture the escapees.

It was not long before Aaron and his cousin Meyer Vesterman found each other. Meyer had been hiding in the same forest as Leo and his wife; Meyer's news was heartbreaking. From the Libau Ghetto, Leo and his wife ended up in a work camp near Riga. In July 1944, the camp was liquidated and the Jews were forced to march to Libau. Slow death was a certainty, so Leo and his wife escaped into the dense forest between Valdemarpils and Talsi. They built themselves a well-hidden bunker and the peasants in the area brought them food and water. It was Christmas 1944 when they were inadvertently discovered by the German SD who were searching for a Latvian army deserter who had shot an SS officer he found sleeping with his wife. Leo and his wife were executed in the Talsi police yard on 14 January 1945.

Like the others, Aaron's story was not ultimately about survival, it was about deprival. Other than Meyer, his cousin, Aaron was the only one left of a large extended family. For Aaron, Latvia was but a cemetery. Still, he built a life in Libau, and, after decades of hope and application, he took his family to Israel.

As with Aaron, Riva Zivcon and her small daughter Ada (Adinka) were alone. Riva's husband had been murdered within weeks of the German invasion of Libau and her mother-in-law was murdered after removal from the Riga Ghetto. After a short stay in Liepaja (Libau), Riva and Ada moved to Vilnius (Vilna), Lithuania. Later they returned to Latvia, living in Riga until 1960.

Riva's mother, two sisters and a brother, and their children lived in Israel. They had made their way in 1936. In the cellar and after, Riva was consumed by the desire to join her family. Before Stalin's death in 1953, this was nearly impossible. Beginning in 1954, Riva petitioned every year for emigration; every year it was denied. Riva did not give up. She would plead for family reunification to whomever would listen, even traveling to Moscow to make her case directly. Finally, in 1960, Riva (48) and Ada (20) were given permission to leave for Israel. There Riva lived peacefully, if in brittle health, until she passed away in 1989 at age 77. Ada married Yosef Israeli and together they have four sons, a daughter, and many, many grandchildren. Riva Zivcon's courage and resolution saved a life, a beautiful family, and countless generations to come.

Kalmer Linkimer (first row, second from the right) and friends, Riga

Zelig Hirschberg with sister Bunya (left) and wife Ramsa (right) at the wedding of his son Jacob in Libau (Liepaja)

Aaron Vesterman, Netanya, Israel, 2007

Hilde Skutelsky, Bat Yam, Israel, 2007

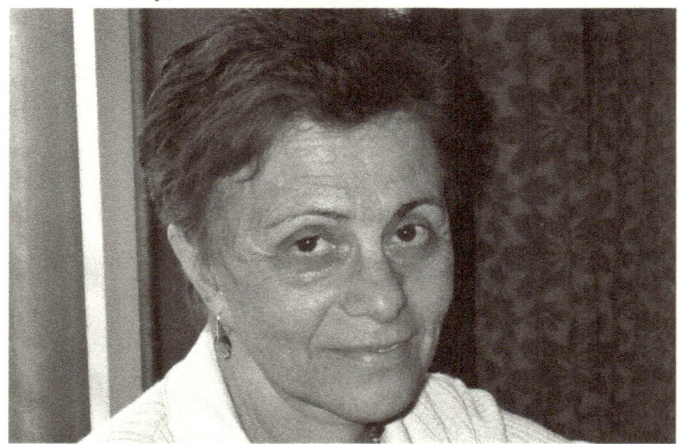

Ada (Zivcon) Israeli, Ra'anana, Israel, 2007

ENDNOTES

1. Aharon Appelfeld, "After the Holocaust," in Berel Land, ed., Writing and the Holocaust, p. 92, New York: Holmes and Meier, 1988.
2. Yosef Hayim Yerushalmi, "Zachor. Jewish History and Jewish Memory." Seattle: University of Washington Press, 1982.
3. Avishai Margalit, "The Ethics of Memory" Cambridge: Harvard University Press, 2002.
4. Anna Akhmatova, "Poems of Akhmatova," translated by Stanley Kunitz, Boston: Little, Brown and Company, 1973.
5. Walter Hahn was a student of the highly regarded composer and conductor Leo Blech (1871-1958). Blech was the principal conductor of the Berlin State Opera until 1937 when he was dismissed because of his Jewish origin. Blech was hired as principal conductor of the Latvian National Opera in Riga. Hahn followed his mentor to Riga in 1938 and was hired as principal conductor of the Libau Opera in 1940. There he staged his opera, "The Blue Mask," as well as a ballet based on Andersen's story "The Little Match Girl." In 1941, Blech fled to Stockholm, Sweden where he conducted at the Royal Opera until returning to Berlin in 1949.
6. Corroborated by Dr. Schwab's son, Professor George Schwab of the City University of New York ("The Destruction of a Family" in *Muted Voices*, G. Schneider, editor, pp 145-156, New York: Philosophical Library, 1987
7. Ilya Ehrenburg (1891-1967) was a Soviet writer and journalist, as well as an apologist for Stalin's bloody terror. A member of the Jewish Anti-Fascist Committee, he was perhaps the foremost anti-German ideologist and propagandist. Ehrenburg's broadcasts must be understood from this perspective. For example, the Vilna Ghetto story is not entirely

factual. In early July1943, two arrested Lithuanian communists betrayed the existence of a communist leader, Itzig Wittenberg, in the Ghetto. Wittenberg was murdered by the Nazis two months *before* the ghetto was completely liquidated, and never did lead the Jewish fighters to the Partisans. Further, the Germans and Estonian police entered the Ghetto on 1 September 1943. The underground, already depleted in number and taken by surprise, did not impede the deportation of 8,000 Jews (2/3 of the total). The underground determined it was more prudent to flee, and within days 200 fighters joined the Partisans in the forest.

8. The tragic story of Kovno was reworked for dramatic effect and Soviet propaganda needs. In reality more than 5000 Kovno Jews were transported to Germany, the men to Dachau and the women to Stutthof. Few survived. About 1500 Jews were hiding in the underground bunkers that were fire-bombed. Ninety managed to escape and join the Partisans in the Lithuanian forest.

9. Moscow Radio propaganda was often shamelessly false, far beyond merely self-serving. Majdanek was liberated by Soviet forces on 23/24 July 1944. Léon Blum died in France in 1950. After the capitulation of France in 1940, Blum was indicted by the Vichy government, tried, and sent to Germany for imprisonment. Over the next 5 years, Blum and other high profile "prisoners" did tours in Buchenwald and Dachau. On 1 May 1945, Blum and the others were moved from Dachau, southward, to keep them from the advancing Americans. They relocated to a Gestapo hotel in Neiderdorf, a village high in the mountains of southern Tyrol. At 2 PM on 4 May, American soldiers overwhelmed the Gestapo guard and freed Blum and the others. The irony of the Soviet propaganda is that Blum returned to France to lead the Socialist defeat of the Communists and greatly influenced France's pro-Jewish vote on the U.N. decision to partition Palestine, in 1947.

10. Cardiazol is a drug which stimulates brain, spinal cord, and lung function. An antagonist to barbiturates, it induces epileptic-like seizures. It was used in the late 1930's as convulsive therapy for schizophrenia and bipolar disorder. Cardiazol is not an analgesic, and does not relieve toothaches.

11. Salispils is 12 miles southeast of Riga. The concentration camp, Kurtenhof, was begun in late 1941 and completed in September 1942. It was guarded by German SD units and selected SS men. It was a typical German camp with several subdivisions encircled by a double barbed-wire fence. The precise number is unknown, but upwards of 100,000 men, women and children were murdered there, mostly Jews from Latvia and other European nations. In 1944, as the Red Army approached Riga, the SS sought to hide the evidence of their crimes and inmates were forced to exhume and burn the bodies originally placed in pits on the periphery of the camp. During the last year of the camp, the majority of prisoners were Latvian resisters, draft-dodgers, and deserters. The camp was set ablaze when the Germans retreated from Latvia. (See testimony in Gertrude Schneider's "The Hangman of Camp Salaspils" in *Muted Voices*, G. Schneider, editor, pp. 137-144, New York: Philosophical Library, 1987)
12. I Samuel 2:3-8
13. Jeremiah 31:15-16
14. Jonah 2:6-7
15. September 28 on the Russian calendar; add 12 days for the equivalent on the Western calendar (October 10). It is unclear why they celebrated on September 28.
16. Weizmann's secular birthday was 27 November, 8 Kislev on the Hebrew calendar, corresponding in 1944 to 24 November. The free immigration promise was hollow.
17. "Battle of the Bulge": began 5:30 AM, 16 December 1944; by New Year, the German Army was broken and in retreat.
18. After the deportation in August, 1944, the Germans left behind 700 people to clean up the evacuated ghetto. When the ghetto was liberated by the Soviet Army, there were 877 Jews, including those who had come out from hiding, a mere remnant of the hundreds of thousands who occupied the ghetto (L. Dobroszycki, "The Chronicle of the Lodz Ghetto 1941-1944." New Haven: Yale University Press, 1984).
19. According to Albert Speer (*Inside the Thrid Reich*, 1970, p.504), this was Hitler's final radio address.
20. Deut. 8:2-3.
21. Eccles. R. 5:10:1.

22. Eccles. 7:12.
23. Psalms 142:1-8
24. Legend has it that Anton Bruckner wrote the cymbal clash at the precise moment he heard the news of Wagner's death. For this and other reasons, Hitler placed Bruckner alongside Wagner in veneration. Indeed, Hitler declared that Bruckner's Seventh was the equal of Beethoven's Ninth. The recording broadcast that evening was probably that of Oswald Kabasta conducting the Munich Philharmonic Orchestra in a live performance in 1942.
25. Hitler actually died on the afternoon of 30 April 1945, and by his own hand.
26. Genesis 12:1 God tells Abram to go forth (*lech lecha*) to a new land.

BIBLIOGRAPHY

Akhmatova, Anna, *Poems of Akhmatova*. Stanley Kunitz and Max Haywards, eds., Boston: Little, Brown and Company, 1973.

Ambrose, Stephen E., "*Citizen Soldiers. The U.S. Army from the Normandy Beaches to the Bulge to the Surrender of Germany June 7, 1944-May 7, 1945.*" New York: Simon and Schuster, 1997.

Anders, Edwards and Dubrovskis, Juris, *Jews In Liepaja, Latvia 1941-1945. A Memorial Book.* Burlingame, California: Anders Press, 2001.

Appelfeld, Aharon, "After the Holocaust," in Berel Land, ed., *Writing and the Holocaust.* New York: Holmes and Meier, 1988.

Babel, Isaac, *1920 Diary*. Carol J. Avins, ed., H.T. Willetts, transl., New Haven: Yale University Press, 1995.

Babel, Isaac, *The Complete Works of Isaac Babel*. Nathalie Babel, ed., Peter Constantine, transl., New York: W.W. Norton, 2002.

Bergers, Eliass, "Pat navēs briesmās būt cilrēkam" (To be human even in mortal danger). *Diena*, 15 June 1993.

Bergs, E. and Eiduss, Z. "Kur tu biji, cilvēk?" (Where were you, human?). *Komunists*, serialized in 14 issues, April, 1995.

Bobe, M., Levenberg, S., Maor, I., Michaeli, Z., eds., *The Jews in Latvia*. Tel Aviv: Ben-Nun Press, 1971.

Carden, Patricia, *The Art of Isaac Babel*. Ithaca: Cornell University Press, 1972.

Ezergailis, Andrew, *The Holocaust In Latvia 1941-1944*. Riga, Latvia: The Historical Institute of Latvia, 1996.

Goldberg, Amos, *Holocaust Diaries as "Life Stories."* Jerusalem: Yad Vashem, 2004.

Hampl, Patricia, *I Could Tell You Stories. Sojourns in the Land of Memory*. New York: W.W. Norton., 1999.

Kim, H and Cabeza, R., "Trusting Our Memories: Dissociating the Neural Correlates of Confidence in Veridical versus Illusory Memories." *J. Neurosci* 27: 12190-12197, 2007.

Kotre, John, *White Gloves. How We Create Ourselves Through Memory*. New York: Free Press, 1995.

Langer, Lawrence L., *Holocaust Testimonies. The Ruins of Memory*. New Haven: Yale University Press, 1991.

Linkimer, Kalman, *Diary 1941-1945*. Edward Anders, ed., Rebecca Margolis, transl. (from Yiddish original). Burlingame, California: Anders Press, 2004.

Margalit, Avishai, *The Ethics of Memory*. Cambridge: Harvard University Press, 2002.

Raudseps, Pauls, "The Linkimer Diaries." *Baltic Outlook*, Dec 2004/Jan 2005, pp. 60-64.

Robertson, Edwin M., "From Creation to Consolidation: A Novel Framework for Memory Processing." *PLOS Biol* 7 (1) : e1000019. doi:10.1371/journal.pbio.1000019.

Schneider, Gertrude, ed., *Muted Voices. Jewish Survivors of Latvia Remember*. New York: Philosophical Library, 1987.

Schneider, Gertrude, ed., *The Unfinished Road. Jewish Survivors of Latvia Look Back*. New York: Praeger, 1991.

Shirer, William L., *The Rise and Fall of the Third Reich. A History of Nazi Germany*. New York: Simon and Schuster, 1960.

Speer, Albert, *Inside the Third Reich*. New York: Macmillan Company, 1970.

Steimanis, Josifs, *History of Latvian Jews*. Edward Anders, ed., Boulder: East European Monographs, 2002.

Torgovnick, Marianna, *The War Complex*. Chicago: University of Chicago Press, 2005.

Weiner, Jon, "History as Moral Obligation: An Interview with Saul Friedlander." *Dissent*, Fall 2007 (dissentmagazine.org/article/?article=882).

Wex, Michael, *Born to Kvetch. Yiddish Language and Culture in All of its Moods*. New York: St. Martin's Press, 2005.

Yerushalmi, Yosef Hayim, *Zachor. Jewish History and Jewish Memory*. Seattle: University of Washington Press, 1982.

ABOUT THE AUTHOR

Dr. Michael Melnick is a Professor of genetics and developmental biology at the University of Southern California in Los Angeles. He has earned degrees at New York University (BA, DDS) and Indiana University (PhD). He established the Laboratory for Developmental Genetics in 1981. Over the past three decades, with support from the National Institutes of Health, Dr. Melnick has investigated the genetic complexities of normal and abnormal embryonic development. Dr. Melnick has published more than 120 peer-reviewed scientific papers and five books. He has been elected a Fellow of the American Association for the Advancement of Science (AAAS). Currently, Dr. Melnick is investigating the cellular genetic response to cytomegalovirus infection as it relates to birth defects and adult tumor formation. Details of Dr. Melnick's scientific work can be found at www.craniodevgen.org.

www.ingramcontent.com/pod-product-compliance
Lightning Source LLC
Chambersburg PA
CBHW020852090426
42736CB00008B/341